Practical social work

Published in conjunction with
the British Association of Social Workers
Series Editor: Jo Campling

Social work is at an important stage in its development. The profession is facing fresh challenges to work flexibly in fast-changing social and organisational environments. New requirements for training are also demanding a more critical and reflective, as well as more highly skilled, approach to practice.

The British Association of Social Workers has always been conscious of its role in setting guidelines for practice and in seeking to raise professional standards. The concept of the *Practical Social Work* series was conceived to fulfil a genuine professional need for a carefully planned, coherent series of texts that would stimulate and inform debate, thereby contributing to the development of practitioners' skills and professionalism.

Newly relaunched, the series continues to address the needs of all those who are looking to deepen and refresh their understanding and skills. It is designed for students and busy professionals alike. Each book marries practice issues and challenges with the latest theory and research in a compact and applied format. The authors represent a wide variety of experience both as educators and practitioners. Taken together, the books set a standard in their clarity, relevance and rigour.

A list of new and best-selling titles in this series follows overleaf. A comprehensive list of titles available in the series, and further details about individual books, can be found online at :
www.palgrave.com/socialworkpolicy/basw

Series standing order **ISBN 0–333–80313–2**

You can receive future titles in this series as they are published by placing a standing order. Please contact your bookseller or, in the case of difficulty, contact us at the address below with your name and address, the title of the series and the ISBN quoted above.

Customer Services Department, Macmillan Distribution Ltd, Houndmills, Basingstoke, Hampshire RG21 6XS, England

Practical social work series

New and best-selling titles

Robert Adams *Social Work and Empowerment* *(3rd edition)*

Sarah Banks *Ethics and Values in Social Work (3rd edition)* **new!**

James G. Barber *Social Work with Addictions (2nd edition)*

Suzy Braye and Michael Preston-Shoot *Practising Social Work Law (2nd edition)*

Veronica Coulshed and Joan Orme *Social Work Practice (4th edition)* **new!**

Veronica Coulshed and Audrey Mullender with David N. Jones and Neil Thompson
  Management in Social Work (3rd edition) **new!**

Lena Dominelli *Anti-Racist Social Work (2nd edition)*

Celia Doyle *Working with Abused Children (3rd edition)* **new!**

Tony Jeffs and Mark Smith (editors) *Youth Work*

Joyce Lishman *Communication in Social Work*

Paula Nicolson and Rowan Bayne and Jenny Owen *Applied Psychology for Social
  Workers (3rd edition)* **new!**

Judith Phillips, Mo Ray and Mary Marshall *Social Work with Older People
  (4th edition)* **new!**

Michael Oliver and Bob Sapey *Social Work with Disabled People (3rd edition)* **new!**

Michael Preston-Shoot *Effective Groupwork*

Steven Shardlow and Mark Doel *Practice Learning and Teaching*

Neil Thompson *Anti-Discriminatory Practice (4th edition)* **new!**

Derek Tilbury *Working with Mental Illness (2nd edition)*

Alan Twelvetrees *Community Work (3rd edition)*

michael oliver and
bob sapey

social work with
disabled people

third edition

First edition 1983
Second edition 1998
Third edition 2006

Published by
PALGRAVE MACMILLAN
Houndmills, Basingstoke, Hampshire RG21 6XS and
175 Fifth Avenue, New York, N.Y. 10010
Companies and representatives throughout the world

PALGRAVE MACMILLAN is the global academic imprint of the Palgrave Macmillan division of St. Martin's Press, LLC and of Palgrave Macmillan Ltd. Macmillan® is a registered trademark in the United States, United Kingdom and other countries. Palgrave is a registered trademark in the European Union and other countries.

ISBN-13: 978–1–4039–1838–3
ISBN-10: 1–4039–1838–4

This book is printed on paper suitable for recycling and made from fully managed and sustained forest sources.

A catalogue record for this book is available from the British Library.

A catalog record for this book is available from the Library of Congress.

10   9   8   7   6   5   4   3   2   1
15   14   13   12   11   10   09   08   07   06

Printed in China

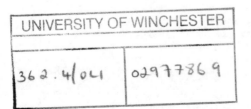

Contents

List of figures and tables

Figures

Tables

Preface to the third edition

When the first edition of this book was published in 1983, social
work appeared to be the occupational group that was best posi-
tioned within the disability industry to change its practice to
support the principles of the social model of disability. The first
edition encouraged social workers to review the individualising and
pathologising knowledge and methods that had dominated their
practice, and to join disabled people in challenging the political,
cultural and professional barriers they faced in their everyday lives.
Fifteen years later, the second edition was published and at that
time, while much had been added to our knowledge of disability by
disabled people, social work had generally failed to take up the
challenge. While the second edition brought much of the context up
to date, the message of the book changed little, and we concluded:

> In this second edition, we have attempted to reconstruct
> [social work] professional practice in the light of . . . chang-
> ing economic and political circumstances. This is because we
> remain committed to the idea of an enabling welfare state
> based upon empowering professional practice. We hope that
> this book will be a vehicle for such a reconstruction because
> if we fail in this task, not only will there be no third edition
> of this book in fifteen years' time, but the idea and practice
> of an enabling and empowering welfare state will itself be
> dead and there will be no professional practice to recon-
> struct.
> (Oliver and Sapey, 1999, p. 184)

It is now five, not fifteen years later, and a third edition is
required because of the significant advances that have been made
by disabled people in changing the ideological underpinning of
disability policy in the UK. We describe this in more detail in
Chapter 1, but in essence it involves a shift from viewing disabled

people as a group deserving of welfare, to fellow citizens with full rights to participate socially, economically and politically in society. In revising this book we have had to reflect on the progress, or lack of it, that has been made by the social work profession towards working with disabled people as citizens within a social model of disability. While this might be described as disappointing, there are more serious consequences. First, it means that many thousands of disabled people continue to live in conditions that would not be acceptable to the social workers and their managers who are charged with administering the welfare system, and this is unacceptable. Second, so much has been achieved by the disabled people's movement in the fight to gain full civil rights, and as those changes come to fruition, it looks increasingly likely that social work, because of its failure to recognise disabled people as citizens, will in the future exclude itself from this area of practice.

Another issue we needed to consider was just how much to revise the text. While we have tried to ensure that the book is up to date in terms of social policy, legislation and new research, we decided to retain older references and quotations where they continue to serve a useful purpose. Even though the language may now seem dated and inconsistent with current terminology, this literature provides the reader with a sense of the length of time over which the disabled people's movement has been fighting for changes in the welfare system, and most importantly, the extent to which too little has changed within social work.

The result is a book that continues to promote the potential for social work with disabled people within a social model of disability, but also clearly states that practice within an individual model is no longer viable. Occupational groups that do not change will soon find they have no role with disabled people.

We continue to hope that the third edition of this book will act as a resource for disabled people and social workers in the continuing struggle to create an inclusive society, in which everyone is recognised and treated as a citizen of our very rich and privileged country.

MICHAEL OLIVER
BOB SAPEY

Key British disability legislation

1948 National Assistance Act
Duty of local authorities to provide residential accommodation (s21); local authorities given the power to provide
certain community services for 'persons who are blind, deaf
or dumb and other persons who are substantially and
permanently handicapped by illness, injury or congenital
deformity' (s29). Amended by LAC 13/74 to include
'persons suffering from a mental disorder of any description'.

1970 Chronically Sick and Disabled Persons Act
Section 1 imposes duty on local authorities to inform themselves of the number and needs of disabled persons in their
areas and; to publicize services provided by the local
authority. This was extended by the Disabled Persons
(Services, Consultation and Representation) Act, 1986 to
include any services known to them.
  Section 2 lists various services that should be provided
to disabled people (defined by s29 of NAA 1948), including:

● Practical assistance in the home;
● Social work support to families; and
● Adaptations to the home and special equipment,
  including telephones.

1974 Local Authority Circular 13/74
Extends s29 of the NAA 1948 to include people with
'mental disorder', which in turn extended the CSDPA 1970
to the same people.

1981 **Education Act**
Introduced idea of children with special educational needs
and led to 'statementing' and improved inclusion within
mainstream schools for some disabled children.

1983 **Mental Health Act**
Provides for the care, detention and aftercare of people
with a mental disorder. Likely to be superseded by a new
Act when the Mental Health Bill 2004 reaches the statute
book.

1986 **Disabled Persons (Services, Consultation and
Representation) Act**
Section 4 made it a duty of local authorities to assess the
needs of a disabled person when requested to do so.

Sections 5 and 6 made for arrangements whereby LEAs
and SSDs had to liaise over the provision of services for
disabled adolescents when they were reaching adulthood.

Section 8 required local authorities to take into account
the ability of carers – the first mention of carers in UK legislation.

1989 **Children Act**
Separate provision for disabled children as 'children in
need'.

1990 **National Health Service and Community Care Act**
Amendments to NAA 1948 to permit local authorities to
purchase services from a third party; transfer of Income
Support payments for residential and nursing homes to
local authorities with the power to spend on community
services; more general approach to what community care
services might be rather than the restrictive list approach of
the CSDPA 1970.

1995 **Disability Discrimination Act**
Unlawful to discriminate against disabled people in relation
to: employment; access to goods, facilities or services; the
management, renting or buying of land or property.
Extended by SENDA 2001 to also cover education.

1996 **Community Care (Direct Payments) Act**
Made it lawful for local authorities to make payments of cash in lieu of community care services if requested to do so by a disabled person.

1999 **Community Care (Direct Payments) Amendment Regulations**
Extended direct payments to people over 65 years.

2000 **Carers and Disabled Children Act**
Extended direct payments to carers and young people.

2001 **Health and Social Care Act**
Gave the Secretary of State the authority to require local authorities to implement the direct payments scheme, rather than leaving it to their discretion. This requirement was implemented in April 2004.

2001 **Special Educational Needs and Disability Act**
Extended the DDA 1995 to cover education. Replaces the idea of meeting special needs on an individual basis to one of schools, colleges and universities having an anticipatory duty and therefore having to be accessible to disabled pupils and students.

Introduction: setting the scene

Historically, British social work could be said to have started with the formation of the Charity Organisation Society in the 1860s. In the late nineteenth century the first hospital almoner was appointed, and it is from that role that social work with disabled people emerged. By the time of the Second World War, social work had become a reserved occupation, but despite its development towards being a profession – the gaining of university status for its training, its proactive stance in terms of child care and health care, and the influence of psychoanalysis on its practice – social work remained essentially concerned with administering welfare on utilitarian principles. The state was concerned to ensure that welfare be distributed on the basis that it would act as a remedy to dependency rather than as a sedative. Theoretically, the role of the social worker was to assess the behaviour and motivations of individuals in need, in order to determine how best to help them become self-reliant. In practice, welfare agencies tended to retain control over the design and management of services, as self-reliance and long-term need were seen as being incompatible.

In the early 1990s, this control was institutionalized as social work was extensively replaced by care management, which was dominated by notions of financial accountability and the rationing of services. Sir Roy Griffiths' (1988) report *Agenda for Action*, the White Paper *Caring for People* (Department of Health, 1989) and the subsequent legislation, the National Health Service and Community Care Act, 1990, introduced care managers into local authority social work and social services departments. Their role was to assess individual needs and then purchase the social care services that were required by disabled people to meet those needs. Social service authorities would be 'enabling authorities' rather than direct providers of care. While the majority of care managers were social workers, this was not a prerequisite, and many occupational therapists and home help organisers also joined them in this new role.

Within social work itself there were, and are, several debates –
genericism versus specialism, community versus individual, material versus emotional concerns, and independent versus state-
sponsored profession – but in the main these were concerned with
increasing efficiency rather than questioning its role in administering welfare. While this role still prevails in local authorities, a
number of new initiatives in social policies have begun to challenge
the need for social work.

Traditionally, both local and national governments have
constructed ideas of what groups of welfare recipients need. This
has led to both the formulated responses of social welfare – that is,
the types of services available – and to the construction of client
groups. However, since the 1960s disabled people themselves have
been campaigning for the right to determine what their relationship
with the state should be, and this includes determining the role of
social work. While the exact meaning of the term 'third way' is still
subject to considerable debate, since 1997 the Labour government
does appear to be supporting an idea of independent living that
takes control of services away from the institutions of welfare and
puts it into the hands of disabled people. Direct payments have been
extended to include all people in receipt of community care services,
the Disability Rights Commission (DRC) has been strengthened and
the Disability Discrimination Act 1995 extended to cover education.

Furthermore, the new Labour modernising agenda has led to
considerable changes in the structure of the institutions that
surround social work. The Central Council for Education and
Training in Social Work (CCETSW) and the National Institute for
Social Work (NISW) have both been disbanded and new organisations have taken their place. The General Social Care Council
(GSCC) and its equivalent in Scotland and Wales are responsible
for regulating standards in social work. Unlike CCETSW, they no
longer award social work qualifications; rather, all social workers
need to be registered with their national social care council and it
is an offence to use the name 'social worker' unless registered.
Other CCETSW activities were handed to the Training
Organisation for the Personal Social Services (TOPSS), in particular setting the national occupational standards for social work.
TOPSS has since been renamed Skills for Care.

NISW's functions have partly gone to the Electronic Library for
Social Care, since renamed Social Care Online, and partly to the

Social Care Institute for Excellence (SCIE). Like its equivalent in the health service NICE (National Institute for Clinical Excellence), SCIE is responsible for identifying and promoting effective practices within social work and social care. The appointment of Jane Campbell, the former Director of the National Centre for Independent Living (NCIL), as the first chairperson of SCIE, and the inclusion of service users on the social care councils' governing bodies, are further indications of a new kind of commitment towards involving disabled people at all levels. This leaves us with the question of what should the relationship be between social workers and their clients, and indeed, what is social work?

The term 'social work' as used here refers to an organized professional activity carried out on behalf of individuals or groups of people. This activity is geared towards the provision of services on an individual, group or community basis. The adjective 'professional' implies that those who provide these services are certified as being competent to do so, and are financially rewarded for doing the work. The provision of such services does not merely involve the matching of need with resources, but also requires professionals to work in partnership with disabled people to help them to ascertain what their needs are, and to argue for adequate resources to meet those needs. The context of such activity may be a community care trust, a social services department, a hospital, residential accommodation, a voluntary organisation or any other appropriate agency. The range of methods involved will include casework, group work and community work, and these may be applied in a variety of settings, including the home, residential care, day care and sheltered accommodation.

This is obviously a very broad definition of social work, and flies in the face of the trend to restrict social work to the management of services. While there may be adequate and justifiable reasons for calls to social work generally to narrow its base of activity, it is not appropriate in the field of disability. It will be argued throughout this book that disability is not an individual problem; rather, it is a social problem concerned with the effects of hostile physical and social environments upon impaired individuals, or even a societal one concerned with the way society treats this particular minority group. As such, the base for social work activity with disabled people needs to be broadened, not narrowed. As has been argued for some time:

Many disabilities are the result of social conditions and amenable to social services intervention. Medical care treatment, for example, is not going to solve the low-income, social isolation, and architectural barriers that are major for the disabled. At issue is the conflict over bureaucratic supremacy between the medical and social service parts of government. The clash involves ideological and theoretical differences concerning the nature of the problem and the response.
(Albrecht and Levy, 1981, p. 23)

There is also the question of the relationship between theory and practice in social work. There is much disillusionment with 'ivory-tower academics' whose theorising is not based on the realities of practice, and again, there may well be some justification for this disillusion across social work generally. The idea of social work as a practical activity is, of course, politically appealing and has led to the promotion of rational models of care management (Social Services Inspectorate, 1991a, 1991b), but in terms of disability this approach is not new. Hanvey (1981) and Bell and Klemz (1981) both epitomised this approach. Both saw the matching of needs and services as being non-problematic: there are x number of disabling conditions brought about by y causes; there is a legal and statutory framework, disabled people have a number of needs and there are these services provided to meet them. This tradition is perpetuated in textbooks on 'social work theory', which assert the importance of methods of intervention over knowledge of social problems or of the impact of such interventions. Such approaches have been institutionalized in the competence framework of occupational standards and evidenced-based practice that dominate current social work training, but they ignore a number of crucial problems: What is 'need'? Are the services that are provided appropriate? As Sapey (2004) has argued, what is the point of developing an evidence base for practice when social workers and disabled people are yet to agree on the aims of intervention?

If only social work with disabled people were as simple as this practical approach implies – the matching of resources to needs within a legal and statutory framework. It will be argued here that the dominant view of disability as a personal tragedy or disaster is an inaccurate one, and may lead to the provision of inappropriate

resources. It will further be suggested that social work as an organised professional activity has either ignored disabled people or
intervened on the basis of the dominant view of disability as a
personal disaster. Chapter 1 will argue this at greater length and
suggest a more appropriate theory of disability – which will be
referred to as the social model of disability – and draw out some of
its implications for practice, particularly the need to recognize
disabled people as citizens, and not clients.

This is not to assert the predominance of theory over practice,
but rather to suggest that there is a symbiotic relationship between
the two: that theory will inform practice and orientate the activities
of practitioners whose very activities will feed back and modify
theory. This view is very close to what Kuhn (1962), in discussing
the history and development of the natural sciences, called a 'paradigm'. A sub-title of this book might well be 'The social model of
disability – a paradigm for social work'.

Chapter 2 will consider various ways of conceptualizing disability and some of the implications that follow from these different
conceptualisations. It will be suggested that the implication stemming from the individual model of disability is to count numbers of
disabled people, compile registers and so on, whereas the social
model suggests that ways need to be developed of measuring the
disabling effects of the physical and social environment instead.

Chapter 3 will focus on the relationship between impairment
and disability in the context of social work practice with individuals, arguing that it is the task of social workers to be primarily
concerned with reducing or alleviating the consequences of disability and not the problems of impairment.

Chapter 4 will widen the discussion and consider these issues in
relation to social work practice with families where there is a
disabled member.

Chapter 5 will consider the role and functioning of residential
care facilities and will suggest that these services further disable
impaired individuals. Suggestions as to how social work can
attempt to prevent this imposition of additional disability, and
work with disabled people to achieve independent living will also
be discussed.

Chapter 6 will consider the legal framework within which
services are provided for disabled people, including the rights that
disabled people have to access such services.

Chapter 7 will pull together some of the issues raised in connection with the relationship of theory to practice, and consider the implications both for service provision and professional practice that the social model of disability raises. Finally, some consideration will be given to ways forward.

1 | Social work and disability: old and new directions

Prior to 1970, help for disabled people and their families was really only available through the health service (medical social workers) or voluntary organizations such as the Invalid Children's Aid Association and the Spastics Society. A few local authority health departments set up professional social work services in the 1950s, staffed mainly by medical social workers, and in some cases by occupational therapists as well. Welfare departments in the pre-Seebohm Report days also offered services to disabled people, but as most did not employ trained social workers, little was done beyond material help and information-giving, while some provision was made for residential care. The Seebohm Report, local government reorganisation and the Chronically Sick and Disabled Persons Act, 1970 was supposed to change all that and usher in a new era. This led to services for disabled people being established as a social services responsibility, but as with many local authority provisions it varied from one part of the country to another. The community care reforms brought in by the National Health Service and Community Care Act, 1990 were intended to bring some level of equity to disability services through transforming the organization of the statutory social services, while the Children Act, 1989 brought in separate provisions for disabled children, but criticisms that services were still based on the wrong approach to disability persisted. More recently, the introduction of direct payments and an emphasis on service user involvement in the delivery of assistance have begun to address some of these criticisms, while the current proposals for the introduction of community care trusts may bring about significant changes in the location and structure of disability services. Finally, as the Disability Discrimination Act, 1995 begins to impact on services provided by local authorities, it is likely to affect the latter's ability to maintain a traditional professionalised approach to the delivery of care; that is, one that places the expertise in the hands of the social worker rather than the service user. What this has meant as far as social work with disabled people is concerned will thus be a major theme of this book.

The role of social services departments

The current role of social service departments emanate from the Seebohm Report, which recommended the development of services for disabled people. Based on Seebohm, the Local Authority Social Services Act, 1970 established social services departments, and its recommendations on disability were incorporated into an additional Act, the Chronically Sick and Disabled Persons Act, 1970. Unfortunately, not only was this Act passed at a time of organizational upheaval when there were also the competing demands of other client groups, notably children, who had also been the beneficiaries of recent legislation, it also suffered from being inadequately resourced through the ambiguity of the money order resolution that accompanied it as a private Member's bill (Topliss and Gould, 1981). The consequence of this was that while the expectations of disabled people were raised, the new generic departments were unable to provide adequate support services, either in terms of practical aid or emotional support (Knight and Warren, 1978; Shearer, 1981a; Topliss and Gould, 1981).

By the mid-1980s, social services were under pressure from two directions – first from disabled people who were dissatisfied with the lack of autonomy they could achieve through the design of personal care services (Shearer, 1984) and its inequitable distribution (Fiedler, 1988), and second, from the government, which was concerned about the spiralling costs of welfare services for adults (Audit Commission, 1986). The first of these resulted in the Disabled Persons (Services, Consultation and Representation) Act, 1986 which attempted to ensure a voice for disabled people in the assessment of their needs. While succeeding at the parliamentary stage, the provisions of this Act were quickly superseded by the government's own proposals in *Caring for People* (Department of Health, 1989) which sought to control expenditure through the introduction of a quasi-market into the social welfare sector. While this reinforced the role of local authorities as the arbiters of need, the disability movement continued to argue its case for greater control by disabled people of their own personal assistance (Oliver and Zarb, 1992; Morris, 1993; Zarb and Nadash, 1994). One of the results of these studies and the case they argued was the Conservative government's Community Care (Direct Payments) Act, 1996 which allowed money to be given directly to clients.

Direct payments, and more specifically what they represent in terms of putting the users of social services in control, became a cornerstone of the 1997 Labour government's social care policies. They argued that social services were going to need direction if they were to serve adults better, and that, in particular, they need to

● seek to promote people's independence while treating them with dignity and respect at all times, and protecting their safety;

● provide services more consistently across the country; and

● make the system more centred on service users and their families, and as convenient and straightforward as possible for people to use.

(Department of Health, 1998, para. 2.4)

In *Modernising Social Services*, the Secretary of State for Health outlined what the government saw as the problems disabled people faced within the care system. First among these was that services were often designed to do things *to* people rather than to support them: 'the guiding principle of adult social services should be that they provide the support needed by someone to make the most of their capacity and potential' (Department of Health, 1998, para. 2.5). The Department of Health noted that, despite increases in funding for services, fewer people were receiving support because of the way that local authorities were focusing on people with higher levels of dependency. This they argued, 'increases the risk that they [people with less dependency] in turn become more likely to need much more complicated levels of support as their independence is compromised. That is good neither for the individual nor, ultimately, for the social services, the NHS or the taxpayer' (Department of Health, 1998, para. 2.6).

Finally, the Department of Health stated that many people were being forced to live in institutions by local authority policies designed to reduce the costs of care, and that this was not desirable. Despite this, between 1996 and 2002 the numbers of 'physically/sensorily disabled adults' under 65 years of age being supported by local authorities in residential and nursing homes in England remained constant, while for other groups there were reductions, and the overall trend saw a fall of 17 per cent (Department of Health, 1996 and 2003). The government had promised to take action to reduce this use of institutional care, through

- better preventative services and a stronger focus on reha-bilitation;
- an extension of direct payments schemes;
- better support for service users who are able to work;
- improved review and follow-up to take into account people's changing needs;
- improved support for people with mental health prob-lems; and
- more support for carers.

(Department of Health, 1998, para. 2.11)

The extent to which social services for disabled people have developed in recent times can be seen by exploring current policies and contrasting them to Seebohm's recommendations. To some extent, the change in government thinking reflects changes of atti-tude towards disabled people in society at large.

Seebohm's first recommendation was that services needed to develop, and more recently, as we have noted, the government are concerned that there are too few services for less dependent people, and that too many disabled people are still being forced into insti-tutions. This has been a persistent pattern of inconsistency. In 1978, one study noted that 'Despite the substantial development of services for handicapped people and the considerable increase of expenditure on these services . . . there were widespread indications . . . that even the most active departments could develop their services further' (Knight and Warren, 1978, p. 70).

Ten years later, Fiedler (1988) described the provision of social and housing services as a 'lottery' in that it would depend on which authority area a disabled person lived in as to whether they would receive the support needed to live independently. Although some authorities might have made much progress, this is certainly not the case everywhere. In 2004, Barnes et al. reported that 'Overall seven years after implementation, direct payments remain marginal as a support option for disabled people. Data so far reveals an inequitable access across the UK, as well as reiterating the divisions between impairment groups, age and ethnicity' (Barnes *et al.*, 2004, p. 11).

In the opening statement of a national inspection of English councils, the Social Services Inspectorate stated that, although independent living had become a reality for a few younger disabled people, primarily through direct payments and other creative schemes, the majority were 'still being offered services in a fragmented way without any obvious consideration of whether they will promote independence' (Fruin, 2000, p. 1). The first two messages of this report were that

1. Most councils and their staff still have fully to absorb and carry through the independent living philosophy.
2. Direct payments schemes are taking off slowly with some councils and some staff still ambivalent. The success of these schemes and of direct payment users' individual benefits needs further publicity so that success can breed success.

(Fruin, 2000, p. 7)

Seebohm's second recommendation suggested that a reasonably accurate picture of the size and nature of the 'problem' should be ascertained, and counting the numbers of people affected by disability was built into the Chronically Sick and Disabled Persons Act as a legal requirement. While all local authorities had conducted their own surveys, the question of accuracy remains. Most of those surveys located only about 50 per cent of the people that the government's own survey (Harris, 1971) suggested there might be. This rapidly changing picture continued with the second government survey (Martin *et al.*, 1988), from which, for example, the numbers of disabled people using wheelchairs was estimated at 360,000, while less than ten years later a survey of Disablement Services Centres found that this figure was closer to 714,000 (College of Occupational Therapists, 1996). Clearly many of the surveys are now out of date and this affects the accuracy of what they are reporting.

It is obvious, therefore, that it is an extremely complex and time-consuming business to maintain an accurate picture of the needs of disabled people in a particular area. Some have questioned the allocation of resources in this way, arguing that it would be more productive to spend money on direct services rather than on counting heads or updating registers. However, Huntington and Sapey

(2003) suggest that collecting information on the needs of social service clients is tending to become the primary objective of many agencies rather than the provision of services. They argue that this is because of the increased importance of information, particularly influenced by new technologies. The government view technology and the ~~~~~~~~~~ on as being important, and as contribu~~~~~~~~ ~~ ~~~~~~ ne respect accorded to disabled people b~~~~~~~

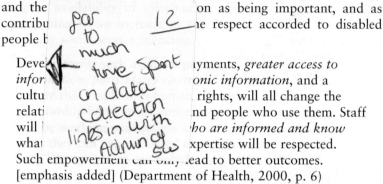

> Deve~~~~~ ~~~~~~~ yments, *greater access to infor*~~~~~ ~~~~~~~ *onic information*, and a cultu~~~~~ ~~~~~~~ rights, will all change the relati~~~~~~~~~ ~~~~ nd people who use them. Staff will ~~~~~~~~~ *ho are informed and know* wha~~~~~~~~~~~~ xpertise will be respected. Such empowerment can only lead to better outcomes. [emphasis added] (Department of Health, 2000, p. 6)

Regardless of whether information empowers people to receive services or acts as a replacement, what is clear is that the head-counting approach has failed. As will be argued later in this chapter, the 'problem' of disablement may be better accounted for by auditing access issues.

With Seebohm's third recommendation, the onus was placed on social services departments to provide a wide range of services, foremost among these being a social work service for disabled people and their families. Few, if any, departments would have claimed to have provided such a service, and since the community care changes of 1993 the focus has moved away from social work. Other services, such as residential and day care, are often criti-ci~~~ ~~~~~~~~~~~~~~~~~~~~ failure to provide, but rather in terms of ~~~~~~~~~~~ what disabled people want. Forcing di~~~~~~~~~~~ stitutions was one of the key problems re~~~~~~~~~~~ ent (Department of Health, 1998) as th~~~~~~~~~~~ f-confidence and a decline in activity' (p~~~~~~~~~~~

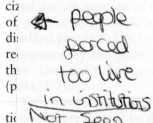

ti~~~~~~~~~~~ s direct payments, and aids and adapta-ti~~~~~~~~~~~ abled people, are often criticized on the gr~~~~~~~~~~~ artments to allocate adequate resources to~~~~~~~~~~~ child, 2002) or to give them sufficient priority (Stainton, 2002). The criticisms of local authorities in this respect also concern the standard of social work practice – the Social Services Inspectorate reports that

> We saw examples across the inspected councils of good elements of the assessment and care management process but we also saw scope for improvement, particularly in the physical disability field. Many assessments were partial with an emphasis on deficiencies, lacking an holistic approach to the person being assessed. Where different assessors were involved with the same person, users often experienced serial and multiple assessments which were not integrated either from the user's perspective or on the case records. Most care plans moved too readily to becoming service plans, with a lack of specification of intended outcomes and with referrals mainly to existing block-purchased services with limited flexibility and tailoring to meet the needs of the individual.
> (Fruin, 2000, p. 4)

The Health and Social Care Act, 2001 introduced care trusts as a new model for the delivery of care. These will be formed by partnerships of local authorities and NHS trusts, and could become the vehicle for the delivery of disability services. If, or rather when, they come into being on a large scale it would effectively end the Seebohm recommendation that services are based in social services departments, but their success would need to be judged on the later modernisation goals of promoting and supporting independent living. Whether social workers will continue to have a key role, and if so exactly what that will be, may depend on their usefulness in achieving this goal – in organisations that are dominated by health concerns it may be important to have personnel who have different priorities.

Seebohm's fourth recommendation was for the development of services for disabled school leavers. Following the recommendations of the 1978 Warnock Report, this had been left to the careers service, with each education authority in England and Wales employing specialist careers officers for disabled people.

Ways of measuring unemployment change quite frequently, and the type of help available also changes, notably the New Deal schemes of the 1997 Labour government. Despite this, in 2004, the Department for Education and Skills' own survey of the main activities of 18-year-olds showed that disabled people were continuing

Table 1.1 Main activities of 18-year-olds, 2004

	Weighted sample	Higher education (%)	Full time job (%)	Out of work (%)
Has a disability or health problem	328	14	18	18
Does not have a disability or health problem	7394	27	31	6

Note: Percentages do not add up to 100 as several other activities have been omitted.
Source: Adapted from Department for Education and Skills, 2004, table B.

to fare less well than their non-disabled peers (see Table 1.1). Two significant activities are those entering higher education, where the percentage for disabled people is about half that for non-disabled people; and in full-time employment, where the percentage is about two-thirds. In terms of non-activity, disabled people were three times as likely to be unemployed.

The importance of employment is recognised by current government policy (Cabinet Office, 2005), as is the importance of welfare services in helping disabled people in this respect. The third national objective of *Modernising Social Services* is

> To ensure that people of working age who have been
> ~~assessed as requ~~iring community care services, are provided
> s in ways which take account of and, as far
> nise their and their carers' capacity to take
> return to employment.

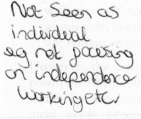

Not seen as individual eg not pacing on independence working etc

ll Services Inspectorate found progress to be
1), particularly for people with physical impair-
ls were criticised for failing to consider employ-
ately and for having charging policies that
d people from seeking employment. Although
re seen as having potential in this respect, the
Social Services Inspectorate found that schemes had either not been introduced or were not promoted.

For many years most social services departments were also reluctant to attempt to identify the non-vocational needs of disabled young people for fear of raising people's expectations, and regarding the increased demands that might be created. This led to the passing of Sections 5 and 6 of the Disabled Persons (Services, Consultation & Representation) Act in 1986 which introduced formal procedures by which social services departments were obliged to communicate with education departments in order to identify and assess the social needs of disabled school leavers. While the actual provision of services remains the subject of rationing, as for other social service clients, it has led to a much greater acceptance on the part of local authorities of their responsibilities, albeit with a high level of formalisation.

Seebohm also called for improved co-ordination between services and this is still a major objective of *Modernising Social Services* and of the Health and Social Care Act, 2001. However, in a review of Seebohm, Phelan stated unequivocally that this may never be achieved:

> Effective co-ordination is as elusive as perpetual motion and if truly achieved verges on acquiring that very characteristic, but frequently social provisions are either organised without acknowledgement of it or administered within a scope which endeavours to eliminate the need for it. *In services for people with handicaps, where generally co-ordination is required more than anywhere else, paradoxically it is to be found the least.*
> [emphasis added] (in Cypher, 1979, p. 56)

Phelan may well have been proved right by the recent history of services since the implementation of the NHS and Community Care Act, 1990. This Act made inter-agency co-ordination mandatory and the emphasis from the Department of Health changed to one of co-operation. A range of guidelines and circulars were issued advising and instructing social services, health and housing authorities on how to ensure they worked together effectively. Critics, including the Audit Commission, would argue, however, that far from breaking down the barriers to co-operation and co-ordination, the introduction of market principles has created more impermeable boundaries determined by budgetary priorities and responsibilities. The Audit Commission described these barriers as being like a 'Berlin wall'. However, co-ordination and co-operation between agencies remains essential to the smooth and effective delivery of services.

The issue of training, which forms the basis of Seebohm's sixth recommendation, was taken up by a Working Party convened by the Central Council for Education and Training in Social Work, whose major finding was encapsulated in its title: *People with Handicaps Need Better Trained Workers* (CCETSW, 1974). Their recommendations were for improved training at in-service, basic and post-qualifying levels. The introduction of the special option on 'handicap' as part of CSS courses, and the considerable number of professionals from social services departments who took the Open University course entitled 'The Handicapped Person in the Community' improved matters a little, but both of these have been superseded by other developments. Following the introduction of the Diploma in Social Work (DipSW) in 1989 and the ending of the CSS and CQSW programmes, CCETSW encouraged universities to develop disability options and to recruit disabled students (Stevens, 1991). Despite pressure from within higher education for courses to be made accessible, Crawshaw (2002) reports that disabled people constitute between 4 per cent and 8.8 per cent of social work students, well below what might be expected in an occupation that has so much to do with disability. Her project at the University of York sought to challenge the 'us and them' divisions in social work, and argued that including disabled students means that social work would 'start to encompass the values of inclusivity it espouses' (p. 512).

The publication of *A Quality Strategy for Social Care* (Department of Health, 2000) and *Requirements for Social Work Training* (Department of Health, 2002) emphasised the need for social workers to be skilled in working in partnership with service users. This has become one of the specific points that the General Social Care Council (GSCC) monitors when accrediting universities to teach social work and when approving their degrees. The Department of Health also made available funds to help universities pay service users to be involved in social work education, in the hope that they might bring disabled people into the classroom as teachers and develop their skills as trainers. This respect for the expertise of disabled people does reflect a considerable shift from the Seebohm approach, which would have seen social workers as having the expertise.

Seebohm's final recommendation was for closer co-operation between the statutory and voluntary sectors. Traditionally, the voluntary sector provision for disabled people extended from residential and day-care services to providing individual volunteers for gardening, driving people to appointments and so on. Hatch, in his study of voluntary organisations in three towns, found

> At the local level most of the organisations for the handicapped worked quite closely with the statutory services. Where they did not do so it seemed in the three towns more a result of statutory neglect than antagonism on the part of the voluntary organisation. Within this kind of relationship the voluntary organisations were able to communicate needs, but seldom did they openly challenge the adequacy of existing provision by taking up an active pressure-group role. (Hatch, 1980, p. 105)

This uncritical co-operation, which has been formalised through purchasing contracts since 1993, has been criticized extensively by organisations made up of disabled people. These groups of disabled people have consistently challenged the structures within which welfare has been provided (see Campbell and Oliver (1996) for a full account of their development). Organizations of disabled people have achieved notable success in campaigning for and demonstrating the advantages of direct payments, and for the involvement of service users in supporting people using direct payments. This support role was clear within Oliver and Zarb's (1992) study of the Greenwich Personal Assistance Scheme. Hasler et al. (2000), in their review of the development of arrangements for independent living, emphasise that local authorities that are implementing direct payment schemes should look to collaborating with disabled people's organisations, which have considerable experience in providing such support.

The Social Services Inspectorate (2000) have also recommended such collaborative arrangements as being essential to the implementation of direct payments, and this is reflected in their standards for inspections of local authorities (Social Services Inspectorate, 1999). Some innovative work in this area was carried out by the King's Fund Centre in their Living Options project. Fiedler (1991) made the point that the involvement of service users within social services could range from information, through consultation and partnership to delegated control. She viewed these as stages in a process that would, and should, result in delegated control rather than being a choice of different models of user involvement. Later the *Shaping Our Lives* project was established as a user-controlled network, with the main aim of 'supporting the development of local user involvement that aims to deliver better outcomes for service users' (www.shapingourlives.org.uk).

In this way, the agenda has moved on considerably since Seebohm's report, with the emphasis being on partnership with service users and a recognition of the value of the support that organisations of disabled people can provide, as opposed to the more traditional services provided by non-user-controlled agencies.

Any attempts to assess progress accurately since Seebohm are obviously difficult, but in the light of what has been said it is not unreasonable to conclude that the modernisation of social services will require a substantial change in the attitudes and practice of social workers. It is in this area of social work services specifically that the least progress has been made, and in the rest of this chapter some of the reasons why this should be so will be considered before going on to outline some of the ways in which social work intervention with disabled people can be made more positive.

Social work services for disabled people

The role of social workers may be affected by organizational developments, but in essence has changed little since 1970. Although in theory their role has been envisaged as being quite broad, including the provision of personal social work help to individuals and families, the assessment of needs, the provision of support and rehabilitation, support and training of social care staff, and co-ordination of care packages (CCETSW, 1974; Stevens, 1991), in practice social workers have had a much more limited role.

There have been a number of studies that have discussed social work in relation to disabled people – but few have been complimentary to social work. Historically, for example, Parsloe and Stevenson (1978) found that the level and extent of social work intervention with disabled people was relatively low, and that occupational therapists or social work assistants provided the most input to disabled people and their families. Goldberg and Warburton (1979) found that social work intervention both lacked depth and fared badly in comparison with work with other client groups. At the time the Barclay Committee reported, these and other studies confirmed that disabled people had less access to skilled social work support, for, as they noted, 'unqualified, inexperienced or assistant social workers carry proportionately more cases of physically handicapped and elderly people' (Barclay Committee, 1982, p. 11).

Social workers also failed to recognise the potential of working with disabled people and 'the preservation of the status quo was all the social workers hoped for' (Goldberg and Warburton, 1979, p. 93). Another study (Phillips and Glendinning, 1981) found that social work intervention could even be positively harmful: 'some people had even been given inaccurate information from social workers which had deterred them from making applications for benefits and caused subsequent financial losses' (p. 43).

Burgess (1982) wrote of a case where, despite regular social work intervention, the disabled client had lost more than £4,000 in unclaimed benefit in the previous few years. Despite the attention that has been brought to this lack of information, Grewal *et al.* (2002, p. 173), in a study involving nearly a thousand disabled adults, conclude that 'a perceived lack of readily available information was frequently cited as an important contributor to the social exclusion that some people described'. Priestley (2004) criticises the core role of social work as being structured to enforce dependency:

> The practice of care assessment and management is not simply a technical 'gate-keeping' mechanism – it defines disabled people's needs in a very particular way. Value-laden purchasing decisions can perpetuate the myth of 'care' over independent living by focusing resources on personal care and limited domestic chores at the expense of support for social integration. Thus, care assessments all too frequently consolidate the social segregation of disabled people in their own homes, rather than challenging their enforced dependency.
> (p. 259)

While many social services departments and voluntary sector agencies undoubtedly established better services for disabled people during the 1980s, these were struggling to survive by the 1990s. The development of advisory (d'Aboville, 1991) or advocacy (Middleton, 1992) services that have been regarded positively by disabled people and their families came under threat through the focus on quantifiable outcomes that have been popularised in the new public-sector management. A particular result of the managerialisation of welfare during the 1980s and 1990s was the conversion of many social work managers to the creed of quality assurance. This doctrine claims that it is of no importance as to who delivers or arranges a service so long as it is provided, but this contradicts much of the evidence from consumers of welfare (Howe, 1987; Morris, 1993; Willis, 1995) that the way in which social workers undertake their duties is important. Not only does this doctrine ignore the wisdom of experience of the Poor Laws – that it was necessary for the administrators of welfare to 'humanise the relationship between the poor and authority' (Albert Evans MP, quoted in Silburn, 1983) if they were to overcome the stigma attached to receiving assistance from the state; it also contradicts evidence from practice. For example, Dawson (2000) found that the take-up of direct payments was affected most by the attitude of social workers, a clear indication of both the positive and negative effects that approaches to professional practice can have on the lives of disabled people.

Furthermore, the failure of social workers to develop an adequate theoretical and practice base for their interventions has led to criticisms, notably by disabled people themselves, who have accused social workers of ignorance about disabling conditions, benefits and rights, failing to recognise the need for practical assistance as well as verbal advice, and to involve disabled people in the training process. They have also expressed resentment at being treated on a less than equal basis in the professional/client relationship (Finkelstein, 1991). In addition, while disabled people have therefore been critical of social workers, social workers themselves have often been reluctant to throw themselves wholeheartedly into work with this particular group. As a measure of social workers' lack of interest, Sapey (2004) reported that in a review of papers on disability relevant to social work, only one in eight were published in social work journals, while more than half were within the disability studies field, led by disabled people. Certainly there are a number of reasons for this, which may include the following. First, low priority is given to work with this group and hence there are restricted career prospects within the statutory social services for anyone wishing to specialise in this type of work. Second, there is a lack of understanding of the potential of working with this group, because, as one writer put it:

Many people believe that work in the field of physical disability must be depressing because they have a vision of custodial care and of crippled lives filled with sadness and lost dreams. In actuality, rehabilitation of the physically disabled is especially rewarding because of the potential that exists in human beings in the face of stress, a potential that has seriously been underestimated.
(Trieschmann, 1980, p. xi)

Third, as has already been said, inappropriate teaching about disability on some training courses may mean that workers feel inadequate or incompetent when working with disabled clients. Finally, personal fears about impairment may mean that workers may be reluctant to get involved in what they perceive to be the personal and social consequences of adjusting to a human tragedy or disaster. But the major criticism is that social workers, like all other professionals, have largely operated with inappropriate models or theories of disability, and it is in a sense perhaps fortunate that social work intervention has been so limited. There have, of course, been several attempts to change this, both from within and outside the profession (Oliver 1983, 1991; Holdsworth, 1991; Stevens, 1991; Middleton, 1992, 1995; Morris, 1993, 1997a; Swain *et al.*, 1993; Thompson, 1993; Cavet, 1999; Oliver and Sapey, 1999; Moore *et al.*, 2000; Read and Clements, 2001; Harris, 2004), but there is little evidence that employers of social workers have made significant changes in the environments in which they practise. As Holdsworth pointed out:

The practice of empowerment social work can thus be seen to entail a radical shift in attitudes on the part of the social worker, and ultimately on the part of Social Services Departments and society as a whole, if continual conflict between individual social worker and employing agency is to be avoided. However, as societal and Social Services Department views are unlikely to change sufficiently rapidly, the individual social worker is likely to experience at least periodic conflict with her employing agency as she aligns herself with her client in an attempt to fulfil a jointly agreed-upon service need.
(Holdsworth, 1991, p. 10)

Before going on to consider an appropriate model of social work intervention, it is necessary to discuss why the current model is inappropriate. For this purpose the inadequate model will be referred to as the 'individual model' of disability.

The individual model of disability

The individual model of disability sees the problems that disabled people experience as being a direct consequence of their impairment. The major task of the professional is therefore to adjust the individual to the particular disabling condition. There are two aspects of this: first, there is physical adjustment through rehabilitation programmes designed to return the individual to as near normal a state as possible; and second, psychological adjustment that helps the individual to come to terms with his or her physical limitations. It is not just that social work had accepted the dominant, individual model of disability that is deeply embedded in social consciousness generally, but that the struggle for professional status and acceptance has also been involved: 'In a search for professional status, social work has emphasised a medical, psychotherapeutic, individualised model of work because that seemed the best way of asserting its expertise and professionalism' (Wilding, 1982, p. 97). It is possible to be critical of both these aspects of adjustment, and it is the latter that will be focused upon as it is of most relevance to social work, though there have been criticisms of the former also (Brechin and Liddiard, 1981; Barnes, 1991).

Starting from the assumption that something happens to the mind as well as to the body when a person becomes disabled, a number of psychological mechanisms of adjustment have been identified, or more appropriately borrowed from other areas such as death and dying. Disabled individuals are assumed to have undergone a significant loss, and as a result depression may set in. In order to come to terms with this loss, a process of grieving or mourning will have to be worked through, in similar manner to those who must mourn or grieve for the loss of loved ones. Only when such processes have been worked through can individuals cope with death or disability. As one Kleinian social work writer put it:

Illness and accidents at any age may confront us with slow or sudden loss of abilities. Denial of the limitations imposed can only lead to a superficial adjustment, which hides underlying persecution and depression. It is only when the work of mourning has been done and the anger, despair, and depression are eventually mitigated by love and courage, that the individual can go forward. If anger and despair predominate permanently, the individual regresses to an earlier stage of development, becoming self-centred, self-pitying, with a chip on his shoulder and begrudging others their freedom, or infinitely demanding of their time and attention. If the loss can be admitted, mourned and accepted with courageous resignation, a heightened appreciation of the remaining gifts and opportunities can lead to development in a different direction. (Salzberger-Wittenberg, 1970, p. 106)

These mechanisms are often seen as a series of stages or steps which have to be worked through. A study by social workers (Weller and Miller, 1977) in New York University Hospital identified a four-stage process by which newly disabled paraplegics come to terms with their disability:

Shock: The immediate reaction to the physical and psychic assault of spinal-cord injury, often characterised by weeping, hysteria, and occasionally psychosis with hallucinations.
Denial: A refusal to accept that complete recovery will not take place.
Anger: Often projected towards those physically active around them, who serve as constant reminders of what has been lost.
Depression: A realistic and most appropriate response to a condition of severe and permanent disability, and a necessary stage if adjustment, rehabilitation and integration are to be achieved.

Thus the social work task is to help disabled individuals through these adjustment stages.

Albrecht (1976) characterised this and various other schemes as developmental models and argued that they all, at least partially, assume that:

(a) an individual must move sequentially through all these stages to become fully socialised;
(b) there is only one path through the stages;
(c) an individual can be placed clearly in one stage by operational criteria;

(d) there is an acceptable time-frame for each stage and the entire process;
(e) movement through the system is one way, that is, the system is recursive.

It is not just in the case of spinal-cord injury that such models are considered appropriate; there are certainly similar ideas in the area, for example, of blindness. According to Carroll (1961, p. 11), 'loss of sight is dying. When in the full current of sighted life blindness comes on a man, it is the end, the death, of that sighted life'. In order to come to terms with this death, Fitzgerald (1970) identified four distinct phases in the typical reaction to the onset of blindness: disbelief, protest, depression and recovery.

There are a number of general criticisms that can be levelled at individualistic theories or explanations. First, these theories implicitly picture the individual as determined by the things that happen to him or her – and the adjustment to disability can only be achieved by experiencing a number of these psychological mechanisms or by working through a number of fixed stages. Second, adjustment is seen to be largely an individual phenomenon, a problem for the disabled person, and as a consequence the family context and the wider social situation are neglected. Finally, such explanations fail to accord with the personal experiences of many disabled people who may not grieve, mourn or pass through a series of adjustment stages. As Clark states; 'The loss of sight need not and usually does not touch the core of a man's intellect and emotional being. What has changed is his relationship with the external world, a relationship with which he had grown so familiar that he scarcely thought of it' (Clark, 1969, pp. 11–12).

However, it is not just in the field of disability that the 'stages' approach has been rejected. Thompson (2002a) draws attention to developments in the sociology of loss and grief that are a reaction to the over-prescriptive nature of psychological explanations of how people respond to death and dying. The dual process model is an attempt to understand why people do not follow these stages, but instead move between a loss and a restoration orientation. Rather than being a process that results in acceptance, the dual process model describes the way that people fluctuate in the way they deal with loss. Thompson argues that the advantages of this approach are that it 'moves us away from the narrow, psychologistic approach which presents grieving as a (largely biologically-based) natural process and alerts us to the complex web of psychological, cultural and socio-political factors which interact to make loss experiences far more complex than traditional approaches would have us believe' (Thompson, 2002a, p. 7).

Similarly, the meaning reconstruction approach of Neimeyer and Anderson (2002) also rejects the stages model. This model argues that there are three important aspects to reconstructing meaning after a loss: sense making, benefit finding and identity reconstruction. The ways in which people reconstruct meaning varies according to their individual psychological dispositions, spiritual beliefs and social support systems rather than through some predetermined psychological process.

Despite these criticisms, it would be true to say that the stages approach has made up the dominant, individual model of disability and this in itself needs to be explained. A major factor in this is that these theories are in accord with 'the psychological imagination', in that theorists have imagined what it would be like to become disabled, assumed that it would be a tragedy and hence decided that such an occurrence would require difficult psychological mechanisms of adjustment. Wilson (2003) for example, draws on Kleinian psychoanalysis to argue that we can distinguish certain commonalities amongst people with congenital impairments. In discussing one man who has been troubled by his difficulty with women not finding him sexually attractive, she concludes that

> Unlike non-disabled children, who try to deny that their existence is due to their parents' lovemaking, children born with an impairment feel connected to that sexual act. Their hatred of parental sexuality is often displaced onto themselves or others. Society's negative and often denigrating reaction to disability contributes to their perception that they must be the result of bad intercourse.
> (p. 100)

There is no foundation for this assertion; rather it is Wilson's application of a particular way of thinking in which she chooses to pathologise disabled people for the responses of others. The psychological imagination is clearly not an appropriate starting-point for such theorising or research – it is surely a value judgement to assume that disability is a tragedy rather than a phenomenon that might be explained in a number of ways.

Another factor is that these explanations, being individualistic, are thereby politically convenient. When a disabled person fails to internalise the rehabilitation goals set by the professionals, or persistently pesters his or her local social services department, he or she can be characterised as having problems in adjusting to the disability. This conveniently leaves the existing social world unchallenged; the goals of the rehabilitator remain unquestioned and the failure of the welfare department to provide the right assistance can be ignored.

While these and other factors may explain the adherence to these psychological theories, they do not explain why the theories have been validated empirically by a number of studies (Berger, 1988). In fact, these theories may become self-fulfilling in at least two ways. At a methodological level, having conditioned themselves in the sense that they posit adjustment to disability as a problem, researchers then ask questions relevant to that problem and get answers that are then presented as findings – valid social facts. Prior to the criticisms of this model by disabled people there had been few, if any, studies which started out from the assumption that disability was not an individual problem. The following quote illustrates the point nicely:

> Reflection on the many problems to which the cord injured person must make an adjustment impresses one with the gravity of the psychological processes which occur following cord injury.
>
> Such an individual is confronted with grieving over his loss, coping with pain and phantom sensations, alternations in sexual functioning, loss of bladder and bowel control, the frustrations of immobilisation, loss of vocational goals and earning capacity, feelings of uselessness, role reversals in the family and the attendant loss of self-esteem and the social stigma of being 'different' in the public eye. *It is an amazing tribute to the flexibility and magnificence of the human spirit that so many people whose lives are thus devastated survive and function at the level of physical and social independence which most cord injured people achieve.*
> [emphasis added] (Ibbotson, 1975, p. 5)

This quote accurately reflects the process of 'sanctification' of disabled people that is deeply embedded in the social consciousness and reinforced through stereotyped media presentations.

There is a polar opposite of this image which presents disability as a tragedy and personal disaster. As Shearer suggests:

The 'norm' demands that people whose disabilities are obvious and severe must be at least 'sad' and even 'tragic'. And if that defence breaks down in the face of individual reality, it is ready with its own flip-side. The reaction of people who break out of the mould becomes: 'Aren't they wonderful?' (Shearer, 1981b, p. 21)

In view of these images it is understandable that social workers are reluctant to get involved, as the scope of professional intervention with super-heroes or tragic victims must appear to be somewhat limited. However, the basic point remains: instead of questioning social reality with regard to disability, researchers simply proceed on the basis of taken-for-granted everyday meanings. But as so many disabled people are able to function at a reasonable level, it is surely more logical to assume that this is a normal, everyday reaction. To put the matter simply, adjustment may be normal and not a problem at all.

There is a second way in which these theories may become self-fulfilling, in that they may in fact create the reality they purport to explain. In the case of mental illness, it has been shown that psychiatrists impose their own definitions of the reality of particular problems on their patients. Similarly in the study of criminal behaviour, it has been shown that criminals will often verbalise theoretical explanations picked up in sessions with psychiatrists, psychologists and welfare workers as excuses for their behaviour even in compulsive crimes such as pyromania, kleptomania and child molestation. With regard to disability, many disabled people will have contact with the theories described above, not through meeting academic psychologists or participating in research projects, but through everyday contact with professional workers who are also internalising these theories.

Finkelstein has argued that the use of such concepts is nothing less than the imposition of standards of able-bodied normality on the meaning of disability for disabled individuals, engendered partly by the 'helper/helped' relationship:

The attitude that a disabled person has 'suffered' a personal loss is a value judgment based upon an unspoken acceptance of the standard being able-bodied normalcy. But attributing loss to disabled people is not just the whim of certain helpers. The existence of helpers/helped builds into this relationship normative assumptions. 'If they had not lost something they would not need help' goes the logic 'and since it is us, the representatives of society doing the help, it is this society which sets the norms for the problem solutions'. (Finkelstein, 1980, p. 17)

What is being suggested is that the psychological mechanisms and processes that research has identified and described are themselves the product of that research activity, both as a result of its methodological predispositions and the spread of this knowledge to professionals, who are then able to impose this definition of reality upon their clients. This is captured by Trieschmann, who asks:

Have professionals been describing phenomena that do not exist? Have professionals in clinical interactions placed disabled persons in a 'Catch 22' position? If you have a disability, you must have psychological problems: if you state you have no psychological problems, then this is denial and that is a psychological problem. And because this is so, have psychologists, psychiatrists, social workers and rehabilitation counsellors lost credibility with other rehabilitation personnel and with persons who have spinal cord injury, and rightly so? (Trieschmann, 1980, p. 47)

And it is not just a matter of losing faith, but, as she points out, disabled people 'have felt victimised by professionals who write articles about the reactions to spinal cord injury that are based more on theory than fact' (Trieschmann, 1980, p. xii).

The use by social work of psychological and physiological explanations of disability has been reinforced by the use of technology, a focus on quantifiable outcomes and the behaviourist nature of much evidence-based practice. The process of compartmentalising and coding 'abnormality' that is derived from the individual model is administratively convenient. The introduction of new technology with an algorithmic basis of analysis leads naturally to the selection of explanations that permit some quantifiable form of linking behaviour and need. Rather than seeking to understand the nature of the relationship between impairment and disability, the ⌐ instrumentally-driven bureaucratic processes that prevail (Blaug, 1995) seek an analysis that is compatible with the technology, and therefore it is of little surprise that the use of such classification systems are promoted as the way forward for social welfare (Ypren, 1996). ⌐

Despite the long-standing criticisms, it is clear that the individual model remains the dominant one with regard to disability and it has perhaps taken on the attributes of what Kuhn (1962) has called a 'paradigm' – that is, a body of knowledge to which all those working in the field adhere. However, the same writer has shown that paradigms are sometimes replaced or overthrown by 'revolution', and this revolutionary process is often sparked by one or two criticisms of the existing paradigm. Only then can a new paradigm develop to replace the old. Having provided one such criticism, it is now worth considering what a new paradigm – a 'social model' of disability – might look like.

A social model of disability

This new paradigm involves nothing more or less fundamental than a switch away from focusing on the physical limitations of particular individuals to the way the physical and social environments impose limitations upon certain groups or categories of people. Shearer captured the need for this change in paradigm in her criticism of the International Year of Disabled People:

⌐ The first official aim of the International Year of Disabled People in 1981 was 'helping disabled people in their physical and psychological adjustment to society'. The real question is a different one. How far is society willing to adjust its patterns and expectations to include its members who have disabilities, and to remove the handicaps that are now imposed on their inevitable limitations? (Shearer, 1981b, p. 10) ⌐

⌐ Adjustment within the social model, then, is a problem for society, not for disabled individuals. ⌐

For some, however, it is not just a matter of society's willingness to adjust its patterns and expectations, but one of removing the social oppression that stems from this failure to adjust. The Union of Physically Impaired Against Segregation (UPIAS) stated:

> In our view, it is society which disables physically impaired people. Disability is something imposed on top of our impairments by the way we are unnecessarily isolated and excluded from full participation in society. To understand this it is necessary to grasp the distinction between the physical impairment and the social situation, called 'disability', of people with such impairment. Thus we define impairment as lacking part of or all of a limb, or having a defective limb, organism or mechanism of the body: and disability as the disadvantage or restriction of activity caused by a contemporary social organisation which takes no or little account of people who have physical impairments and thus excludes them in the mainstream of social activities. Physical disability is therefore a particular form of social oppression.
> (UPIAS, 1976, pp. 3–4)

While both Shearer and UPIAS are advocating a social model of disability, there are differences in their views that need to be acknowledged. Shearer is asking society (that is, able-bodied society) to remove the disabilities imposed on impaired individuals, whereas UPIAS argue that such disabilities will only be removed by disabled people themselves who engage in active 'struggles'. Thus the former sees the reduction or removal of disability as something which may be given, whereas the latter sees it as having to be fought for. There are obviously different implications for professional practice stemming from these views, which can be encapsulated in asking professionals whether they wish to work for disabled people or with them.

This social model of disability, like all paradigms, has a fundamental effect on society's world view and, within that, the way particular problems are seen. If the problem of housing for disabled people is taken as an example, the individual model focuses on the problems that disabled people encounter in terms of getting in and out, bathing, access to the kitchen, the bedroom, and so on. In short, the approach focuses on the functional limitations of individuals in attempting to use their own environment. The social model, however, sees disability as being created by the way housing is unsuited to the needs of particular individuals. Thus we have 'housing disability'. A housing research project in Rochdale (Finlay, 1978) attempted to operationalise this concept by taking as given the 'reduced performance capabilities' of particular individuals and measuring instead the restrictions that unsuitable housing environments placed upon the individuals concerned. The implications of this approach for professionals involves a switch in emphasis away from the provision of personal aids (most of which are not used in any case) and remedial therapy and a move towards adapting environments so that they do not unduly restrict people with functional limitations.

The longer-term policy implications of this approach centre on

whether the policies most suited to their needs should adopt a preventative approach, in the form of more suitable housing provided in the community, or a remedial approach in the form of paramedical support provided either in the home or special institutions by people whose very intervention, if made unnecessarily, is by itself a disabling factor in the lives of physically handicapped people. **)**
(Finlay, 1978, p. 15)

(Applying a social model approach to housing is not just about physical access. In the case of disabled children it is also about issues such play space, safety, location and housing quality (Beresford and Oldman, 2002); it is about design that enables families with a disabled child to live together rather than resorting to institutional solutions such as respite care. In the case of visually impaired children, environmental factors become important and those living in more deprived areas find it more difficult to gain confidence and independence (Allen *et al.*, 2002). **)**

The same perspective can provide important insights in other areas: the well-known problems of finding out about benefit entitlements are examples of 'information disability' (Davis and Woodward, 1981). They argue that

(Information disability is a specific form of social oppression. In practice, it results in the disadvantage or restriction of activity caused not by the impairment of the individual – but by the way in our society we present, or withhold, information and prevent opportunity for full participation in the mainstream of social life. **)**
(Davis and Woodward, 1981)

When applied to the world of work, the social model of disability provides equally valuable insights:

The world of work (buildings, plant, machinery, processes and jobs, practices, rules, even social hierarchies) is geared to able-bodied people, with the objective of maximising profits. The growth of large-scale industry has isolated and excluded disabled people from the processes of production, in a society which is work centred.

(Swain, 1981, pp. 11–12)

This is crucial in late capitalist society, where individuals are still judged on what they do and appropriate social status is accorded. Hence it is not difficult to see that the dominant social perception of disabled people as 'dependent' stems not from their inability to work because of their physical limitations, but because of the way in which work is organised in modern industrial society.

According to Finkelstein (1980), this social model of disability may be applied most appropriately to physical impairments, but can also take in sensory impairments. For example, Deaf people may be disabled by the increasing use of the telephone, which restricts people who can communicate perfectly adequately at a face-to-face level, or meetings may be held in badly-lit rooms, so that they cannot see other participants adequately and follow the movements of their lips. Harris (1995) suggests that Deaf people who use British Sign Language (BSL) suffer a disadvantage because of linguistic isolation in employment situations where the majority of workers are hearing. In fact, pressure is exerted on Deaf workers to behave as much like hearing workers as possible – in effect, to 'deny' and make invisible their deafness. She argues that many Deaf people work in situations where there is a complete lack of meaningful communication between themselves and colleagues. The disadvantages suffered by Deaf people stem from a lack of tolerance and respect for linguistic difference by management and co-workers, and as such become individualised as a problem for Deaf workers to solve, rather than for hearing people to view as a challenge (Harris, 1997). However, Harris suggests that such a change in attitudes by hearing people and a willingness to learn BSL could radically alter the pattern of disadvantage and provide an empowering environment for Deaf people.

Sayce (2000) and Beresford (2004) both argue that the social model of disability has relevance for people with mental distress. Sayce describes a disability-inclusion model in which she calls for a two-pronged attack on the causes of stigma and social exclusion; first, strong anti-discrimination legislation; and second, the assertion of a positive identity by saying 'no to shame'. Both she and Beresford also recognise that there may be tensions, not least because the social model accept the notion of impairment, whereas many people labelled as 'mentally ill' would not see their 'distress' as an impairment.

Similarly, learning difficulties can be seen as less the problem of the intellectual impairment of certain individuals, but more related to general expectations about levels of social competence (Marks, 1999). As Dexter wrote:

> In our society, mental defect is even more likely to create a serious problem than it is in most societies because we make demonstration of formal skill at coordinating meanings (reading, writing and arithmetic) a requirement for initiation into adult social status, although such skills are not necessarily related to the capacity for effective survival or economic contribution.
> (in Boswell and Wingrove, 1974, p. 294)

Since its development there have been criticisms of the social model. Morris (1991) raised the concern that the social model might be oppressive if it is imposed in such a way as to deny the experience of individuals. Drawing on feminist criticisms of male theorising, she suggests that the danger lies in attempting to compartmentalize the personal feelings and experiences of people rather than grounding the political analysis in them. Crow (1996) supports this position and calls for the inclusion of impairment in the theorising of the social model:

> We need to take a fresh look at the social model of disability and learn to integrate all its complexities. It is critical that we recognise the ways in which disability and impairment work together. The social model has never suggested that disability represents the total explanation or that impairment doesn't count – that has simply been the impression we have given by keeping our experiences of impairment private and failing to incorporate them into our public political analysis.
> (Crow, 1996, p. 66)

Some disabled people do experience the onset of impairment as a personal tragedy, which, while not invalidating the argument that they are being excluded from a range of activities by a disabling environment, does mean it would be inappropriate to deny that impairment can be experienced in this way. Such reactions may themselves be caused by the extent to which the norms and values attached to the individual model have embedded themselves within our psyche. Drawing on Thomas's (1999) work about the psycho-emotional dimensions of disablism, Reeve (2002) discusses the way in which oppression becomes internalised for disabled people, not as a result of an individual psychological deficiency, but as a consequence of their treatment within a disabling society. The values of the social model have been shown to be effective in combating these effects. Tate *et al.* (1992) reported on a study which showed that people with spinal injuries who were put on an 'independent living program' at the time of their acute rehabilitation were able to adjust to their new circumstances with fewer negative psychological effects than those who received a more traditional, medically orientated service. Furthermore, many individual disabled people have borne, and continue to bear testament to the value of the social model to them personally:

> My life has two phases: before the social model of disability, and after it. Discovering this way of thinking about my experiences was the proverbial raft in stormy seas. It gave me an understanding of my life, shared with thousands, even millions, of other people around the world, and I clung to it. (Crow, 1996, p. 56)

Some researchers have attempted to incorporate a model of impairment that is consistent with the social model of disability. Creek *et al.* (1987), in their study of the social implications of spinal injury, used the theoretical approach of viewing impairment as a significant life event. As with other life events, individual reactions are related to a range of social and personal factors. This interactionist approach takes into consideration the prior experience of individuals, and acknowledges the impact this will have on the adjustment they make to change, while also being consistent with the social model of disability.

A further criticism of the social model was raised by Stuart (1994), who suggests that the social model has tended to be an exclusive analysis that had failed to acknowledge the multiple oppressions of black disabled people. He explains:

> The oppression of medicalisation and the potential for empowerment of the social model is as relevant to black disabled people as it is to any other disabled people. The legitimate point of view of this group should be perceived as, perhaps, broadening our understanding of the disabling process and the methods of achieving empowerment. It should also be acknowledged that these people might not accept that the social model, as it is currently theorised, will provide the intended liberation. To do so, it is important to acknowledge that disability itself has been racialised. In other words, the perception of disability differs depending upon the colour of an individual's skin or his or her ethnic identity.
> (Stuart, 1995, p. 372)

This experience of black disabled people suggests that racism is operating within the disability movement just as it is operating within other institutions in Britain and that organisations of disabled people are not in some way exempt or immune from acting oppressively towards black people. Ahmad (2000) argues that the social model may 'seem over-westernised' as it has come from a political movement that is historically and culturally specific. Furthermore, given the ways in which black disabled people experience the provision of social work services as racist (Begum et al., 1994), it is clearly necessary for the social model of disability to incorporate an understanding of these differing perceptions of disability if it is to provide an analysis that is inclusive.

As we explain further in Chapter 2, a key reason for understanding disability within a social model and rejecting individual explanations is that historically, experiences of disablement have been located culturally in responses to impairment (Gleeson, 1999; Borsay, 2005). Furthermore, the social model of disability is just that, a model, not a social theory. Therefore it has the capacity to be used to understand a range of different experiences rather than necessarily dictating to disabled people what their experiences should be; those experiences will undoubtedly be culturally located and reflect differences of class, race, gender and so on.

The overriding importance of this social model of disability is that it no longer sees disabled people as having something wrong with them – it rejects the individual pathology model. Hence, when disabled people are no longer able to perform certain tasks, the reasons are seen as the poor design of buildings, unrealistic expectations of others, the organisation of production, or an unsuitable housing environment. This inability therefore does not stem from deficiencies in the disabled individual. As Finkelstein (1980, p. 25) points out, 'The shift in focus from the disabled person to the environment implies a shift in the practical orientation of workers in the field.' What does this mean for social work? It is this question that will now be considered briefly.

The social model and its implications for social work

The social work profession has failed to give sustained consideration to physical disability, in terms either of theory or practice. However, as was suggested earlier, it is perhaps fortunate that there has been this lack of sustained interest, as social work has adopted the wrong model of disability. Outlining a social model of disability before going on to discuss some of its implications for social work practice goes against the current conventional wisdom, which suggests that theory should be practice-based rather than the other way round. Nevertheless, to rely on practice to inform theory when practitioners may have already internalised an inappropriate model is to invite disaster, as it would merely result in reinforcement of the individual model of disability at a theoretical level. Therefore, an attempt has been made to lay the theoretical base before considering some of the practice implications. This discussion will inevitably be brief, because it is for practitioners themselves to work out, in conjunction with their disabled clients, the full implications, and not for academics to extract practice blueprints from their theories.

If consideration is first given to the three main traditional social work approaches (casework, group work and community work), it is possible to make a number of statements relevant to practice. For example, the switch from an individual to a social model of disability does not signify the death of casework. Rather, it sees casework as one of a range of options for skilled intervention. It does not deny that some people may grieve or mourn for their lost able body, but suggests that such a view should not dominate the social

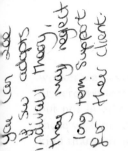

nt of what the problem may be. Thus grief work
ounselling may be appropriate in some instances,
even in most. Some disabled people, particularly
ssive diseases, may need long-term support of the
asework relationship can provide, and indeed the
whole family may become the target for casework intervention (see
Lenny, 1993; Oliver, 1995; Reeve, 2000, 2004; Lago and Smith,
2003, for a discussion of counselling). Equally, a casework
approach may be used to provide support to disabled people while
they are learning to use direct payments effectively.

Similarly, groupwork need not focus solely on the need to create
a therapeutic environment in which individuals or families can
come to terms with disability. Groups can also be used to pool
information on particular benefits, knowledge on where and how
to get particular services, and even on a self-help basis to give individuals the confidence to assert that their disability does not stem
from their impairments, but from the way society often excludes
them from everyday life. In addition the group can be used as the
major means of giving disabled people back the responsibility for
their own lives, as is described in a discussion on residential care:
'meetings in the small residential groups were a forum for staff and
residents to plan their activities and to determine priorities. They
gave the opportunity for residents to take responsibility for themselves and also for the staff to do "social work" ' (Dartington *et al.*,
1981, pp. 52–3).

The potential for intervention using community work methods is
also exciting. There are many local access groups that focus on the
way the physical environment disables people, and numerous
access reports and guides have been produced. Sometimes community workers have organised 'forum' meetings of all organisations
of, and for, disabled people in a particular locality and these have
proved useful in confronting local authorities about cut-backs, and
in ensuring that the needs of disabled people are taken into account
in pedestrianisation schemes and so on. Marian Barnes (1997)
argues strongly that community care needs to include community
participation:

> it has to involve rather more than the production of individ-
> ualised care packages, based on professional assessment of
> needs. It has to involve enabling people to participate in

decision making processes about services, and in social, economic and political life more broadly. The concept of 'care' is an inadequate one to describe what it is that needs to be delivered in order to enable people to live their lives within communities.
(Barnes, M., 1997, p. 172)

And if the definition of 'community' is expanded beyond its strictly geographical meaning to take in the idea of moral communities (Abrams, 1978) or psychic communities (Inkeles, 1964), or what the Barclay Committee (1982) referred to as 'communities of interest', then it is possible to see community work methods being used in disability organisations. For example, as far back as the 1980s the Spinal Injuries Association employed a welfare officer whose job was to enable its members to work out their own problems and solutions by utilising the collective wisdom and experiences of its paraplegic members through mutual support, peer counselling and the provision of information and advice (d'Aboville, 1991). This has since expanded into a comprehensive peer support service (see www.spinal.co.uk). Disabled people have also set up and continue to run centres for independent living (CILs) which undertake a community development role based on a social model (Barnes *et al.*, 2000a). CILs offer a range of services including mutual support in the use of direct payments (see www.ncil.org.uk).

In suggesting that theory should inform practice with regard to disability rather than vice versa, a number of developments in social work practice compatible with the social model of disability have obviously been ignored. There have undoubtedly been initiatives by individual social workers or departments that are not based on the individual model, and are indeed perfectly compatible with a social model of disability. For example, Essex County Council set up independent living teams, but these are described as islands of social model practice within the authority (James and Hutchins, 2003). But social work as a profession has not given systematic attention to developing a theoretical perspective on disability. Even within the vastly growing literature on anti-discriminatory practice, there is little evidence, with the notable exception of Thompson (1993, 2001), of a sustained application of the combating of oppression in relation to disability. Neither is there any sign of this in the USA, where Gilson and DePoy reach a similar conclusion: 'for the most part, the academy has taken the diagnostic approach to disability, viewing disability as a medical phenomenon to be understood by professionals and treated through the provision of services and supports that counterbalance personal deficits' (Gilson and DePoy, 2002, p. 157). Such theory has been developed elsewhere, notably by disabled people and their organisations. As a consequence, theory and practice have proceeded separately and have not merged into what was earlier called a 'paradigm' in respect of the individual model. It is crucial, however, that in future there is a merger between theory and practice in order to create an alternative paradigm to the one based on the individual model.

A useful framework for analysing the theoretical basis of services that can be used by social workers and their managers is that developed by Oliver and Bailey (2002) in a review of services in one local authority. The framework identifies three approaches to the provision of services: the humanitarian; compliance; and citizenship approaches.

The humanitarian approach

Under this approach, services are provided out of goodwill and the desire to help individuals and groups perceived as less fortunate. This leaves producers in control of these services, and users are expected to be grateful for receiving them. The outcome of this is often that producers think they are doing a good job, but users, when asked, are critical and are seen as being ungrateful.

This approach is set out in summary form below:

Providers:

● we know best;
● individual model – whereby the disabled person is the problem;
● doing clients a favour; and
● clients should be grateful.

Disabled people:

● don't like being patronised;
● reject individual model;
● not valued as people; and
● services not reliable.

Result:

- conflict;
- lack of trust;
- inadequate services; and
- poor levels of satisfaction.

The compliance approach

Under this approach, services are driven by government policy and legislation. Obviously the Disability Discrimination Act, 1995 is of prime importance here in respect of services to disabled people, but other legislation such as the Community Care (Direct Payments) Act, 1996, the NHS and Community Care Act, 1990 and the Chronically Sick and Disabled Persons Act, 1970 are also relevant. This often means that producers adopt a minimalist approach, to both to the principles and practice of service delivery, and do only what is necessary to comply with the law or government regulations. Service users often feel disgruntled because they think they are being denied something they are entitled to.

This approach is set out in summary form below:

Providers:

- meet laws, rules and regulations;
- check list approach;
- minimum standards; and
- lack of commitment or partnership.

Disabled people:

- rights not fully met;
- going through the motions;
- still service- rather than needs-led; and
- staff tend to own the task not the aim of the service.

Result:

- conflict;
- denial of entitlements and expectations;
- inadequate services; and
- poor levels of satisfaction.

The citizenship approach

This approach requires disabled people to be seen as full citizens, with all the rights and responsibilities that are implied. There are three dimensions to this approach:

● disabled people are seen as contributing members of society as both workers and valued customers (users);
● disabled people are recognised as empowered individuals (voters); and
● disabled people are seen as active citizens with all that implies in terms of rights and responsibilities.

Only when all three dimensions are met will the relationship between providers and users of services be a truly harmonious one. This is summarised below:

Economic dimension:

● disabled people as contributors/workers; and
● disabled people as customers.

Political dimension:

● disabled people (plus relatives and friends) as voters; and
● disabled people as powerful groups.

Moral dimension:

● disabled people are people too and have human rights.

Services to disabled people are still largely provided under the humanitarian and compliance approaches, and as some local authorities are already moving in the direction of a citizenship approach for other minority groups – for example, by setting quotas for the employment of people from ethnic minorities (Oliver, 2004) – there is no reason why they cannot do the same in respect of disabled people.

This has much in common with the 'paradigm' change being sought by Nelson *et al.* (2001) in relation to mental health in Canada. They argue that within the traditional paradigm, which includes medical-institutional and community treatment-rehabilitation approaches: people are treated as patients or clients, rather than citizens; the professionals remain in control; stigma, while recognized, is explained by individual deficits; and services are segregated. On the other hand, the new paradigm they see emerging from within user-controlled services places an emphasis on: consumer/survivor participation and empowerment; integration and support; and social justice. There is a strong sense of people being 'cared about', rather than 'cared for' and this is shown in their adoption of a feminist concept of power 'that is no longer based on individualism and "power over", but instead emphasizes "power with" ' (p. 22).

The citizenship approach, which appears to have support within the rhetoric of current government policies, is the only one that is compatible with the social model of disability. We shall be making use of this framework in revising this book, we hope we shall be making some initial recommendations for changing and adapting the more traditional approaches to professional social work.

Conclusions

To conclude this critical overview, it has been suggested that the track record of social work involvement with disabled clients has not been good. Social workers have either ignored disabled people and their needs or, when they have been involved, their interventions have been based on inappropriate assumptions about the nature of disability. Certainly, social work has failed to develop its theory and practice in terms of even the Seebohm view of seeing the disabled person in the context of family and community, let alone taking on board the implications of a fully developed social model of disability. There are, of course, reasons for this. Social work, like all other professions, has been unable to shake loose from the individual model generally embedded in social consciousness. It is also, of course, politically convenient to have the problem located in the individual — repeated requests for assistance can be explained away as signs of having a 'chip on the shoulder' or of a 'failure to adjust to disability'. More recently, the institutional structures within which social work operates have been organized to focus on the provision of services within strict budgetary limits. The rhetoric of 'needs-led' services has been outweighed by the instinct of organisations to ensure they are above criticism from a judicial review of their activities that would interpret need from an individual model.

The social model of disability has been articulated not just by individual disabled people, but by organisations of disabled people. As these developed in the 1960s and 1970s, it was possible to identify three distinct approaches adopted by these groups: the incomes approach; the self-help approach; and the populist approach. All these approaches, to a greater or lesser extent, built on the social model of disability, and such activities have tended to become consolidated, further exposing the contradictions between the individual and social models of disability. Today, some of the leaders from these organisations have moved into influential positions within the institutions set up to govern social work, and the message of the social model can no longer be ignored.

The social work profession has made some attempts to join with disabled people and their organisations – for example, the BCODP–BASW conference in Birmingham in 1986, though few formal links have been sustained. For many years it appeared to be the occupational group best placed to play a supportive role in the development of a new paradigm as, despite criticisms, it is possibly less tied to the individual model of disability than are paramedical professions such as occupational therapy, and it has a range of methods of work, skills and techniques that are well suited to working within the social model of disability. The rewards for social workers would arise from the enhanced professional and personal satisfaction that stems from both the increased range of tasks in which to exercise professional skills, and the greater potential for achieving change. In working with disabled people the social work task can no longer be one of adjusting individuals to personal disasters, but rather in helping them to locate the personal, social, economic and community resources to enable them to live life to the full.

In the following chapters, some of the themes developed will be pursued in relation to issues concerning social work practice. It should be re-emphasised, however, that this does not mean that what follows will be a practical manual on 'how to do social work with disabled people within the social model of disability'. Rather, it will be an orientating perspective enabling social workers to develop their practice in conjunction and in partnership with their disabled clients.

putting it into practice

Exercise 1

It has been argued in this chapter that the individual model of disability has dominated social work. One factor in this domination is the language we use. A useful exercise is to examine the language being used to describe disabled people in conversation, in newspapers or on the TV. For example; what does the term 'wheelchair-bound' mean? Why are people referred to as 'sufferers'?

1. Make a list of all the words or phrases you find or have heard and decide if they are negative, positive or neutral.
2. Ask yourself how they influence the way you think about disabled people.
3. Ask yourself if these terms make you more or less fearful of impairment.

Exercise 2

Take the characteristics (below) of the Humanitarian and Compliance approaches to welfare attributed to providers and use them to examine the approach of a welfare society with which you are familiar.

Humanitarian
- we know best
- individual model – whereby the disabled person is the problem
- doing clients a favour
- clients should be grateful

Compliance
- met laws, rules and regulations
- check list approach
- minimum standards
- lack of commitment or partnership

Discuss and decide what changes would have to be made for that agency to move to the Citizenship approach.

Further reading

Oliver, M. (1996) *Understanding Disability, From Theory to Practice*, London: Macmillan. A collection of essays which explore the implications of the social model of disability across a range of topics.

Oliver, M. and Barnes, C. (1998) *Disabled People and Social Policy*, Harlow: Longman. An accessible introduction to the analysis of social policy from the perspective of the social model of disability.

Sayce, L. (2000) *From Psychiatric Patient to Citizen*, Basingstoke: Palgrave. Utilises the social model of disability as an alternative approach to overcoming the stigma associated with mental ill-health.

2 | Thinking about disability

A major theme of this book is that social work, as an organised professional activity, has given little thought to the problems of disability, and where it has, it has merely reproduced traditional thinking in its application to social work practice. A second theme of the book is that much of this traditional thinking about disability is inaccurate and incorrect, at least in that it is incongruent with the personal experiences of many disabled people. A third theme will be to develop more appropriate thinking about disability, and to draw out some of its implications for the practice of social work.

There are three main sources upon which to draw when considering the question 'What is disability?' There is social consciousness generally, there are professional definitions of disability, and there are personal realities, as articulated by disabled people themselves. Each of these sources needs to be considered separately.

General views of disability

It has already been suggested that the now-dominant view of disability is one of personal tragedy or disaster. However, this is not true of all societies, and some may regard disability as a sign of being chosen, of possession by God or the devil. In short, disability does not have meanings that are similar in all cultures, nor indeed within the same culture is there always agreement about what disability actually is. As two anthropologists have noted:

> A class of persons grouped together under the term 'physically handicapped' is at best difficult to treat as ethnological data. Here for us is a category of persons with social liabilities peculiar to the conditions of our society. It represents no logical or medical class of symptoms. For example, carrot-colored hair is a physical feature and a handicap in certain social situations, but a person with this characteristic is not included in this class. Nor is the symptom itself the only criterion, for though the person afflicted with infantile paralysis

may limp as a result of the disease and be deemed to be handicapped, yet the person with an ill-fitting shoe or a boil on his foot who also limps will be excluded.

When one introduces the concepts of other cultures than our own, confusion is multiplied. Even assuming the existence of such a class in other societies, its content varies. The disfiguring scar in Dallas becomes an honorific mark in Dahomey.

(Hanks and Hanks, 1980, p. 11)

Variations in cultural views of disability are not just a random matter, however, but differences may occur as a result of a number of factors, such as the type of social structure; for example, restricted mobility is less likely to be a problem in an agricultural society than in a hunting and gathering one. And the way production is organised also has implications for 'the speed of factory work, the enforced discipline, the time-keeping and production norms – all these were a highly unfavourable change from the slower, more self-determined and flexible methods of work into which many handicapped people had been integrated' (Ryan and Thomas, 1980, p. 101).

Gleeson (1999), who from a social model perspective undertook an historical geographical analysis of disability, concluded that this approach 'recognises the material reality of impairment while stressing the specific ways in which this form of embodiment is socialised in different times and places' (p. 195). Thus the social structure and values of a society are important in shaping cultural views of disability. A hierarchical structure based on values of individual success through personal achievement means inevitably that most disabled people will be low in the hierarchy on the basis of their reduced ability to compete on equal terms with everyone else. Societies whose central values are religious may well interpret disability as punishment for sin or possession by the devil, or conversely as a sign of being chosen by God.

These and other factors shape social attitudes to disability. The point is that the general view of disability as a personal disaster – an individual tragedy – is a culturally specific one, and not necessarily the only view. Certainly, the view of disability as a personal disaster is a common one in modern industrial societies, but there are considerable variations in professional conceptions of disability and their implications for the provision of services and for professional intervention. Scott (see Douglas, 1970) has demonstrated this clearly in his analysis of blindness in the USA, Sweden, Britain, Italy and France. The rest of this chapter is concerned with the way this general view is translated into professional conceptions of disability in Britain, and the implications of this for social work.

Current professional definitions of disability

Brechin and Liddiard (1981) have suggested that there may be as many as twenty-three different professionals involved with a disabled individual, though they do not, of course, all use different definitions. Townsend (1979) has suggested that these definitions can be divided into five broad categories: abnormality or loss; clinical condition; functional limitation; deviance; and disadvantage. No single one of these is right or wrong, but rather they are developed for specific purposes or situations, and all can be criticised on various grounds.

1. *Abnormality or loss*   This may be anatomical, physical or psychological loss, it may refer to loss of a limb or part of the nervous system, or of a sense modality (for example, deafness or blindness). The existence of either may not necessarily be disabling. Someone who has lost both legs may well have a very hectic social life, whereas someone else with a minor facial blemish may never go out because of it.

2. *Clinical condition*   This will refer to diseases or illnesses which alter or interrupt physical or psychological processes. Arthritis, epilepsy, bronchitis and schizophrenia are examples of such definitions, although the very existence of schizophrenia is challenged as part of psychiatric folklore (Bentall, 1998). Diagnosis, however, is often difficult with conditions like schizophrenia and epilepsy, and there has been controversy over whether a number of former miners had bronchitis or pneumoconiosis. If they had the former, they were not entitled to compensation; whereas, if they had the latter, they were. Learning difficulties is another difficult area, for there is often no clinical diagnosis, but rather attempts to assess social competence, or possibly measure IQ.

3. *Functional limitations of everyday activities*   This refers
   to the inability, or at least restricted ability, to perform
   normal personal or social tasks such as washing and dressing, doing the shopping, negotiating steps or going to the
   cinema. There are obvious difficulties in establishing objective standards against which abilities can be measured and
   which take into account other factors such as age, sex and
   motivation. External factors are also important: someone
   in a wheelchair in a non-adapted house may be limited
   functionally, but not so in an adapted one. Additionally,
   this definition often leads to the debatable assertion that
   'we will all be disabled one day', in that everyone becomes
   functionally limited by the ageing process. This is normal
   and expected, and while various professional definitions
   may regard many old people as disabled, it does not follow
   that they themselves, or society at large, agree with this
   definition.
4. *Disability as deviance*   There are two separate aspects of this
   that need to be considered: first, deviation from accepted physical and health norms; and second, deviation from behaviour
   appropriate to the social status of particular individuals or
   groups. In seeing disability as deviation from particular norms,
   the problem arises in specifying what those norms are and who
   defines them. A similar problem arises with regard to deviant
   behaviour: who specifies what normal and appropriate behaviour is, and with reference to what? Deviation from behaviour
   appropriate to the non-disabled, or behaviour appropriate to
   disabled normality?
5. *Disability as disadvantage*   This refers to the allocation of
   resources to people at specific points in the social hierarchy,
   and in the case of disabled people they often receive less than
   their non-disabled counterparts. This broadens the concept of
   disability considerably, as it is not just those with physical
   impairments who are socially disabled – so are illiterate
   people, alcoholics and one-parent families, plus, perhaps,
   ethnic minorities and women.

Since 1995 a new definition has begun to emerge, particularly in
government research and policy documents – that of 'DDA
disabled'. This refers to people who qualify for legal protection

under the definitions of the Disability Discrimination Act, 1995, which defines a disabled person as someone who has a mental or physical impairment that has an adverse effect on his or her ability to carry out normal day-to-day activities. The adverse effect has to be substantial and long-term, which means of at least twelve months duration. However, as this gives people certain rights, contesting whether someone is disabled has become the first line of defence of many employers whose actions have been challenged under the Act (Gooding, 2003), adding further layers to the confusion of definition.

Thus there are a number of definitions of disability, none of which presents the whole picture or is the right answer, because, as Townsend puts it:

> Although society may have been sufficiently influenced in the past to seek to adopt scientific measures of disability, so as to admit people to institutions, or regard them as eligible for social security or occupational or social services, these measures may now be applied in a distorted way, or may not be applied at all, or may even be replaced by more subjective criteria by hard-pressed administrators, doctors and others. At the least, there may be important variations between 'social' and objective assessments of severity of handicap. (Townsend, 1979, p. 688)

In the remainder of this chapter, functional definitions will be considered in more detail, particularly in view of the fact that these are currently the definitions upon which access to social services departments and the services they provide usually depend.

Functional definitions of disability

There have been various piecemeal attempts to gather statistics about disabled people, beginning with the census of 1851, which asked questions about blindness and deafness. However, these questions were dropped in 1921, and for seventy years no census attempted to gather information about disability, largely on the methodological grounds that it is too difficult to frame appropriate questions in such a general survey. Since 1991, the census has included a question asking respondents if any member of their household had a limiting long-term illness, and other surveys have included questions about work-limiting disability, or whether people are disabled in terms of the Disability Discrimination Act.

Legislative measures, such as the repealed Disabled Persons (Employment) Act, 1944 and the National Assistance Act, 1948, required that registers be kept, but only for those in receipt of services, not as any systematic attempt to estimate numbers and establish needs. By the 1960s it was obvious that there was not much data available to facilitate the expansion of services for disabled people as part of the general programme of increased welfare expenditure. Accordingly, the then Ministry of Health instigated a research programme that was to culminate in the mammoth study by the Office of Population Censuses and Surveys (OPCS) (Buckle, 1971; Harris, 1971) whereby nearly a quarter of a million households were surveyed. The exercise was repeated, with some methodological changes, in 1986 (Martin et al., 1988), when 100,000 private households and an unstated number of communal establishments were screened. From the first survey, 8,538 households were followed up and interviewed in depth, while the second involved approximately 10,000 adults in private households and 4,000 in communal establishments. In 1996/7 the Department of Social Security (Grundy et al., 1999) conducted a survey of 7,000 people using very similar questions to the 1986 survey, and more recently, in their current guise as the Department for Work and Pensions, they have attempted to estimate the numbers of people covered by the Disability Discrimination Act (Grewal et al., 2002).

Functional assessments of disability were used in each of these studies, and while there was some change in the wording of the definitions, the first three were all based on the World Health Organization's (WHO) International Classification of Impairment, Disability and Handicap, as follows:

Impairment
'Any loss or abnormality of psychological, physiological or anatomical structure or function.' [Here we are dealing with parts or systems of the body that do not work.]

Disability
'Any restriction or lack (resulting from an impairment) of ability to perform an activity in the manner or within the range considered normal for a human being.' [Here we are talking about things people cannot do.]

Handicap
'A disadvantage for a given individual, resulting from an
impairment or disability, that limits or prevents the fulfilment of a role (depending on age, sex and social and cultural
factors) for that individual.' [This is in relation to a particular environment and relationships with other people.]
(Martin *et al.*, 1988, p. 7)

The measurement of the extent of 'handicap' in the first study
was based on a series of questions regarding people's capacity to
care for themselves. The response to each question was graded
according to whether the activity could be managed without difficulty, with difficulty, or only with help. Some activities were
regarded as being more important than others, and measurements
were weighted accordingly. The most important items were:

(a) getting to and using the toilet;
(b) eating and drinking; and
(c) doing up buttons and zips.

Other items were:

(d) getting in and out of bed;
(e) having a bath or all-over wash;
(f) washing hands and face;
(g) putting on shoes and stockings;
(h) dressing other than shoes or socks;
(i) combing and brushing hair (women only); and
(j) shaving (men only).

The responses to these questions were collected, and as a consequence disabled people were divided into four categories: (i) very
severely handicapped; (ii) severely handicapped; (iii) appreciably
handicapped; and (iv) impaired. According to this functional
measurement, it was estimated that there were just over 3 million
impaired people, or 7.8 per cent of the total population. The Harris
survey also highlighted two other important facts: that disablement
increases with age; and that disabled women begin to outnumber
disabled men in the older age groups (see Figure 2.1).

Overall, there were considerably more disabled women in the
population than there were disabled men, but within the age structure there were significant variations. In fact, up to the age of 50,

Figure 2.1 Prevalence per 1,000 men and women in different age groups, with some impairment, in private households in Great Britain, 1971

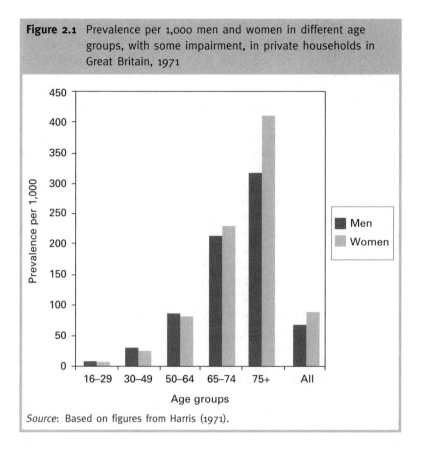

Source: Based on figures from Harris (1971).

both in sheer numbers and prevalence, more men were likely to be defined as disabled than women. Two possible reasons are: (i) many more men risk disablement through accidents at work and work-induced illnesses; and (ii) many more young males take part in dangerous sports and leisure activities – for example, motorcycle riding, rugby, mountaineering and so on. Consequently, these figures reflect sexual divisions within society whereby certain activities, in both work and leisure, are dominated by males. But after the age of 50, not only are there more disabled women in total, but their prevalence in the population is also greater. This is a reflection of the fact that women live longer than men, coupled with the fact that prevalence of a significant number of impairing conditions increases with ageing. Additionally, of course, functional definitions of disability use measures of physical capabilities, and as these inevitably decline with ageing, more and more elderly people are defined as disabled.

The gender differences are more pronounced when looking at particular groups of disabled people. Sapey (1995), for example, found that there were twice as many women as men in receipt of NHS wheelchairs from one Disablement Services Centre (DSC) in 1993, a pattern confirmed by the College of Occupational Therapists (1996) and Sapey *et al.* (2004a). While most of this difference was made up of people over 65 years of age, it begins in the 35 to 40 age group. Below this age there is a slightly higher incidence of wheelchair use among men. It should also be noted that the College of Occupational Therapists (1996) found that about two-thirds of those over 60 years did not use their wheelchairs all the time, usually because they were ambulant indoors.

The Harris study formed the basis for much subsequent thinking about disability, and played an important role in the planning and development of services. However, there are a number of important criticisms that can be levelled.

Townsend has suggested that the Harris study adopted too narrow a definition of disability and therefore grossly underestimated the numbers of disabled people in the population: 'disability itself might be best defined as inability to perform the activities, share in the relationships and play the roles which are customary for people of broadly the same age and sex in society' (Townsend, 1979, p. 691). In operationalising his broader definition in his massive survey of poverty, he concluded that there were three times as many 'handicapped' people as Harris suggested. Table 2.1 illustrates the differences in numbers produced by these two surveys.

There are two points of clarification that need to be made. First, the Harris figure of 1,297,000 individuals with 'no handicap' refers to people who have impairments but are not restricted, at least according to this particular definition. Second, the Townsend figure of 2,890,000 people with little or no 'handicap' includes 180,000 children between the ages of 0–9. Children were specifically excluded from the Harris survey.

The figures produced by Harris did not prove reliable in estimating the cost of introducing new benefits, nor indeed did they always match with data collected by government for other

Table 2.1 Disabled people in Great Britain: two national surveys

Harris (1971)		Townsend (1979)	
Degree of handicap	Total numbers	Degree of incapacity	Total numbers
Very severe	161,000	Very severe	325,000
Severe	366,000	Severe	780,000
Appreciable	633,000	Appreciable	1,990,000
Minor	699,000	Some	3,915,000
No handicap	1,297,000	Little or none	2,890,000
Total	3,146,000	Total	9,900,000

purposes. According to Jaehnig (in Boswell and Wingrove, 1974, p. 449, n. 2), on the introduction of the attendance allowance it was estimated from the Harris survey that there were approximately 25,000 people entitled to it – yet in the first year alone there were more than 72,000 successful applicants. And Topliss pointed out:

> From the government survey in 1969 it was estimated there were 697,000 impaired men and women in the labour force or temporarily off sick or actively seeking work. Only 176,000 of these were classified as substantially handicapped by their impairments. On the other hand, there were in 1978 over half a million names on the Disabled Persons Employment Register, kept by the Employment Services Agency, and yet it was thought that only one third of those eligible to register in fact were registered. This would suggest that there are substantially more than the estimated 697,000 impaired people in the work force.
> (Topliss, 1979, p. 48)

She went on to suggest that this discrepancy is 'undoubtedly due to the different definitions of disability employed', in that many people who may have few or minor functional limitations may nevertheless be severely disabled in obtaining employment.

Functional definitions were not acceptable to all, and Finkelstein suggested that these definitions located the causes of disability at the level of the individual, whereas 'the cause of handicap lies within the society which disadvantages impaired people . . . handicap is caused by having steps into buildings and not inability to walk' (in Finlay, 1978, app. 7). Finkelstein then proposed a reversal of the Harris terminology along the following lines:

> Firstly, that the cause of handicap lies within the society which disadvantages impaired people by taking no, or very little account of their physical condition and consequently does not provide the solutions, for example providing ramps for wheelchair users who are unable to walk up steps . . . Secondly, I suggest changing the definitions of the words handicap and disability around. In this way a person is disabled when he or she is socially prevented from full participation by the way society is arranged.
> (in Finlay, 1978, app. 7)

While there were very real and important criticisms of the Harris work, it did at least attempt to obtain the extent of the problems of disability in a coherent and systematic way. Unfortunately, while the Harris survey recognised the social dimension of disability, it still attempted to utilise an individual measure and to locate the problems of disability within the individual. Bury (1996) argues that this resulted in the identification of the consequences of disability, but not in any greater financial compensation or consideration of disabled people's views. He suggests that

> In part this arose from the continuing part that medicine played, within administrative circles, in adjudicating access to benefits. In order to tackle this problem, and provide new estimates of disability based on a broader definition, a new national study was commissioned by the OPCS in 1984, and several surveys, including one on children, were carried out between 1985 and 1988. The main purpose of this new initiative was to inform a review of social security in the disability field, and pave the way for such benefits to be based on a more systematic appreciation of the relational character of disability.
> (Bury, 1996, p. 21)

These new surveys continued to make use of the World Health Organization (WHO) definitions of impairment, disability and handicap, but attempted to be more sensitive than their predecessors. This time the surveys produced ten categories of severity

Table 2.2 Estimates of the numbers of disabled adults and children in Great Britain, by severity category

Severity category	Adults	Children
10	210,000	34,000
9	365,000	25,000
8	396,000	31,000
7	486,000	46,000
6	545,000	38,000
5	708,000	43,000
4	704,000	43,000
3	750,000	48,000
2	840,000	19,000
1	1,198,000	33,000
Total	6,202,000	360,000

Sources: Martin *et al.*, 1988; Bone and Meltzer, 1989.

rather than the four used by Harris. Pen pictures of people who had been categorised were provided in the reports to illustrate the meaning of each of these. Table 2.2 shows the results of the surveys in terms of their estimations of adults and children into the different severity categories.

What is immediately apparent is that these surveys revealed twice as many disabled adults (6,202,000) as had Harris, and a further 360,000 disabled children. However, as Abberley (1992) has argued, if the people in the least severe categories (1–3), who would probably not have qualified for inclusion in Harris's 'impaired' category, were to be removed, then the total remains similar to that in the earlier study. One of the results of this is that the surveys underestimated the additional costs of disablement, as the respondents were predominantly in the lower categories. In their own surveys of severely disabled adults, the Disablement Income Group found the average extra weekly expenditure to be 58 per cent higher than the OPCS estimates (Abberley, 1992).

Martin *et al.* (1988) confirmed Harris's earlier findings concerning the prevalence of disability among different age groups (see Table 2.3), and as Bury (1996) argues, they should be commended

Table 2.3 Estimates of prevalence of disability among adults, by age and severity category, men and women (cumulative rate per 1,000 population)

Severity category	Men, age group				Women, age group			
	16–59	60–74	75 and over	Total	16–59	60–74	75 and over	Total
10	1	5	21	3	1	4	45	6
9–10	3	17	64	9	4	18	102	17
8–10	6	31	107	16	8	31	154	28
7–10	10	46	150	24	13	50	224	42
6–10	14	62	191	32	19	73	293	58
5–10	20	87	250	45	28	106	369	78
4–10	27	117	309	58	36	136	431	97
3–10	34	155	369	73	44	172	495	115
2–10	41	207	442	92	51	213	561	135
1–10	56	283	533	121	64	264	631	161

Source: Extracted from Martin *et al.*, 1988, p. 22, table 3.7.

for not identifying the age of respondents initially and therefore not making the assumption that certain functional limitations were caused by old age and, by implication, therefore were not an impairment. The surveys confirmed that disability was far more prevalent in older age groups, with almost 70 per cent being over 60 years of age.

However, the OPCS estimates were notably lower than the estimates of prevalence from the 1985 General Household Survey (GHS) in all age groups below 75 years. Martin *et al.* (1988) explain this by the design of their survey, which only included people who were limited in specific activities, whereas the GHS counted limitations to any activity. The lower incidence in the GHS estimates after 75 years of age is accounted for by the probability that many older people might not perceive themselves as being limited by illness, disability or infirmity, but by age, and therefore would not have been counted by the GHS. The follow-up to this survey in 1996/7 estimated that the numbers of disabled adults living in private households in Great Britain was 8,582,200, or 20 per cent of the adult population (Grundy *et al.*, 1999).

There are clearly some key methodological and definitional problems in trying to estimate the prevalence of disability through functional definitions. This is reinforced by the 2001 Census, which found yet another figure of 9,484,856 adults and children in England and Wales with a 'limiting long-term illness'. This represented 18.2 per cent of the population, and the variance between regions ranged from 23.3 per cent in Wales to 15.4 per cent in the South East of England (neighbourhood.statistics.gov.uk). These variations are very similar to those identified on the Labour Force Survey of 2003 (www.statistics.gov.uk), which is used by the Disability Rights Commission (www.drc-gb.org). According to this source there are 6.86 million disabled people of working age, or 19 per cent of the population. Bajekal *et al.* (2004) have made comparisons of different methodological approaches to counting disabled people, and find that while most of the main surveys are reasonably close when it comes to adults of working age, there are wide variances with other groups, particularly older people. The problem, however, is more than one of accuracy, as Barnes states: 'this approach creates artificial distinctions and barriers between disabled people and the rest of society which, at best, prolong ignorance and misunderstanding and, at worst, nourish and sustain ancient fears and prejudices' (Barnes, 1991, p. 25).

The International Classification of Impairment, Disability and Handicap (ICIDH) definitions upon which the OPCS studies were based, was published in 1980. Widely regarded as the most comprehensive catalogue of its kind, it was used as a basis for government initiatives on disability in both the developed and developing world. However, the ICIDH was not successful as a tool to classify disabled people, and there have been very few studies that have managed to operationalise it properly. Even the United Nations (Despouy, 1993) failed to make use of it. Consequently, the WHO sought to revise the whole scheme and to add a fourth, environmental, dimension. This has resulted in the International Classification of Functioning, Disability and Health (ICF), endorsed by the World Health Assembly in 2001.

Through the ICF the WHO seeks to create a biopsychosocial model which, they argue, should incorporate what is right from both the social and 'medical' models of disability. Furthermore, they sought to end the distinction that existed between illness and disability by use of two separate classification systems. To achieve this, the ICF makes a distinction between a health condition, impairment, activity limitation and participation restriction (World Health Organization, 2002). However, this effectively continues the distinctions of the ICIDH with activity limitation replacing disability, and participation restriction replacing handicap, with the difference that the causes of these are explained as arising from socially constructed barriers. While in the ICF, the environment is specifically included, the basic methodological approach remains one that assumes that not only can the components of each level be reduced to numbers, so also can the complex relationships between them. Hence the scientific rationality on which the medical approach is founded remains unchanged in the new scheme and there is every reason to suppose that the ICF will be even more difficult to operationalise than its predecessor. Thus, while the ICF is likely to provide more work for research, social and medical scientists, it is unlikely to contribute any more to improving the lives of disabled people than did the ICIDH.

The ICIDH conceived the social dimensions of disability as arising from the 'abnormality' of impairment. The argument for the social model of disability is that the causal relationship begins with the reactions of mainstream society to people with impairments that oppress and exclude them. Part of this oppression is the imposition of an understanding of disability that blames the individual. Oliver (1990) has argued that this was clearly apparent in the face-to-face interviews within the 1986 OPCS Disability Surveys. By rewording some of the questions used by the researchers, he demonstrates the way in which respondents were influenced to consider themselves as inadequate:

Questions from 1986 Disability Surveys

- What complaint causes your difficulty in holding, gripping or turning things?
- Are your difficulties in understanding people mainly due to a hearing problem?
- Do you have a scar, blemish or deformity which limits your daily activities?
- Have you attended a special school because of a long-term health problem or disability?
- Does you health problem/disability mean that you need to live with relatives or someone else who can look after you?

Alternative questions (Oliver, 1990)

- What defects in the design of everyday equipment like jars, bottles or tins causes you difficulty in holding, gripping or turning them?
- Are your difficulties in understanding people mainly due to their inabilities to communicate with you?
- Do other people's reactions to any scar, blemish or deformity you may have, limit your daily activities?
- Have you attended a special school because of your education authority's policy of sending people with your health problem or disability to such places?
- Are community services so poor that you need to rely on relatives or someone else to provide you with the right level of personal assistance?

Bury (1996) is critical of this approach to the analysis of the OPCS surveys, and points out their positive role in highlighting the predominance of chronic illnesses such as arthritis and hearing loss as causes of impairment. He argues that this helps to explain not only the higher prevalence among older people, but also the gender differences, and goes on to suggest that

> no matter how justifiable the attempt is to influence the direction of the operation of welfare, and notably social security, away from medical adjudication, a full picture of disablement in contemporary populations inevitably exposes its health and illness dimensions. From the viewpoint of everyday experience, therefore, different aspects of health and welfare needs may be relevant. Moreover, these dimensions have implications for different forms of intervention on the impairment, disability and handicap continuum.
> (Bury, 1996, p. 22)

Both the criticisms from Oliver and Barnes and the support of Bury for the OPCS surveys have at their heart a concern for the impact of the research on the lives of disabled people. It is helpful in examining this to look at the ways in which research has been operationalised within social work. While the results of the Harris survey were being published, the Chronically Sick and Disabled Persons Act, 1970 was making its way through Parliament. Its very first section stated:

It shall be the duty of every local authority having functions
under section 29 of the National Assistance Act 1948 to
inform themselves of the number of persons to whom that
section applies within their area and of the need for the
making by the authority of arrangements under that section
for such persons.

So it was not just a matter of counting heads, but also of making
provision to meet need.

The main reason for including this section was not merely to
identify the numbers of disabled people in particular local authority areas, as that could have been done by reference to the Harris
survey, which had analysed its data in this fashion, but rather to
identify each disabled individual in a particular area. As Topliss
and Gould (1981, p. 90) put it, 'There can be no doubt, therefore,
that the original intention of Alf Morris was that local authorities
should identify, person by person, the handicapped individuals in
their respective areas.' However, under guidance from the DHSS,
local authorities were directed towards making assessments of
numbers rather than attempting to identify specifically every
disabled individual. All local authorities complied with this duty
either by carrying out house-to-house surveys or sample surveys, or
by using other methods.

These surveys provided a picture of disability, at least in terms of
age, gender and severity of disability, at the local level that was
broadly similar to the national picture found by Harris. However,
in numerical terms, the numbers of disabled people on local authority registers in England in 1980 was 900,669. Thus it is clear that
social services departments had located only one in three disabled
people, at least according to the Harris estimate of numbers.

Nowhere in the Chronically Sick and Disabled Persons Act,
1970 was the idea of a register mentioned, but as the keeping of a
register of disabled people was made a requirement of the National
Assistance Act, 1948, many local authorities decided that keeping
one was the way to meet their duty under section 1. There are problems in keeping registers, however. First, some people may feel that
inclusion on a register is an invasion of privacy and may be stigmatising. While all sorts of actions may be taken to reduce the
stigma, it cannot be removed entirely as these registers represent the
control and dominance of the administrative model of welfare,

which, as Finkelstein has argued, assumes 'that disability means social death necessitating interventions by able-bodied professionals and lay workers who then 'administer' the cure or care solutions' (Finkelstein, 1991, p. 27). Second, it is difficult to keep registers up to date and in line with the changing circumstances and capabilities of those registered. Finally, Warren *et al.* (1979) showed that registers are likely to be extremely inaccurate (by up to 30 per cent or more). Even with the help of new technology and its promise of efficiency in record-keeping, the level of accuracy has changed little, and the problems of updating information remain (Glastonbury, 1995). The most telling criticism of registration, however, is that there is only a tenuous link between it and the provision of services (Topliss and Gould, 1981). Registration is not a requirement for receiving a service, and neither has it guaranteed that disabled people are informed about what services are available. The lack of information that disabled people receive remains a key issue (Department of Health, 2000) as it is central to ensuring that people are able to seek the assistance to which they may be entitled.

Finally, the criteria for registration offers considerable discretionary powers to those doing the registering, both in terms of the resources available in a given area and the personal whims of those undertaking the registration process (Satyamurti, 1981).

Despite the clear problems that had been identified, the keeping of registers of disabled children became a requirement under Schedule 2 of the Children Act, 1989. Middleton (1995) made a similar point, about these being an infringement of civil liberties, as Barnes had of the large-scale surveys of disability; it amounts to a process of problematising all disabled children in a way that would be totally unacceptable if it were any other identifiable group of the population. Middleton also made the point that where local authorities attempted to defend this practice, they did so on the grounds that it would help their planning of services. This she described as

chilling in the extreme, since it suggests that they have some preconceived notion of what the future holds in terms of needs of disabled children, and adults, for services. Given the apparent lack of imagination of many local authorities this can only mean pre-programming children either for day care of for its current substitute of everlasting segregated education.
(Middleton, 1995, p. 7)

The problem of registration for social work, particularly when viewed from a social model of disability, is a false one. It starts from the assumption, built into the Chronically Sick and Disabled Persons Act, that all disabled people have special needs, and that statutory provision should be made to meet them. The resource implications of such a view have become apparent and need not be dwelt on here. However, it is the assumption that all disabled people should be identified in order to meet their needs that is false.

It has been estimated variously that perhaps as many as three in four disabled people may not wish to be known to social services or have any needs that statutory provision might meet. One study (Owen, 1981) found that only 40 per cent of those interviewed had in fact used the services of a social worker. Given that registers appear to identify only a third of disabled people, it is clear that the idea of providing a comprehensive service for all disabled people has proved to be unattainable. In addition, the underlying assumption locates the problem within the individual and fails to take into account the way that the physical and social environments are disabling. Services are therefore geared to the problems of individual limitations rather than to alleviating the restricting effects of physical and social environments. Social services departments and social workers, then – most of whom have regarded registration as a crucial issue – have in fact been operating in the wrong area.

The social work task is thus not to identify and register impaired individuals; it is rather (i) to identify ways in which disabilities are imposed upon impairments with a view to remediation; and (ii) to provide a flexible and accessible service to meet such individual needs as may arise. It is for planners and policy-makers, not social workers, to identify the likely extent of such needs. Of course, some will say that this is all very well, but central government at present allocates funds to local authorities on the basis of head counts; however, there is no reason why local authorities should not suggest that this is an inappropriate way to proceed, and that alternative ways of estimating and meeting needs should be explored. Sutherland, for example, suggested that new definitions of disability needed to be developed:

> The most useful basis for such a definition is the fact of stigmatisation itself. If we make no attempt to create a definition based upon some type of physical incapacity, but simply

define this group as consisting of all people who are stigma-
tised or discriminated against on the basis of their physical
condition, we have an extremely practical rule of thumb
definition.
(Sutherland, 1981, p. 20)

Whether a definition based on stigma would prove adequate is
perhaps debatable, but it is certainly clear that any definitions need
to move away from personal physical incapacity or functional limitation as their base-line.

Self-definitions

It is not just individual disabled people such as Finkelstein and
Sutherland who have articulated different definitions of disability,
but a growing number of organisations of disabled people are also
demanding the right to define the problems faced by their own
members. More will be said of this later, but it is worth noting at
this point that the inaugural meeting of Disabled People's
International, a congress representing disabled people from over
fifty countries, rejected the ICIDH on the grounds that it was allied
too closely to medical and individual definitions of disability.

Self-definitions are not only important at the level of the
disabled individual. Professionals have often been reluctant to
accept a disabled person's own definition and have used terms like
'denial' and 'disavowal' to account for contradictions between
definitions. The assumption that has usually followed from this is
that it is the disabled person who is mistaken or misguided, and
the professional who is correct. It follows logically from this
perception of a given situation that the social work task is to facilitate a more realistic assessment of the situation by disabled
persons themselves. Indeed, Corker and French (1998) warn that
when disabled people attempt to talk about their experiences,
professionals may use it as an opportunity to reinterpret that experience and to say, 'I told you so.'

What this may amount to in practice is the social worker impos-
ing the professional definition upon the disabled person, and it is
certainly true that the only way to gain access to certain benefits and
services is to 'act disabled'. However, as Blaxter's study showed, in
situations where professional and self-definitions conflict, this was

much more likely to give rise to long-term problems than when these definitions were in accord: 'One of the circumstances in which the problems of adjustment and rehabilitation were very likely was when the patient's own view of his condition differed from that of his doctors' (Blaxter, 1980, p. 221).

The problem for professionals generally, and for social workers in particular, is not working out the correct or right definition of disability, for part of the argument here is that there is no such thing. Definitions depend on a number of factors, some of which have already been identified and some of which have not. Albrecht and Levy argue that definitions of disability are socially constructed, and such social constructions often reflect vested professional interests:

> Certainly it is in the interest of medical professionals, hospitals, nursing homes, and medical supply companies to find treatable, chronic disabilities. Yet, the disabilities identified, discovered, and treated may reflect professional and occupational exigencies rather than actual consumer need. For these reasons, disabilities can be seen as socially constructed entities regardless of their physiological bases.
> (Albrecht and Levy, 1981, p. 21)

Thus social workers need to recognise that disability is a social construction and not necessarily a fixed physical entity, and need to plan their strategies of intervention accordingly. Some of the ways in which they might do this are considered in following chapters.

---

putting it into practice

Exercise 1

Taking the approach that Oliver (1990) used to reword the questions in the 1986 disability surveys, examine the questions being asked in community care assessments. These assessment forms should be available from social services departments:

1. Do the questions focus on individual inadequacies and if so, how could you reword them to focus on social inadequacies?
2. What differences might this make to a social worker's assessment?

→

> →
> **Exercise 2**
> The Deaf community have asserted that Deaf people often consider themselves as members of a linguistic minority rather than seeing themselves as disabled or impaired. However for hearing people this is usually treated as a denial of an obvious impairment.
> 1. Discuss this in a small group and in particular ask yourselves what personal or professional beliefs you would have to change in order to accept this self-definition.
> 2. How would acceptance of this self-definition change the approach social workers might take in working with Deaf people?

Further reading

Campbell, J. and Oliver, M. (eds) (1996) *Disability Politics*, London: Routledge. A history of the modern disabled people's movement including the struggle for self-representation.

Priestley, M. (2003) *Disability: A Life Course Approach*, Cambridge: Polity Press. Integrates a social model understanding of disability with a sociological understanding of the ways in which different life phases are constructed.

Swain, J., French, S., Barnes, C. and Thomas, C. (eds) (2004) *Disabling Barriers – Enabling Environments*, 2nd edn, London: Sage. A revised edition of the classic Open University reader, with chapters by leading writers in disability studies on a wide range of pertinent issues.

Thomas, C. (1999) *Female Forms: Experiencing and Understanding Disability*, Buckingham, Open University Press. This re-examination of the social model of disability helps to reconcile some of the key debates between medical sociologists, feminists and materialists.

3 | The causes of impairment and the creation of disability

The distinction between the individual and social dimensions of disability already referred to are also important in discussing the causes of both impairment (individual limitation) and disability (socially imposed restriction). From a medical point of view, the main causes of impairment can be seen in Table 3.1.

Commenting on previous such studies, Taylor has suggested that this approach is entirely justified in that the major causes of impairments are diseases of various kinds. It follows from this that, 'Unlike the case of most instances of mental handicap, there is a significant medical contribution to be made within the overall pattern of support for physically disabled individuals' (Taylor, 1977, p. 10). In short, most impairments are caused by disease, doctors cure diseases, and even where they cannot effect a cure, medical intervention will often control symptoms. Therefore, doctors have an important, if not crucial, role to play. The question of the relevance of medical knowledge for social work intervention will be discussed later in the chapter.

It is also argued that these diseases are 'residual'; and that their increased incidence is a result of two factors – increased life expectancy, and the growing numbers of elderly people in the population. A consequence of this view is the assumption that these diseases are 'degenerative' and largely a product of the age structure of the population. According to Doyal:

> The new 'disease burden' consists largely of the so-called 'degenerative' diseases, such as cancer, heart disease, arthritis and diabetes, all of which now kill and cripple many more people than they did in the past . . . In addition, of course, many more people are becoming chronically ill for longer periods in their lives than they did in the past.
> (Doyal, 1980, p. 59)

Table 3.1 Frequency in Great Britain of complaints in International Classification of Diseases groups causing disability, by severity category, all adults

ICD groups	Percentage of disabled with complaint in each ICD group (severity category)					All groups
	1–2	3–4	5–6	7–8	9–10	1–10
Infections	1	1	1	1	1	1
Neoplasms	1	1	2	3	6	2
Endocrine	1	2	3	4	5	2
Blood	0	1	1	0	1	1
Mental	11	17	19	19	25	16
Nervous system	4	10	16	24	38	14
Eye	18	19	24	27	32	22
Ear	39	34	35	37	32	36
Circulatory	18	21	21	20	15	20
Respiratory	12	14	14	13	10	13
Digestive	4	5	7	8	5	6
Genito-urinary	1	3	4	5	8	3
Skin	1	1	1	1	2	1
Musculo-skeletal	35	45	53	57	44	45
Congenital	0	1	1	0	0	0
Other/vague	4	6	8	9	11	6

Note: Percentages do not add up to 100 as some people have more than one condition.
Sources: Adapted from Martin et al., 1988, p. 34, table 4.10; Martin et al., 1989, p. 9, table 2.21.

The diseases causing death and impairment are very similar, but whereas Taylor sees the prospects of prevention as being limited and the medical profession as the appropriate agency for dealing with the causes and consequences of such conditions, Doyal has an alternative view more in accord with Finkelstein's social definition of disability. It could be argued that, while Finkelstein suggests that disability has social causes, Doyal sees impairment as also having social causes. This is not simply a feature of industrialised economies; Guelke (2003), for example, takes a similar view in relation to the use of new technologies and their role in the cause of repetitive strain injuries.

Using the work of Powles (1973), Doyal argues that these degenerative diseases occur almost exclusively in advanced industrial
societies and, regardless of their individual causes, they result from
the fact that the environment to which humans are biologically
adapted has changed fundamentally. The living conditions of
advanced industrial societies produce diseases of 'maladaptation'.
The implications of this view differ from those derived from the
view of Taylor, in that, if the causes of these diseases are ultimately
environmental (social) rather than individual, then perhaps the
medical profession is not the crucial agency that should be
involved. In short, if these diseases are the consequence of a
dysfunction between human beings and the environment, then it is
to the material environment that programmes of treatment (or
prevention) should be directed. Indeed, some writers, notably Illich
(1975), have suggested that the disappearance of a number of
diseases such as typhoid, cholera, polio and tuberculosis is solely
due to changes in the material environment, and the role of medicine has been irrelevant or even positively harmful. He develops his
argument through usage of the term 'iatrogenesis', by which he
means 'doctor-induced illness', which he defines as 'illness which
would not have come about unless sound and professionally recommended treatment had been applied'.

Prevention

A major reason for considering the causes of both impairment and
disability is that it raises the possibility of prevention. As Albrecht
and Levy put it:

> The major causes of mortality and morbidity today – heart
> disease, cancer, stroke, diabetes and accidents – can be
> prevented partially by changes in the environment and
> lifestyle . . . Disability and the costs of rehabilitation could
> be partially controlled if those precipitating events that are
> preventable were eliminated. To avoid blaming the victim,
> preventative efforts should be directed at the industries and
> governmental agencies that promote disability-causing
> behavior rather than by merely faulting those individuals
> who become disabled.
> (Albrecht and Levy, 1981, pp. 26–7)

However, the term 'prevention' as used by the medical profession is not necessarily the same thing as the concept of 'prevention' used by social workers. Leonard (1966) attempted to distinguish between three levels, which he calls primary, secondary and tertiary. For him, primary intervention is aimed at preventing the causes of certain events, secondary intervention is aimed at preventing the immediate effects of events, and tertiary intervention is aimed at preventing the consequences of these events. This threefold distinction is very similar to the classifications of disability produced by Harris and Finkelstein discussed in the previous chapter. The ideas discussed so far can be summarised – see Table 3.2.

This perspective therefore sees the medical profession and health educators as being largely responsible for primary prevention; that is, reducing the numbers of disabled babies being born, providing information about the prevention of accidents at work and so on. Secondary prevention – that is, the reduction of the personal limitations that may be imposed by impairments, falls to rehabilitation staff in particular. Tertiary prevention – that is, the reduction of socially imposed restrictions on impaired individuals, forms a large part of the social work task in working with people with disabilities,

Table 3.2 Definitions and scope for intervention

Professional intervention	Individual model (Harris 1971; Martin et al., 1988; Taylor, 1977)	Social model (Finkelstein in Finlay, 1978)	Type of prevention (Leonard, 1966)
Medical profession and health education	**Impairment**	**Impairment** (Treatment and care)	**Primary**
Paramedics and rehabilitation staff (e.g. OTs, physios)	**Disability**	**Impairment** (Therapy)	**Secondary**
Social workers, politicians, pressure groups	**Handicap**	**Disability**	**Tertiary**

though as Holdsworth (1991) has pointed out, this also requires the support of the social work institutions and society.

Leonard (1966, p. 12) has suggested, in respect of social work generally, 'Much of social work has concentrated, necessarily, on tertiary intervention; for example, the intervention involved in the whole field of the care of adults and children in residential institutions, foster homes and hostels.' Leonard's description of the social work task with disabled people contains an interesting contradiction that illustrates the argument of this book. If, on the one hand, intervention at a tertiary level involves the reduction of socially imposed restrictions on impaired individuals, it follows that this would amount to the prevention of disability, thereby making it a form of primary intervention from a social model perspective. However, the example given by Leonard, of care within institutions, forms one of the more obviously disabling responses of society towards people with impairments, rather than a preventative one. What is preventative is therefore clearly relative to the perspective from which the issue of disability is being analysed.

From an individual model perspective, social work has probably also been involved at the primary and secondary levels in providing antenatal advice to pregnant clients or in helping to locate rehabilitation services. These are also not without their problems in terms of the way that Leonard sees them. It is only from an individual model analysis that assumes a eugenicist concept of 'normality' that it can be concluded, for example, that aborting a foetus that is impaired is preventative of disability. From a social model perspective, the disability is caused by the reactions of the society into which the child is born. As Dona Avery put it, when describing how she had been expected by hospital staff to follow the five stages of the Kubler–Ross model (Denial; Anger; Bargaining; Depression; and Acceptance): 'I have seen a 5th stage, and it is not Acceptance or Hope of a Cure. It is learning that an unborn perfect child was one conceived by society, not me, and that the actual child I *was* gifted with is perfectly fine' (Avery, 1997).

Equally, the organisation of rehabilitation services can be viewed as being helpful in functional terms, or it may be seen in quite a different way: 'Our first concern is that disabled people are faced with impossible social, financial, housing and environmental difficulties, and are then offered a piecemeal welfare system of professionals and services to help them adjust to and cope with their unacceptable circumstances' (Brechin and Liddiard, 1981, p. 2). Traditionally, however, social work has been concerned essentially with the tertiary level within an individual model of disability. Although there may now be considerable administrative limitations placed on those who are employed as care managers in highly regimented organisations, it remains that intervention at this level holds out the best starting point for changing to work within a social model of disability. It is necessary, therefore, to explore the range of knowledge and skills needed to carry out this task.

Medical knowledge and the social work task

One immediate question posed by this conceptualisation of the social work task concerns how much knowledge of medical conditions social workers in fact need. In suggesting that it is the social rather than the individual model within which social workers should operate, it does not follow logically that they should have no knowledge of medical conditions. Indeed, without such knowledge it may well be impossible to consider the personal, interpersonal or social consequences for the client concerned. Such knowledge may be acquired from other professionals or through reference books of various kinds. However, in most cases the major source of such knowledge is the disabled person. Thus, one young social worker, when allocated to work with a tetraplegic woman, approached her new client by telling her that she knew nothing about tetraplegia, but was willing to learn. They agreed to spend a complete day together from the time before the woman woke up until after she fell asleep in bed. The social worker learned more about tetraplegia from that particular experience than she could ever have done from books or other sources, and as a consequence was able to provide the client with satisfactory services.

It is important to extract other aspects from the medical facts: whether the condition is visible or non-visible, static or progressive, congenital or acquired, whether the impairment is sensory or physical, will all have important effects on the personal, interpersonal and social consequences of particular impairments. Hicks spells this out in the case of visual impairment:

> Because of the inabilities to acquire information through
> sight and to make eye contact with other people, the visually

handicapped, and particularly the functionally blind, may encounter relationship and sexual problems which are not common to other disabilities. These problems differ for those whose visual impairment is congenital (from birth or infancy) or adventitious (occurring after some visual concepts have been formed). They apply to initial encounters, to the range of potential partners, to sexual relationships and they have clear implications for education and counselling and for professional relationships with the client. (in Brechin *et al.*, 1981, p. 79)

What is being suggested, for visual impairment in particular and for all disabled people in general, is that such aspects are more important for the social worker than to know than whether the impairment was caused by glaucoma, cataracts or retinitis pigmentosa.

Disability, then, is neither simply an individual misfortune nor a social problem; it is in fact a relationship between the impaired individual and the restrictions imposed on them by society. This relationship is defined by Finkelstein: 'Society disables people with different physical impairments. The cause, then, of disability, is the social relationships which take little or no account of people who have physical impairments' (in Brechin *et al.*, 1981, p. 34). Thomas (2004) describes Finkelstein's understanding of disability as being distinctive because of 'its *social relational* character, making it a new form of social oppression associated with the relationships, at both macro and micro social scales, between the impaired and the non-impaired' (p. 578).

A framework for intervention

We have already argued that traditional approaches to service provision are inadequate, as they are based on an individual model of disability, and the approach that needs to be adopted by social workers and their agencies should be one that acknowledges disabled people as full and active members of society; the citizenship approach (Oliver and Bailey, 2002). The economic, political and moral dimensions of this approach require social workers to regard disabled people as 'contributing members of society as both workers and valued customers or users'; to recognise disabled people 'as empowered individuals and voters, and a powerful, interest group'; and to see disabled people 'as active citizens with all that implies in terms of rights and responsibilities' (Oliver, 2004, p. 28). Admitting people to services as a service-user is itself problematic as it can limit their inclusion and restrict them to a particular role. The Derbyshire Centre for Inclusive Living, which takes a social model approach, argues that

> The people it supports are not to be constructed as 'users', because such a role has constraints on what people might want to say about the purpose, direction and inclusiveness of public services. And it does not purport to 'involve users', because historically it's an organisation in which disabled people 'involved workers'.
> (Gibbs, 2004, pp. 157–8)

Two examples of how the citizenship approach could be achieved are (i) increasing the accessibility of social work as an occupation for disabled people; and (ii) supporting the use of direct payments and extending the principle to self-assessment of need.

Sapey *et al.* (2004b) undertook a review of research concerned with the recruitment of disabled people to social work, and concluded that the most significant barrier was the attitude of those non-disabled people already employed in social work agencies, particularly social workers. This institutional disablism manifests itself through social workers

> who are unable or unwilling to see disabled people as their colleagues rather than their clients. While the actual terminology may vary – consumer, service-user, patient – the sentiment is the same, that disabled people are at times expected to remain in the position of being helped, rather than becoming a helper.
> (Sapey *et al.*, 2004b, p. 15)

With regard to the direct payments system, Oliver (2004) argues that it stresses the following points:

● the user makes direct payments to the person of their choice to provide personal support;
● the support worker identifies the disabled person as the person with the power to end the relationship and the income source;

- the support worker identifies with the overall aims of the relationship not specific tasks, like getting someone to bed;
- the user expects the support worker to turn up on time and therefore can take on work and other commitments;
- the user makes the decisions about how they want to be treated by support staff.

(Oliver, 2004, p. 28)

Both the recruitment of disabled people as social workers and the move towards direct payments and self-assessment require social workers and their managers to review and fundamentally change the way they think about disablement and their own role. As Finkelstein and Thomas have argued, disability is a social relationship between people with impairments and the rest of society; it is a form of social oppression.

Social workers perhaps occupy a unique position in the welfare system in which, although employed directly or indirectly by the state to implement its welfare policies, they are also the human face of that system. They not only have to represent the welfare services; they are often the only people with whom service users have direct contact and they therefore play a key role in feeding-back the needs, desires and ambitions of their clients to their agencies and the broader welfare system. This clearly requires that social workers are skilled communicators, but if they are to utilise the idea of disability as a relationship, some way of linking the individual and the social is needed.

One such attempt was made through the development of the concept of 'career', which originally developed in American sociology (Becker, 1963; Goffman, 1963), but later came to be used on both sides of the Atlantic in discussions of disability (Safilios-Rothschild, 1970; Blaxter, 1980). Carver argued that the 'concept of career is a broadly comprehensive one and implies that the individual is actively and repeatedly involved in the definition of his own problems and in the search for solutions, and like any other career, it will comprise a succession of interactions with his environment, both physical and social' (Carver, 1982, p. 90).

In working with individuals, the concept of career provided a link with social structure and offered the social worker the possibility of conceptualising disability as a social relationship. On its own, the idea of a 'career' provided a useful basis for short-term work or crisis intervention, in that support and help may be needed when a career in disability begins. But in order to make use fully of the concept of 'career' it needed to be harnessed to the notion of 'life-cycle events': that is, that there are key transition stages in life through which everyone passes, such as birth, starting and leaving school, puberty, going to work, marriage, retirement and death. These transition stages are often marked by uncertainty as individuals move from one role or status to another, and this can give rise to adjustment problems, both for the individuals themselves, and for family, friends, peers, and so on. Disabled people will also move through key life-cycle events, though disability may exacerbate some of the problems involved and enhance the need for professional intervention. For example, anxious parents may well seek to help their disabled offspring at a childhood stage well into the period when disabled people feel they should be treated as adults.

From other social scientific research it is possible to predict certain occurrences at particular stages in the life-cycle. For example, poverty is more likely to occur when a family is bringing up young children and around the point of retirement; personal relationships are often fraught around the time of puberty; unemployment can be particularly severe during adolescence; and family crises may occur during the early years of marriage, when parents are adapting to having young children in the home.

However, it is important not to reduce the concept of career to a series of losses or crises. Creek *et al.* (1987) made use of a concept of significant life events in their study of the social implications of spinal injury in order to explain how people experienced the onset of impairment. This was argued on the basis of the inadequacy of the personal tragedy theory with its behavioural analysis of how individuals are expected to react. Quoting from Silver and Wortman, they put the case for this approach:

We have found little reliable evidence to indicate that people go through stages of emotional responses following an undesirable life event. We have also reviewed a substantial body of evidence suggesting that a large minority of victims of aversive life events experience distress or disorganization long after recovery might be expected. Current theoretical

dels of reactions to aversive outcomes cannot account for
variety of responses that appear.
lver and Wortman cited in Creek *et al.*, 1987, pp. 20–1)

This implies that social workers need to view the concept of a 'disabled career' not as being predetermined, but as entirely personal. As the causes of disability lie in the social responses to impairment, the ways in which any individual might react to that process or to the onset of impairment will be determined by their own unique set of experiences and circumstances. The social worker therefore needs to understand the actions of each person in terms of their subjective meaning to that individual – it is an interactionist rather than behavioural understanding that is required.

One key limitation of the career approach to understanding the experiences and needs of disabled people is that while it recognizes that the individual is passing through certain life-cycle events, it does not emphasise sufficiently the extent to which roles within those periods of their life are socially produced. As a result, the concept of career may focus too much on the individual and insufficiently on the social. On the other hand, the 'life course' approach to understanding disability (Priestley, 2003) starts with an examination of the construction of those different periods of life and offers a more complex analysis of the social relationships between culture, role and disability:

> Adopting a life course approach raises a number of significant questions. Why, for example, have states gone to such lengths to limit or prevent the birth of disabled children? Why have disabled children been so often excluded from mainstream education? What is the significance of youth culture and youth transitions for young disabled people? How does the expectation of an 'independent' adulthood – for example, in relation to employment or parenting – contribute to the production of disability in modern societies? Why are older people with impairments rarely seen as disabled in quite the same way that younger adults often are? Why are different moral standards applied to the death and dying of disabled and non-disabled people?
> (Priestley, 2003, p. 1)

It is necessary now to say something about the applicability of these ideas to the environment of social work practice. With limited resources, pressures on time from other work, departmental management not being sympathetic to this kind of work and so on, most social workers may feel that they are unlikely to have the 'luxury' of working in collaboration with disabled people and their families. Collaborative working and a properly planned long-term intervention strategy is not a luxury, but is justifiable economically in that planned intervention can be preventative and alleviate the need for more costly crisis intervention at some later stage.

Assessment

Whatever kind of intervention strategies may be used, there is a long-standing legal requirement for an assessment of the problem or problems. According to Bell and Klemz, 'In social services departments, the purpose of assessing the needs of physically hand-icapped clients is to bring to them the appropriate services which councils provide and to advise on other services that may be required' (Bell and Klemz, 1981, p. 117). Today, of course, many services are purchased by councils, and we would need to add that the purpose should include ascertaining the cost of services that are needed in order to allocate an appropriate level of direct payment.

With the implementation of the NHS and Community Care Act, 1990, the focus moved from assessing eligibility for services provided by councils to a needs-led assessment. This was enshrined in *Caring for People* (Department of Health, 1989) and in the subsequent policy and practice guidance (Social Services Inspectorate, 1991a and 1991b) which requires that social workers and other assessors of need look at what services may have to be purchased or provided in order to enable that individual to live more independently. The implementation of this needs-led approach was heralded with criticisms of the service-led approach. In his foreword to Ellis's study of user and carer participation in assessment, the chief inspector of the Social Services Inspectorate likened the latter to the methods of Procrustes:

> Their assessment procedures are rather more sophisticated than those of the Greek robber Procrustes, 'who placed all who fell into his hands upon an iron bed. If they were longer than the bed he cut off the overhanging parts, if shorter he stretched them till they fitted it.' Even so the report demonstrates how

the workers' preconceptions of policy, resources and values precluded that dialogue with users and carers which should be the foundation of joint assessment. Occupations which trade in non-judgementalism are shown to be as moralistic in their approach as any lay person. The ways in which some workers discouraged 'dependency' should impress the most fervent advocate of Victorian values, and shows that the spirit of the Poor Law is alive and kicking nearly 50 years after its official internment.
(Utting, in Ellis, 1993, p. 3)

However, the introduction of a needs-led system of assessment has not been seen by all as the solution to the ills of the past. Sapey (1993) argued that the NHS and Community Care Act, 1990 is the continuation of an ideological tradition within social policy that started with the Poor Laws in that it maintains that it is local authorities, rather than disabled people, who know best what is needed by the latter. In this sense, it is hardly surprising that Utting should find those values being implemented within social services departments, but he is remiss to blame only the practice of the individuals employed, when the policy structure itself demands such behaviour of them. Morris (1993) also questioned the meaning behind the rhetoric of the Act and the compatibility of local authority Community Care Plans with independent living: 'this compatibility is actually a superficial one. The aim of independent living is held back by an ideology at the heart of community care policies, which does not recognise the civil rights of disabled people but instead considers them to be dependent people in need of care' (Morris, 1993, p. 38).

Thompson (1993) also had doubts about the model of disability that lay behind community care: 'The current emphasis on "care management" as a key part of the development of community care also retains the influence of the medical model, for example in the assumption that the professional experts know best what the needs of disabled people are' (Thompson, 1993, p. 114). Thompson (2002b) argues that the social model of disability has had little effect on disability services. This is not surprising when we consider the content of a care management training package from the main social work trade union at the time, NALGO (now part of UNISON). NALGO specifically argued against placing too much value on the views of service users (Meteyard, 1992). While acknowledging the problems of paternalism and subjectivity associated with normative assessments of needs, Meteyard nevertheless equated felt needs with 'wants' and argued the case in relation to community care, with negative examples of drug addiction in which felt needs are damaging. By associating the demands of community care service users with those of drug users, he diminished the value of felt needs and yet purported to be working from a value base of empowerment. This position was reinforced by the government guidance that defined needs as 'the requirements of individuals to enable them to achieve, maintain or restore an acceptable level of social independence or quality of life, *as defined by the particular care agency or authority*' [emphasis added] (Social Services Inspectorate, 1991a, p. 14). As Morris (1993) has pointed out, there is clearly a gap between the rhetoric and reality in community care policies.

Therefore, the problems here are twofold. First, we need to be able to distinguish between the rhetoric and reality of assessment policies, and second, we need to ensure that assessments reflect accurately the needs of the client concerned, and not professional commitment, consciously or unconsciously, to one or other model or view of the world. Philips (2004) argues, in relation to people with learning difficulties, that it is difficult to implement partnership approaches aimed at inclusion in an environment where 'professionals are still locked in medical discourses and where the policing of bodies still prevails' (Phillips, 2004, p. 172).

Borsay (2005) identifies this discourse as one that focuses on loss, and finds examples of it occurring as early as the eighteenth century. This professionalised view of disability as loss acts as a barrier to people seeking help. Rummery *et al.* (1999) looked at what frontline workers, disabled people and carers had to say about their experience of accessing community care assessments and identified some specific ways in which the barriers materialise:

- the lack of accessible advice and information on the services available, the eligibility criteria used to assess people's needs, and the assessment process
- the use of jargon by front-line workers (such as the way they refer to services)

● the unfavourable treatment of older people in accessing assessments, compared to younger people with a disability and those with sensory impairments.
(Rummery *et al.*, 1999, p. 300)

While the problems of poor assessment are easy to identify, it is perhaps more difficult to locate a particular model for good practice. Sapey and Hewitt (1991) have argued that social workers and other social services personnel stand between disabled people and their rights derived from various welfare enactments. Because the provision of services is dependent on the local authority assessment of need, this places the assessors of that need in a position, not simply of gatekeeping scarce resources, but of sanctioning the rights to services prescribed by Parliament. They go on to suggest that if assessments are to be needs-led they must also be undertaken by the disabled person. Self-assessment has received some official sanction. When drawing up guidelines on working with disabled people, CCETSW argued that 'Self-assessment should be central to the assessment process and subsequent planning and evaluation should start from the same stand-point; in other words, disabled people are the best definers of their own needs' (Stevens, 1991, p. 19).

Self-assessment, while potentially causing alarm among budget holders, has the advantage of making clear the separation between need and the ability or willingness of any particular agency to meet that need. Doyal and Gough (1991) describe the professional assessment of need as a 'colonialist' approach in that it involves one group determining what is best for another, less powerful, group of people. They argue for an objective and universal approach to the notion of needs, and suggest that one of the principal benefits of this is to separate clearly the arguments over what needs exist from the issue of how and to what extent any society may be willing to meet those needs.

The Social Care Institute for Excellence (SCIE) is now actively promoting self-assessment of need. At a SCIE seminar on independent living in November 2004, each if the speakers, including those from the Disability Rights Commission and the government, made it clear that self assessment for social care needs should be the next step in ensuring that disabled people have real access to independent living.

Middleton had some concern about self-assessment. She argued that the idea that disabled people always know best may be a 'simplistic rhetoric' that 'not only represent[s] an avoidance of responsibility by professional helpers, but can be deeply disempowering for people who find themselves in new situations and need help' (Middleton, 1997, p. 73). However, she also emphasises that a professional role in assessment must be more than a one-to-one activity that comes up with a plan:

> Assessment is the art of managing competing demands, and negotiating the most reasonable outcome. It means steering between the clashing rocks of organisational demand; legislative dictates; limited resources; political and personal agendas. It includes having to keep one's feet in an inter-agency setting when the ground beneath them is constantly shifting. It is about making sense of the situation as a whole, and working out the best way to achieve change.
> (Middleton, 1997, pp. 3–4)

Thus assessment and self assessment are complex tasks that will involve much more than the ticking of boxes on a prescribed form. Middleton's argument is that social workers have much more to offer to working in partnership with disabled people.

Harris (2004) takes the argument a stage further and says that if we are to stop processing disabled people into being service users, we need to change the focus of assessment from needs as defined by agencies, to outcomes as desired by disabled people: 'There are a number of reasons why focusing upon "needs" is problematic, both conceptually and practically. The identification of "needs" is no mean feat, since theoretically these are subjective, potentially endless and relative to one's immediate situation' (Harris, 2004, p. 117). She goes on to explain how the supposed objectivity of professionals creates hierarchical relationships with disabled people, who will have a more subjective view of their own needs. Furthermore, as needs change over time and as one need is met, another may materialise, disabled people become locked into a service-user role in which they are dependent on the professional assessor. Harris's argument arises from an attempt to implement a social model approach to assessment through making significant changes to its focus. In this study, assessors focus on the outcomes that disabled people want from the services, rather than on a normative view of their needs. In this way needs become self-defined as they arise from the aspirations that disabled people have, and not from the responsibilities that local authorities believe they might have to decide how to ensure clients' safety and comfort, or to act as arbiters in a 'needs versus wants' debate.

As we discussed earlier, there has been a change in the focus of government policies that includes a greater commitment to disabled people being empowered through the types of social services they receive. In *A Quality Strategy for Social Care*, the Department of Health point to an outcomes-led approach when they say:

> We must focus on *what people want from services*. There is now a strong body of evidence pointing to the qualities people value in social services:
>
> ● high standards at all levels in service delivery throughout the whole workforce
> ● responsiveness, speed and convenience of service delivery
> ● appropriateness – *services tailored to individual need*, with respect for culture and lifestyle
> ● services that build on peoples' abilities and *enable them to participate fully in society*
> ● *services that involve the user*, so that choices are informed and respected
> ● strong safeguards for those at risk
> [emphasis added] *(*Department of Health, 2000, p. 6)

From a social model perspective, the idea that assessment should be empowering seems clear and receives a lot of support, both in terms of the involvement of disabled people as full participants within the process of assessment, and in terms of the outcomes. While structural barriers to such an approach may remain, practitioners can nevertheless begin to work in a more participatory way. Good advice on this comes from Morris (1997a; 2002) who first focuses on the skills required by individual practitioners if they are to implement a needs-led assessment in ways that are compatible with the independent living movement, and latterly on communication skills. While Ellis (1993) also highlighted the institutional and attitudinal barriers to user participation, she argued that despite the powerless position professionals may perceive themselves to be in, they do have the discretion to choose between competing models of practice in assessment. It is they who will implement the assessment procedures of their agencies, and it is they who will reinterpret them against the interests of their clients if they choose to do so. Good practice in assessment will involve a clear understanding of the power dynamics that operate between the social worker and disabled person, as these are central to an incorporation of the social model of disability. Thompson (1998) also provides some very practical ways in which social workers can think about how they practise in both oppressive and empowering organisations.

Similarly to Harris (2004), Holdsworth argued that the principal outcome of an assessment should be geared to 'needs for empowerment':

> what might be the characteristics of an empowerment model of social work with physically disabled people? Probably the most important of these, having accepted the implications of the social model of disability and the concept of disability as oppression, is the ability to start where the client is, as any individual disabled person could be at any point along a continuum of power and powerlessness and will therefore need *a service geared to her specific needs for empowerment.* [emphasis added] (Holdsworth, 1991, p. 27)

While empowerment may be central to the assessment and service provision processes, it is important that it is understood from a social model perspective. For some years it has become part of the rhetoric of central government, local authorities and the social work profession, and has reached the point where it is an organizing principle for institutional change in the public and private sectors (Baistow, 1995), but this does not mean that it will result in any benefit for disabled people. We discuss this in more detail in Chapter 7, but suffice to say at this point that empowerment is not something that should be thought of as the gift of social workers. Freire (1972) has argued the case that empowerment is a process in which powerless people themselves take power away from the powerful. Social workers are in a position of power, as are their employing agencies and the various levels of government. If social workers have a role to play in the process of disabled people empowering themselves, it will be as allies and as people who are prepared to give up and share their own power.

It would not be appropriate at this point to make more detailed suggestions about how assessments should be done, but in conclusion two points need emphasis. Assessments that take into account individual and social aspects of disability and the relationship between them need to be undertaken by competent and knowledgeable professionals in collaboration with disabled people, to ensure that they consider the wishes, concerns and goals of their clients. Most important, if the social dimension is included, then it is social workers who need to be involved, because they are concerned with the tertiary level of intervention which, when approached as an issue of empowerment, has the potential to become a primary-level intervention in terms of a social model of disability. To finish as the chapter began, the social model needs to be applied to both impairment and disability, otherwise the criticism levelled by Corrigan and Leonard will remain unchallenged:

> In the field of physical handicap, for example, symptomatic treatment at the individual level is still the primary response, in the case of bronchitis, structural responses would require a substantial indictment of methods of economic production, in the case of mental disorder, medical models of treatment are still dominant, a dominance which allows the neglect of structural factors in the creation of mental disorders. Poverty itself, and the stigma associated with it, is indissolubly linked in both definition and service delivery to individual pathological conceptions.
> (Corrigan and Leonard, 1979, p. 101)

putting it into practice

Exercise 1

Most of us are able to exercise a great deal of autonomy in deciding what we need to enhance our own lives. Consider why the state has decided it is necessary to have trained professionals to decide this for disabled people. Try to answer the following questions:

1. Why is it necessary for a social worker to assess the needs of a disabled person?
2. What problems would arise if disabled people assessed their own needs?

→

→

Now apply your answers to yourself and consider what difference it would make to your life if someone else was making these decisions for you.

Exercise 2

Make a list of three medical conditions with which you are familiar. Make nine further lists of the range of social needs that might arise for people from three different socio-economic backgrounds with each of these conditions. Examine the lists and think about whether the needs which arise are more likely to be linked directly to the medical condition or to the socio-economic backgrounds.

Further reading

Barnes, C. and Mercer, G. (eds) (1996) *Exploring the Divide: Illness and Disability*, Leeds: The Disability Press. Papers exploring the medical sociological and social model perspective of impairment and disability.

Thompson, N. (1998) *Promoting Equality*, London: Macmillan. Guidance on strategies for developing anti-oppressive practice with organisational cultures that may encourage discrimination.

4 | Disability in the family

The social model of disability can be a useful and sensitising perspective in considering the implications of disability for family life. There are three ways in which the 'disability relationship' discussed in the previous chapter is important here. To begin with, the disablement of an impaired individual may be exacerbated by the way he or she is treated by the family, as, for example, the way that some disabled children are overprotected by their anxious parents. In addition, family structure and stability may be affected adversely by one of its members becoming disabled, though it is important to note that such an occurrence may strengthen rather than weaken familial ties in some situations. Finally, there is the question of the way society treats families, through social policy provision, where there is a disabled member.

These themes will be interwoven in this chapter, but to begin with it is necessary to consider the consequences of disability within the family and the scope and possibility for social work intervention. To locate the family in its appropriate social context it needs to be recognised that it is a universal social group which in one form or another occurs in all societies and at all times.

In Britain, there has been a tendency to over-romanticise historical aspects of family life, seeing families in the past as being much more capable of looking after their own, particularly weaker members, and coping in times of stress. However, it is sometimes argued that, since the start of the twentieth century, family size has reduced considerably and the extended family of the past has become the modern two-generation nuclear family. Also, the family has lost many of its functions to the state, which provides education for all children, care and treatment for sick members, and economic support in times of unemployment.

The accuracy of this picture of family life is still the subject of much debate. Some writers have argued that the nuclear family has always been the basic family unit, while others have suggested that there is little evidence to support the notion that the family was better able and more willing to support other family members in the past than it is now – there were more old people in institutions, for example, in 1900 than in 1980. Certainly, it is true that there have been a number of very important changes in the nature of the family. First, there has been a rapid increase in marital breakdown: the numbers of couples in the UK divorcing rose from 33,074 in 1950 to 156,814 in 2001, peaking at 180,018 in 1993 (*Social Trends*, 2004). Much of this increase occurred in the early 1970s following the Divorce Reform Act, 1969. The Family Policies Study Centre (1997) estimated that on the current trends at that time, 28 per cent of children would experience their parents divorcing before they were 16 years old. Second, and as a consequence of this, there are many more one-parent families, though some are of short-term duration because people remarry: in 2001, remarriages accounted for 40 per cent of all marriages. The proportion of households with dependent children headed by a lone parent rose from 7 per cent in 1972 to 23 per cent in 2003 (*Social Trends*, 2004). Finally, the increasing numbers of elderly people in the population at large has placed additional caring responsibilities on many families. While the numbers of children under 16 years of age has decreased, from 14.25 million in 1971 to 11.85 million in 2001, the numbers of people over 65 years of age increased, from 7.41 million to 9.36 million over the same period. By the year 2021 it is estimated that the under-16s will have fallen further, to 11.21 million, while the over-65s will have increased, to 12.28 million (*Social Trends*, 2004).

Young and Willmott (1973) characterised the present-day family as 'symmetrical'; that is, where often both the husband and wife work, but family life is centred on the home, and family members share most of the domestic tasks. This is, however, to some extent an idealisation of the family because in 1996 official figures put the number of people unemployed at just over 2 million, and during the 1997 election campaign, the Labour Party claimed that this meant that one in five households had no earned income. In 2003 the number of unemployed was still put at 1.5 million (*Social Trends*, 2004), but the government remained concerned that a significant proportion of the 2.7 million people claiming Incapacity Benefit could be working (Department for Work and Pensions, 2005). Furthermore, while people tend to agree that household tasks should be shared, it remains the case that in the majority of families, these fall to women. Indeed, in the 16 to 44 age group who are most likely to have dependent children, women are likely to spend twice as much time undertaking household chores than men (*Social Trends*, 2004). When there is a disabled child in the family, mothers are also likely to take on the major tasks associated with their child's impairment and disability (Read, 2000). It has been recognised for some time that when disability occurs within the family, this does limit the possibility of sharing tasks and may also exacerbate other internal and external pressures on the family. As Topliss puts it:

> Although the precise impact of disablement upon family life depends upon the position within the family of the disabled person, a growing body of literature suggests that whether it is a handicapped husband, wife, child or elderly parent who is affected, disablement has an important effect on the relationship and opportunities of the family as a whole.
> (Topliss, 1979, p. 129)

What is being suggested is that, in considering the consequences of disability within the family, external economic and social pressures on family life need to be taken into account, as well as the impact of impairments on individual members and the family as a unit. Families with an impaired member may be further disabled by poor housing, poverty, lack of emotional support and the lack of social provision generally.

Children with disabilities

The birth of a disabled child can be a traumatic and shattering event for a family, and that is the dominant way that both professionals and researchers have treated the subject. As a consequence, it has usually been assumed that as well as needing appropriate information and practical assistance, parents need skilled help to overcome the loss, grief and bereavement they feel as a consequence of failing to produce a healthy child. This view was summarised by Selfe and Stow:

> Many writers have dealt with the initial emotions experienced by parents. These often include extreme feelings of shock, helplessness, shame, embarrassment and guilt. In

addition there may well be feelings of frustration, and rejection of the child. Some psychologists have seen this as part of the process of grief and mourning for the normal child who was never born. Others conceive parents to be in a state of chronic sorrow because they are faced with the life-long reality of their situation.
(Selfe and Stow, 1981, p. 205)

However, this view does not pass completely unchallenged, and others have suggested that the birth of a disabled child does not automatically promote adverse emotional reactions (Roith, 1974; Avery, 1997), while Baldwin (in Walker and Townsend, 1981) argued that, even where stress is present, it may stem from unresolved practical problems. Thus, in discussing the impact of a disabled child on family life, differing views based on the individual and social models of disability emerge once again.

Lonsdale, who carried out her own study, made sense of these differing views in the following way:

It is known that some parents cope and some do not, but as yet we have little explanation of the reasons for this. It might be that there are links between being able to manage and having adequate finances, or with enjoying secure relationships within the family, or with the nature of handicap itself, or it might be a combination of all three. The nature of the problems suggest that it is an area for social work involvement but of what kind and when it is likely to be most helpful has perhaps been insufficiently considered.
(in Lonsdale et al., 1979, p. 1)

There are thus at least three areas where social work has an important role to play: in providing emotional support when needed; in providing access to practical assistance and resources; and in reducing the negative impact that dealing with an unfeeling professionalised bureaucracy may often have. These need to be considered separately.

In dealing with the emotional impact on the family, it should be stressed that not all families will need professional help. However, for those that do, Jordan issues the following warning:

Social workers do not 'know the right way' for people to react in such circumstances, still less should they impose

their stereotyped formulae on others' suffering. Rather they are there to help people find their own way through their crises, and to provide a substitute for or complement to the fellow-feeling once given mainly by the afflicted to each other.
(in Lonsdale *et al.*, 1979, p. viii)

Despite this warning, Lonsdale, in the first paper in her book, was stuck within the individual model of disability and saw the birth of a disabled child as inevitably being a matter for grieving. As well as neglecting the practical problems that might arise, Lonsdale was too accepting of the universality of grief processes.

While some parents may experience a grief reaction, social work practice should not begin with the assumption that this is always the case. Neither should they assume that grief necessarily follows the pattern of stages popularised by psychologists. Thompson (2002a) argues that social workers would do well to take note of some of the recent sociological developments in this field. Issues concerning assessment, discussed in the previous chapter, are equally important in working with families with a disabled child, and doing so from a social model perspective is just as appropriate.

Middleton (1992) challenges the emphasis put on parents' reactions to the birth and considers what it might mean to the child. She argues that the first two of ten hurdles that disabled children have to overcome are getting born and then getting accepted. Getting born may prove difficult if an impairment is diagnosed during their mother's pregnancy, as this will almost certainly result in the consideration, and perhaps the recommendation, that the foetus be aborted. Oliver and Barnes (1998) highlight the current abortion legislation as one of the ways in which disablism is structural to British society. If this hurdle is overcome, though, the question is how the child comes to be accepted by his/her family as being something more than a disappointment, and how he or she then develops a strong self-identity. However, Read (2000) suggests that children are usually accepted by their parents as children, and it is more likely that it is people outside their immediate family, including social workers, who will view them negatively.

The skills that social workers need to help families are not necessarily different or new, but they have to practise them with an understanding of the causes of disablement. If the child is seen as a problem and as deficient, then it follows that the grief of the parents will be natural and to be expected. If, however, the child is seen as someone who will be disabled by the social reactions towards his or her impairment, it would be the anger and frustration with the social barriers that would be the expected and understandable response. Emotional reactions to such births therefore appear to be the result of the way in which disability has been socially constructed. Barnes (1997) draws on anthropological evidence that children born with impairments are not seen in a negative light in all societies, to support the argument that disability is a product of the material and social forces in Western culture, but even in the West there have been exceptions to this attitude. In her study of deafness in Martha's Vineyard, Groce (1985) describes how the birth of a hearing child was felt to be preferable, but the birth of a deaf child was not in any way a cause for mourning or even regret.

While the need for emotional support can therefore be redirected as a need for help in changing social attitudes, this may, of course, produce anger and frustration within parents at the way in which others in society are reacting towards their children. The social worker may be called upon to help both the child and his/her parents in this respect. By moving from the individual to the social model, what the social worker does is to refocus intervention on the help needed to become aware of and deal with disabling barriers.

What is also clear is that social workers must adopt a flexible approach and not base their interventions on preconceived ideas or theories of how families cope. Elfer (in Lonsdale et al., 1979) describes his experiences of working with families with a terminally ill child, and says that he began with two assumptions: that the child should be told about his or her illness, and the family encouraged to talk about it. These assumptions were soon lost when he found that help had to be geared, not to normative assumptions about a healthy family life, but to the way in which each family coped. Thus he found that there were few, if any, ground rules upon which to structure his intervention, and he concluded:

Perhaps the only one is the importance of offering help quickly – but situations that occur can be so threatening, painful or bizarre that responses have to be those that seem right and appropriate for the situation, however unorthodox.
(in Lonsdale et al., 1979, p. 6)

Thus, in providing emotional support, the appropriate place to start is with the coping strategy of the family itself and it is important not to see some reactions as pathological and others as healthy – rather just to work towards reducing the disablement of the child. This means that the social worker will often be working in a situation of uncertainty, but better this than attempting to impose a professional definition on a personal problem.

A second area in which families with a disabled child may need help is with practical problems. Swain (1981), in his discussion of disability in the family, sees the main practical problems as being suitable housing, a reasonable income, a reduction of the limitations on mobility that may be caused, and perhaps an increase in time and energy spent on the 'normal' child-care tasks that all parents are required to undertake. Beresford and Oldman (2002) found extensive housing poverty among families with disabled children, but argued that unless a social model approach is taken to understanding housing need, then families with disabled children will be subjected to a special-needs approach rather than an inclusive one.

Certainly, it can be part of the social worker's job to help in this organising and adapting; in making sure that the family is receiving all the financial benefits to which it is entitled, contacting organizations such as the Family Fund where necessary, and negotiating with other agencies, such as housing departments. It is also necessary, however, for social workers to assess and provide a range of services from their own agencies, particularly if they are working in the statutory sector.

Since 1989, services for disabled children have been provided under the Children Act, 1989. Although the definitions of disability remain the same, children are no longer subject to the restricted list of services that appeared in the CSDPA, 1970, but can expect that

> Every local authority shall provide services designed –
> (a) to minimise the effect on disabled children within their area of their disabilities; and
> (b) to give such children the opportunity to lead lives which are as normal as possible.
> (Children Act, 1989, Schedule 2, Part 1, Section 6)

Despite its use of the term 'normal' that is indicative of the influence of the individual model of disability, this Act does open up the possibility of services that are innovative and relevant to the removal of disabling barriers. The inclusion of disabled children in this Act should ensure that they are not treated differently from other children, but there are difficulties in that social services do not deal with all children, and this affects their concept of 'normal'. Often this results in placing the responsibility for disability services in teams that are concerned primarily with child protection and it means inevitably the marginalisation of the former. Middleton (1995) suggests that this has been made worse by the separate Department of Health guidance on working with disabled children, which has allowed many social workers to remain uninvolved. Both managers and practitioners need to ensure that the statutory responsibilities towards disabled children are taken seriously if they are to contribute to the removal of disabling barriers and the promotion of inclusive services (Middleton, 1999). The marginalisation of such services is oppressive and part of the process of disabling children that the Children Act sought to minimise.

A final area where families may need help is in handling the stresses created by their dealings with apparently unfeeling professionals and bureaucracies. There has long been evidence that doctors are particularly poor at giving information to parents about their disabled child (Lonsdale *et al.*, 1979; Brechin *et al.*, 1981). Robinson (1978), in his discussion of the relationship between professionals and clients with a disabled child, encapsulated his findings in the title of his book *In Worlds Apart*. He identified a number of dimensions to the problem, including poor communication between the doctor and parents, and the failure of professionals to acknowledge, let alone deal with, parental feelings of discomfort or threat. In addition, he found that parents felt powerless with regard to decisions made about their child's future, and some professionals individually behaved in an autocratic way. Finally, the service offered was itself inadequate.

Additionally, in relation to ethnic minority families, Ahmad *et al.* (2000a) argue that the reductionist approach of health professionals, who view certain problems such as sickle cell disease as being linked to ethnicity, avoids fuller explanations and makes families feel guilty.

Again, social workers can be involved in two important ways: first, as members of teams involved in telling parents, they can try to ensure information is imparted in the most appropriate and humane way possible; and second, they can provide emotional support for parents who may need to resolve their feelings of anger and distress about the way they have been treated.

In this section on families with a disabled child, the fact that most space has been devoted to the emotional reactions of the families concerned does not mean that this is regarded as the most important problem. Rather, it is the problem to which social work has devoted the most attention and it is for this reason that it has been considered at length. However, the need for practical assistance may in many cases be paramount, and social work assistance with locating and providing appropriate resources may be crucial. This once again suggests a shift in focus, away from the individual model and towards a social model of disability.

Abuse of disabled children

Disabled children have remained largely hidden in respect of child abuse and the response of social work, despite this being a major concern regarding non-disabled children. A few writers (Brown and Craft, 1989; Kennedy, 1989; Kelly, 1992; Marchant and Page, 1992; Middleton, 1992; 1995, 1999; Westcott, 1993; Westcott and Cross, 1995; Morris, 1997b, 1998; Read and Clements, 2001; Reeve, 2003) have begun to discuss the issue and to identify a range of ways in which disabled children are abused.

Child protection practice recognises four main forms of abuse: neglect; physical; sexual; and emotional. All of these can happen to disabled children as much as to any other child, if not more so, but they may occur for different reasons in some circumstances, and there are some additional forms of abuse that may be specific to them. The main issues of abuse of disabled children are threefold: first, that child protection services have ignored their abuse, either because they fail to acknowledge that it could happen, or because services that are geared to families miss the abuse that occurs in residential school settings, or because abusive acts towards disabled children are treated as a normal and tolerable reaction of over-stressed parents, or because social workers lack the appropriate communication skills. Second, the institutionalisation of disabled children by the education system in particular leaves them not only vulnerable to abuse by non-family members, but it also denies them a role in mainstream society that other children enjoy. Finally, the imposition of a non-disabled normality through activities such as conductive education and the psycho-emotional effects of disablism can act as a form of identity abuse. While there is insufficient space here to consider the practice of child protection *per se*, the purpose of this section is to highlight the most pertinent issues that affect disabled children, and to consider what the social model might mean in terms of the response of social work, the police and the courts, which tend to see such abuse as unbelievable or the fantasies of disabled children.

The absence of provision for disabled children's welfare by those who operate within child protection services is obviously a major cause for concern, precisely because it appears not to be of concern to those services. Middleton reports that, in the volumes of research into child abuse that were commissioned by the Department of Health following the Cleveland enquiry, there is only 'one passing reference to disabled children as special victims which relates to the special problems facing some parents'. She goes on to explain that this research

> conceptualises child abuse as socially constructed, reflecting the values of society. If this is essentially true, it follows that the official failure to deal with the abuse of disabled children reflects a cultural lack of concern for their welfare. Disabled children will only be better protected when we learn as a society to value them equally.
> (Middleton, 1995, p. 70)

There is no doubt that disabled children are abused (Westcott, 1993; Westcott and Cross, 1995) despite the official denial of the problem. Understanding why this is the case is key to changing the situation, both in terms of reducing the level of abuse and in terms of getting the child protection services to act. Middleton (1995) suggests that the situation arises from a combination of factors, and while these interact in a complex manner, it is worth separating them in order to consider how they have failed disabled children.

First, it is paradoxical that non-disabled adults, who operate the protection services, find it difficult to believe that the children they see only as vulnerable could ever be the target of an abuser, despite the evidence that abusers prey on vulnerability. This reflects the social norm of viewing disability as a personal tragedy and seeing disabled people only in terms of the help and assistance they need, rather than as having the same potential for abuse as non-disabled people, even when that potential may be greater.

Next, social workers, as representatives of the welfare system, may consider that much of the abuse that disabled children suffer is acceptable. The dominant ideology that sees the disabled child as a burden on an otherwise happy family is forgiving of lapses in the patience of parents and carers. While this certainly arises from the failure to see disabled people as anything more than dependent and as the cause of the problem, it also reflects some collusion on the part of social workers and their agencies, by their failure to provide adequate support to families with disabled children.

Third, some abuse may not be recognised as such because it does not happen to non-disabled children. Rough handling of children requiring personal assistance, or the failure to ensure that certain aids and equipment are changed as the child grows, or are fitted carefully, are common. This is reframed in terms of the treatment of the child rather than as a form of abuse and reflects the strength of the process of medicalising disability that is integral to the individual model.

Fourth, for some disabled children, the problem arises because the child protection services generally have no means of communicating other than with non-disabled children. This is both in terms of the general lack of communication skills such as sign language, but also a result of the tendency to understand the world, including abuse, in terms of a non-disabled culture. Throughout the welfare system and society at large, the issue of communication is seen as a problem of the individual who cannot talk or hear, rather than as society's failure to be inclusive of other communication systems. This results in disabled children being unable to give evidence or even to be heard.

Finally, abuse may be considered as an acceptable price to pay for otherwise resolving an administratively difficult problem. Many children are, for example, sent to residential schools, or may be placed with foster families in which they are subsequently abused. These resources may be quite scarce because of the reluctance of other foster parents or of mainstream schools to accommodate disabled children, so the additional problem to the social services authority of placing the child if he or she were to be removed serves to outweigh the abuse. While this may be the least bad option from an administrative perspective, it is not, in the language of child care, in the best interests of the child.

These reactions to impairment in children illustrate the depth of the influence of the individual model within social work. The institutional structures of social services agencies and the cultural beliefs of social workers both tend to mitigate against an approach that treats disabled children appropriately. The problem, however, is not simply one of an inadequate response, but also possibly one of collusion.

Morris (1997b), in a review of literature on the placement of disabled children in boarding schools and care homes, found that social services departments may be using such placements as a means of avoiding intervening in child care issues, and this may include cases of abuse to disabled children. This not only reflects discrimination against individual children, but on an institutional level it is qualitatively different from the response to non-disabled children. These problems are not resolved by simple policy changes, although these are important, and ideas such as replacing child protection conferences with children in need conferences might go some way to breaking down the organisational barriers. What is also required is for the culture of understanding to be changed. This can only be achieved by challenging the assumptions on which it is based and which have been internalised by many social workers and agencies, or they will continue to curtail those who seek to practice appropriately.

Middleton (1995) argues that social workers must respond to the challenge of child abuse as part of an anti-oppressive practice that leads to a breakdown of artificial institutional boundaries and that does not seek to polarise the interests of the child and his/her parents on the basis of one being the victim of the others who are totally bad. However, child protection services are facing their own political and practice problems that often mitigate against the inclusion of disability issues. The other components of an anti-oppressive strategy would therefore need to include disability equality training and awareness-raising regarding the nature of disablement. These are training issues that will be discussed further in Chapter 7, but two factors should be stressed. First, social work practice will not progress unless it is modified to incorporate the social model of disability. This is not simply an academic debate, as what we see in examining child abuse is that it is the individual model of disability that causes the child protection services to ignore disabled children. Second, it is insufficient simply to direct training at those specialists who express an interest. The lesson of child protection's failure to protect disabled children is that any disability equality and awareness training must include the majority of social workers and their managers, while recognising that the role of specialists is complex and must not be sacrificed.

The issue of abuse of disabled children also needs to consider the cultural and structural barriers that exclude them, or try to control and limit their identity as disabled people. Finkelstein and Stuart (1996), for example, seek an ending of the treatment of disabled children as children with 'special needs', arguing that this arises out of a cultural belief that their lives have a lesser value than those of non-disabled children. The changes they seek start at conception, with an end to screening programmes. They argue that the impairment of a foetus causes no additional risk to the mother during pregnancy or at birth, and that the future quality of life of the child is not a ground for abortion. They highlight instead the need for family support and the right of the child not to be over-protected on some false assumption of their inability to take responsibility for themselves, as well as the ending of segregated education. Morris (1997b) also identifies the lack of family support as a factor in causing a correlation between severity of impairment and the likelihood of residential care being considered an option by social services. Abbott et al. (2000) report widespread variations between authorities in this practice:

> in one inner London authority there were 8 disabled children per 100 pupils with a statement of special educational needs placed at residential school by the education authority; in a North East England metropolitan authority the equivalent figure was 0.2 per 100.
> (Abbott et al., 2000, p. 2)

For Abbott et al. there was a second issue, which was the extent to which children were not consulted, particularly by education authorities, but also by social workers if children were perceived to be difficult to communicate with. However, being put into care as a disabled child not only means a segregated childhood, but often a segregated adulthood. Not only does placement in residential homes lead to an increased risk of recognised forms of abuse, it is a level of deprivation that is not experienced by non-disabled people.

The final issue here is concerned with emotional abuse and the denial of self-identity. We have already referred to conductive education, which while being the subject of considerable debate (Beardshaw, 1993; Oliver, 1993), nevertheless serves as a good example of what emotional abuse might mean in relation to disabled children's identity. In a society that is dominated by the individual model in which normality is seen as the lack of any impairment, it is difficult for anyone who deviates from this norm to develop a positive self-identity, as they are treated as being abnormal. Yet this has been identified as an important element of the struggle of disabled people to remove the barriers that confront them. This is quite different from overcoming difficulties in the functional sense. The development of a positive self-identity is necessary to individuals seeking to assert their own value and citizenship alongside others. What is problematic about conductive education is that it aimed to train people to conform to a non-disabled normality, and in the process devalued diversity.

This is also the case when deaf children are prevented from learning sign language by being sent to special schools that allow only lip-reading. They are being denied the right to become part of a linguistic culture and are expected to conform to the hearing norm. Morris describes the importance of pride to disabled people:

> When a mother says that she loves her child 'in spite' of that
> child's disability, she is saying that she does not love the
> disabled part of her child. When the Spastics Society urges
> the public to 'see the person and not the wheelchair', they
> are being asked to ignore something that is central to our
> experience. And when our achievements are applauded as
> 'overcoming all odds', the disabled part of us is being denied
> and diminished.
>
> Valuing us as people should not mean ignoring the things
> about our bodies which make us different. In asserting our
> rights we also want to take pride in ourselves. We cannot do
> this unless this pride incorporates the way we are different.
> (Morris, 1992, p. 6)

Childhood is a formative period of life and the impact both then and later in adulthood of having one's life devalued can be enormous. Emotional abuse is not usually considered to be as important as other forms of abuse – physical, sexual and neglect – but the

to occur within a society that devalues impairment
/e, 2003), so it is a matter that should underpin social
/ disabled children, both within child protection and else-

Growing up with a disability: making relationships

Certainly, many disabled young people experience difficulties in
making relationships of either a social or a sexual nature, and there
are a number of factors in this, some of which may be related to
individual problems and others that may be a consequence of the
social and physical environment. Stewart sums this up when he says
that 'Disabled people sometimes have severe relationship difficulties, either through sheer lack of opportunity for meeting and
involvement with other people, or through deficiency in the
emotional and social skills which enable adequate development and
maintenance of friendships and love affairs' (Stewart, 1979, p.
201). However, there is a problem with the assumption that the
lack of opportunities and deficiency in skills are two separate
issues, as the former will certainly lead to the latter. In other words,
it is the experience of special schools and overprotection during
childhood that fails to equip people with the ability to develop relationships alongside their peers rather than the presence of an
impairment. Furthermore, the reactions of non-disabled people,
who have themselves had an education away from disabled children, are unlikely to ease the process. Specific aspects of these problems need to be discussed in a little more detail in order to clarify
areas where social work intervention may be appropriate.

Disabled people may not have the same opportunities to meet
other people. Many social gatherings, such as clubs and discos, may
simply be physically inaccessible, and in a wheelchair it may not
always be possible to participate in that favourite teenage pastime
of hanging around on street corners. Disabled people may also find
it difficult to initiate contact in pubs or at parties. To take the initiative and take a seat close to someone may be very difficult for
wheelchair users or for visually impaired people. Parents of
disabled youngsters are sometimes overprotective and reluctant to
allow their children to take the usual teenage risks. Furthermore,
disabled teenagers may also find it difficult to do things that
perhaps they should not (when they go out they probably have to

be transported by their parents). They therefore can't lie to their parents about where they have been or who they have been with.

Special schools are often criticised for exacerbating these problems in a number of ways. For a start, they usually take disabled youngsters away from their own home environment and peers for most of the year, and by the time they eventually leave these segregated establishments, peer relationships have often been formed in their local community on a lasting basis and they find themselves excluded. For ethnic minority families, the problems also include the lack of culturally sensitive Deaf education which leads to difficulties for Asian Deaf children in learning about culture and religion (Ahmad *et al.*, 2000b). This is summed up in the title of their paper, 'I sent my child to school and he comes back an Englishman.'

Criticism is often levelled at these schools, not only in terms of the educational standards they provide, but also because they fail to provide remedial social skills programmes to alleviate the negative effects of segregation. Hence special education may further disable impaired adolescents and offer nothing 'special'. This non-education approach to schooling dates back to the beginning of the twentieth century, for while disabled children were seen as educable prior to that time, the influence of eugenics appears to have led to policies of containment (Borsay, 2005). These criticisms are very serious when it is borne in mind that there has been little change since then in the proportion of disabled children who are educated in special schools. Barnes (1991) examined the educational statistics from the Department for Education and Science which showed that between 1977 (the year of the Warnock Report) and 1989, the proportion of schoolchildren in special schools had fallen by only 0.06 per cent, from 1.41 per cent to 1.35 per cent. Furthermore, he argues that, in itself, this figure is misleading, as many local authorities had in fact increased their segregated education over this period, a few by as much as 25 per cent. The trend over a longer period (Table 4.1) shows that the proportion of all children attending special schools rose from 1.01 per cent in 1970/1 before the Warnock Report, peaking in the decade after this and then reducing to 1.11 per cent in 2002/3. It is perhaps too early to assess the impact that Part IV of the Disability Discrimination Act, 1995 will have on this trend, though any move towards inclusive education would appear to be slow.

Table 4.1 Percentage of schoolchildren attending special schools, 1970–2003

1970/71	1980/81	1990/91	2000/01	2001/02	2002/03
1.01	1.40	1.23	1.12	1.11	1.11

Source: Adapted from *Social Trends* 34, table 3.2.

Another major problem for disabled people in making and sustaining relationships is the reaction of other people. There are two aspects to this. Other people may be prejudiced towards the disabled individual or indeed may simply be uncertain about how to treat him or her – should the disability be ignored, or spoken about openly, and, if the latter, at what stage in the relationship should such questions be raised? Lenney and Sercombe (2002) suggest that avoidance of communication with disabled people, which

> is often interpreted as hostility, either because of the way that people with able bodies look at those with disabilities or because of their avoidance of interaction, may more frequently be due to uncertainty about how to interact, about reluctance to draw undue attention to themselves or the person with a disability or to invade their privacy.
> (Lenney and Sercombe, 2002, p. 17)

Such uncertainty is a product of the lack of contact caused by segregated education. On the other hand, disabled people may be unsure or simply lack experience about how to present themselves to other people. This may occur as a consequence of over-protection by parents, or again through segregation during their education. Thus disabled people may be too intense in their personal relationships, or may want to move to different stages in a given relationship too quickly. It is certainly clear that other people are part of the problem, because, as American sociologist Edwin Lemert has commented:

> Although physical handicaps partially restrict opportunities for achievement, the more critically operating limits come from an overlay of interpersonal and formal social barriers

founded upon cultural stereotypes about physical defects. As many physically disadvantaged people say, the problem is less the handicap than it is the people.
(Lemert, 1967, pp. 1617)

Stewart shows how making relationships for disabled people may be more of a problem for disabled young people than for others:

> Our relationships, including our sexual relationships, are formed mainly within our circle of established acquaintances, and the smaller the circle, the less the opportunity. The part which unsuitable ingress to premises plays in limiting social – and hence relationship – activities for handicapped people is incalculable. Admittedly, some disabled people will make use of this excuse to withdraw from social life, but for others it remains the main problem.
> (Stewart, 1979, p. 36)

So the main problems involved in making relationships with disabled youngsters are the physical environment, the response of others, segregating educational practices, over-protection and the lack of experience that some disabled people themselves have in coping with the demands of an able-bodied world. Sensitive social work intervention should take into account the possible presence of some of these factors, and should encourage disabled youngsters to take their place in the world and not be segregated from it in schools, day centres and residential units.

On an organisational level, the problem has been identified as one of transition between different services; that is, between the education services which provide support for disabled children and adolescents, and social services which provide services for disabled adults. And with children's social work services having moved into education departments, the need for communication is not diminished. The Disabled Persons (Services, Consultation and Representation) Act, 1986 addressed this issue specifically in sections 5 and 6, which lay down a framework for these two agencies to communicate with each other in order to ensure the transfer of responsibility and a smooth transition for disabled adolescents.

However, as the Social Services Inspectorate (SSI) (1995, 1997) project into this issue has shown, it requires more than administrative procedures. These reports also place an emphasis on the need for interrelated policy-making between children's and adult services; for the inclusion of disabled youngsters in that policy-making process; for the development of social work skills in working with families with disabled children; and for the use of disability equality training as a means of promoting the social model of disability. Despite the rhetoric of joined-up services since 1997, there has been little change in practice.

Furthermore, the SSI recognised the need to go beyond the two agencies that are by statute required to communicate, and to involve GPs, health authorities, housing departments and employers in the process. Each of these contribute to the production of a disabling environment, and therefore needs to make changes to its own practices if disabled children are to be enabled to enter adult life with the opportunities available to non-disabled people.

Sex and disability

The attention paid to sex and disabled people has tended to focus on problems, and the manner in which subsequent interventions have occurred have often been 'unhelpful because they are mechanistic, depoliticised, and outdated' (Shakespeare, 1997, p.183). In fact, it could be argued that this aspect of disabled people's lives has received too much attention and that it should be returned to where it belongs – to people's private lives. Certainly, it is true to say that the attention attracted by the 'sex and disability industry' reveals as much about society's own values as it does about the sexual aspects of the lives of disabled people. Once again, then, the individual and social models of disability need to be considered in relation to sex – the individual sexual problems that some disabled people may have (individual model), and value judgements concerning appropriate and acceptable ways of expressing sexuality in present-day society (social model).

Stewart provided some of the earlier material on the sexual problems of individual disabled people. In his own survey he found:

> Over half the disabled people interviewed (searchingly and at some length) were found to be subject to current, personal, significant sexual problems: the precise proportion was 54%.

A further 18% had experienced such problems since the onset of their disorders (whether at birth or later) but these had become less significant – having been solved by personal effort, infrequently resolved by suitable advice or counsel, all too often fading into insignificance only with time and custom.

(Stewart, 1979, p. 39)

There is little other empirical evidence about whether the proportion of disabled people experiencing sexual difficulties is greater than the rest of the population or not, though Morris (1989) does add a more qualitative dimension to the meaning of that experience for women with spinal injuries, while Shakespeare *et al.* (1996) have contributed significantly to the literature with their biographical and analytical account of sexuality focusing on gay and lesbian relationships. McCarthy (1999) interviewed a number of women with learning difficulties, and for most of them their experience of sex was negative; they perceived it as an activity in which men were always in control. Stewart's findings also need to be qualified by the fact that the numbers in his sample were fairly small, and as a sexual counsellor it is likely that he would be sensitive to this particular aspect of disabled people's lives. Certainly, the assumption made by some professionals that sexual relations are an inevitable problem for disabled people and their partners is unwarranted.

The relevance of this discussion for social work intervention is that it would be wrong to assume that all disabled people have unresolved sexual problems of one kind or another, but that when it is apparent that there are sexual problems it might be useful to have some understanding of possible causes. Pain or lack of sensation may be factors that make it difficult to achieve satisfactory sexual fulfilment for both parties, as may impotence, depending on the particular medical condition. Real or imagined physical danger can also affect sexual performance, as can the side-effects of some medication. Incontinence and incontinence devices may also inhibit or affect sexual relations. Finally, it has been clearly established that psychological factors such as fear, anxiety and a poor self-image can also adversely affect sexual performance.

It would be foolish to deny that most disabled people are impaired in sexual performance if we take the dominant cultural values of completed coitus and orgasm as the standard. However, that does not imply that it is not possible for the vast majority of disabled people to achieve satisfactory sexual relations. The problem, then, may be one of social expectations and cultural values rather than impaired individual performance, though, of course, the discrepancy between social expectations and individual performance may be experienced as personal inadequacy. Shakespeare explains how these expectations operate:

> In the realm of sex and love, the generalised assumption that disability is a medical tragedy becomes dominant and inescapable. In modern western societies, sexual agency is considered the essential element of full adult personhood, replacing the role formerly taken by paid work: because disabled people are infantilised, and denied the status of active subjects, consequently their sexuality is undermined. This also works the other way, in that the assumption of asexuality is a contributing factor towards the disregard of disabled people.
> (Shakespeare, 1996, p. 192)

The social model of disability may also throw light on the sexual problems of disabled people in day centres and residential establishments, in that often these problems are in the minds of professionals rather than in those of disabled people themselves. They stem from decisions made about segregating disabled people in particular kinds of institution and the rules made in them to regulate all behaviour, including sexual. These rules often extend to disabled people's own homes when they are dependent on community care services. That is not to deny that there are genuine moral dilemmas to be resolved concerning issues such as helping disabled people to masturbate if they are unable to do it for themselves, or putting them in a bed of their choice and not where staff think they should be. These issues are not only related to sex, however, but also to things such as smoking cannabis and other activities. The point is that problems created by non-disabled people organising services in particular ways are often turned around and located at the level of individual disabled people. The practice of social work within a social model would require an end to this process of pathologising and the development of an awareness of the support that individuals might need when faced with such barriers.

Furthermore, it requires individual social workers to examine their own prejudices, which may contribute to the negative stereotypes that see the sexuality of disabled people, whether heterosexual or homosexual, as being perverted and limited to relationships with other disabled people.

Disability, marriage and partnership

Sex may or may not be a problem in long-term relationships where one or both of the partners is disabled. But certainly there may also be practical problems of housing or mobility, and most of the aids and adaptations are geared to the single person: ripple mattresses are not made in double sizes, and extensions to houses are often only built to accommodate the disabled person, regardless of whether there is a partner or not. This not only causes practical problems to many people, but also reflects the dominance of a social attitude in which disabled people are not seen as being part of a family or other relationship.

However, what little evidence there is on the break-up of marriages where there is a disabled member is conflicting. Topliss (1979), in a survey in Southampton, found that 16 per cent of disabled women were divorced or separated compared with a national divorce rate of 7 per cent at the time. However, only 4 per cent of disabled men were divorced. Sainsbury (1970) suggests that marriages are more likely to break up when the wife rather than the husband is disabled. On the other hand, Blaxter (1980), in her study in Scotland, found that the divorce rate among disabled men exceeded that among disabled women. In Morris's (1989) study of women with spinal injuries, which may not necessarily be representative of other disabled people, 17 out of 102 who were married at the time of their injury had subsequently divorced (over varying time spans) and while some account for this by individual reactions to their impairment, social expectations also played a role: 'Samantha blames her divorce partly on her consultant who told her husband that "75 per cent of marriages go bang and to get rid of the double bed. I am sure this stayed with him and did not give our personal life a chance. He left 15 months after I came home"' (Morris, 1989, p. 83).

Again, social work intervention should not proceed on the assumption that impairments may create relationship problems;

even where such problems are present, they may stem from outside rather than from individual defects and hence form another aspect of the process of disablement. One way of highlighting possible stresses brought about by social expectations is through the concept of 'role'. When sociologists talk about roles, they usually mean 'behaviour oriented to the patterned expectations of others' (Merton, 1957). This provides the link between the individual and social structure, and suggests that people's behaviour takes into account social expectations, and failure to behave (or failure to be able to behave) in this way may create stress and conflict.

In particular, this expectation is often applied to gender and in the past has suggested that where a man is impaired he may not be able to take on the roles expected of him in the sphere of work, and hence his economic role may be affected. On the other hand, the social expectations of a woman have been seen as different, and the presence of an impairment may be thought to have less effect on her role performance. Today, this makes inappropriate assumptions about role performances based on gender, but does recognise the historical reality of dominant social expectations.

People do not, however, perform roles simply based on external social expectations, and when they do, these expectations are both socially constructed and subject to change. Each individual relationship may produce its own internal expectations about the roles for each partner, and these will reflect contemporary lifestyles. It is important, therefore, for social workers to be aware of the range of role expectations on individuals, to avoid stereotyping people themselves, and to be conscious of the impact of disability from the perspective of the way people see themselves.

Disability in relationships may thus give rise to three kinds of problems: individual problems of a personal or sexual nature; problems related to lack of resources or practical provisions; and, linking the two, discrepancies between individual behaviour and social expectations. Social work assessments will need to take into account the possibility of any or all of these factors being present in order to avoid the situation described by Blaxter (1980, p. 219), where 'Social work support for emotional and family problems tended to be available only after a crisis situation had developed, when help might be too late.' But, again, social workers should avoid assumptions that any or all of these problems must be present. In many relationships where there is a disability no help may be needed at all. Shearer quotes one description of what is an entirely 'normal' marriage:

> My wife goes about her daily chores. I earn the living; we have friends who accept us; our bungalow is indistinguishable from the neighbouring bungalows except that possibly ours is a little better kept. My wife helps me to dress; I help her to bath; we have sexual intercourse frequently; we row about my driving; she never has enough housekeeping money; she always lacks something to wear for the special occasion; in fact, it's all very normal.
> (Shearer, 1981b, pp. 29–30)

Parenting

Despite preconceptions of asexuality, the normality of life for many disabled people includes parenting: according to Goodinge (2000) there are somewhere between 1.2 and 4 million disabled parents in the UK, more than two-thirds of them women, and this number is growing. In her inspection of eight social service authorities she identified 621 disabled parents receiving services, the majority of whom (61%) had physical impairments, while 12 per cent had learning difficulties. However, about one in five of all these families were treated as child protection cases, and this rose to about two-thirds when the parents had learning difficulties. Both these figures are high, and seem to suggest that social workers are not that likely to provide support for disabled parents without an element of concern for the protection of the child. None of the authorities Goodinge inspected had any system for identifying families with disabled parents, and as such offering support was not routine.

Wates (2004) argues that the dominant cultural attitudes in which disabled people are depicted as vulnerable, incapable and dependent lead to child care policies in which 'the (mainly non-disabled) children of disabled parents come to be seen as the primary "clients" and the potential recipients of services, rather than the disabled adults with parenting responsibility for those children' (Wates, 2004, p. 137). She also points out that when disabled parents have been involved with social services, the provision of services improved (Wates, 2002).

Throughout the twentieth century however, there were consider-able attempts in many Western countries, ranging from segregation to sterilisation, to prevent disabled people, especially those with learning difficulties, from having children, and this eugenicist impulse contin-ues to dominate the concerns of many in the welfare field. While it is quite obvious that some disabled people will need support to be able to parent a child, just as they may need support to work or to cater for their personal care, services are geared towards a concept of dangerousness. A very clear example of this is the criteria by which a disabled parent would become eligible for the care component of Disability Living Allowance (DLA) – they have to demonstrate that they are a risk to their child without the supervision of another person.

Goodinge comments on the inappropriateness of social services being provided outside of a social model:

> We were concerned to find that although, according to
> senior managers, the social model of disability guided the
> council's work this did not follow through into their staff 's
> actions. The focus of staff appeared to be either on the chil-
> dren in the family or on the impact of the adults' disability
> on their personal needs. Workers rarely looked beyond this
> and seldom focused on the whole family and how to support
> and help the parents in the discharge of their parental duties
> in their social setting.
> (Goodinge, 2000, p. 2)

She goes on to make recommendations on the principles of services that should be provided:

> A philosophical and practical shift in the approach to work-
> ing with disabled parents is required. It needs to be under-
> pinned by:
> ● a recognition of the right of disabled people, within the
>   bounds of current legislation, to be supported in fulfilling
>   their roles and responsibilities as parents.
> (Goodinge, 2000, p. 2)

Although her report concentrates on the ways in which practice might be enforced administratively, it is worth noting the extent to which the social model analysis of disability issues is accepted by those in authority, and their expectations that this should be the guiding principle for social work interventions.

Priestley (2003) argues that disabled people have not just been considered as incapable of parenting, a situation which might explain why their needs are so poorly met by social workers, but that people with learning difficulties in particular are subjected to surveillance rather than support. He points to a number of user-led initiatives that do offer support to disabled parents in non-intrusive ways. These include advocacy and direct payments, which will be discussed in more depth in Chapter 5. The challenge for social workers is quite clear in respect of parenting; they need to respect disabled people's rights while providing sufficient support in a manner that will enable disabled parents to take full responsibility for child-rearing, without the necessity for surveillance based solely on the presence of impairment.

Growing old with a disability

Any consideration of disability has to take into account that, by adopting a functional definition, the majority of disabled people are, in fact, old. It is not the intention to deal separately with the topic of social work with elderly people, for this has been covered by a number of other writers (for example, Rowlings, 1981; Scrutton, 1989; Froggatt, 1990; Hughes, 1995; Marshall, 1996; Marshall and Dixon, 1996) and as the principal responsibilities of social services towards older people arises through their disablement, this literature tends to deal with the issue of impairments that come with ageing. Rather, it is ageing with a disability needs to be considered.

Until recently there was virtually nothing known about the effects of growing old on disabled people, mainly because, in the past, few people with impairments would have survived into old age. However, the numbers who now do so have increased and some researchers (Morris, 1989; Zarb, 1991; 1993; Zarb et al., 1990) have begun to examine the issues and the consequences for the provision of supportive environments. Zarb (1993) argues that it is important to have a conceptual framework for understanding this issue, as traditional psychological concepts of ageing and policy analyses tend to be inadequate to explain the personal, physical and social consequences of ageing with a disability.

The concept of career has been used as it is capable of taking into account the different experiences and resources that individuals may bring to similar processes, and thus it helps to explain the variations in the way ageing will be experienced. However, while each individual will experience ageing differently, there are certain commonalities in terms of both individual problems associated with impairment, and social problems that result from the way society has responded to this phase in the careers of disabled people. Zarb describes some of the individual issues:

> First, many people's experiences are consistent with the notion of 'premature' physical ageing; for them, ageing is characterised by a process of 'general deterioration' which appears to be more closely associated with the length of time since the onset of the impairment than with age itself. Typically there is a noticeable 'downturn' in physical well-being and health status around 20 to 30 years from onset, regardless of chronological age.
>
> Second, many of the physical changes that people experience are perceived as being long-term effects of their original impairments. For some groups, there are also common secondary impairments caused either by the original impairment, or the long term effects of medical treatment or rehabilitation. The most common of these is the high incidence of arthritic and rheumatic problems; other specific examples include blindness and neurological problems associated with long-term diabetes; chronic pain resulting from building up immunity to certain drugs, such as morphine (various groups); chronic respiratory problems caused by spinal deformity (scoliosis); and a variety of physiological problems coming under the heading of 'post-polio syndrome'.
> (Zarb, 1993, p. 190).

It is clear, therefore, that as a result of ageing, individual impairments may be exacerbated and as a consequence the need for personal assistance will increase. However, current social policy tends to assume the opposite, because it reflects the role expectations of society which are themselves linked artificially to chronological age. In this way, the spending limits of social service authorities on community care, which are set relative to residential and nursing home payments, are considerably lower for people over retirement age than for those of working age, while direct payments may be discouraged if the person is over 65 years of age.

Similarly, social security payments are usually reduced at retire-ment age, and some allowances, such as the mobility component of DLA, disappear altogether, causing a real drop in income to people who may have had very restricted opportunities to earn personal pensions in the same way as the non-disabled population.

The difficulties of ageing can be emotional as well as physical. Becoming older often causes people to reflect more on their earlier lives, and for some disabled people such reflections may amount to a reminiscence of unfulfilled potential. MacFarlane (1994) argues that, for disabled women in particular, this may be a time when they recall a lifetime of being deprived of the right to enjoy fulfill-ing relationships, of being aware of one's own sexuality and of experiencing childbirth, and that this can prove to be a daunting time. Furthermore, while this is itself a result of the social responses to impairment over a lifetime, it can be compounded by policy and institutional reactions to age: 'It is agonising to look forward to the struggle of reaching the age of sixty and to know that hard fought for services and other provision will be reassessed and probably changed because of the ageing process' (MacFarlane, 1994, p. 255). Ageing may therefore be experienced as a time of threat, not simply from the difficulties caused by deteriorating health or emotional distress, but also by the reactions of welfare agencies, in particular their readiness to view residential care as a more appropriate response to the need for personal assistance. Zarb suggests that this threat to lifestyle may be so great as to cause some people to consider euthanasia or suicide, which is a terrible indictment of the role that social services play in providing 'care' to disabled people as they grow older. Clearly, then, the task for social workers as agents of such authorities must be to assist individuals to access the services that will permit them to maintain independence and choice within their own lives. Once again, it is necessary to have an aware-ness of the individual problems that disabled people face, but it is more important to understand how these become barriers when policy responses follow an individual model of disability.

Disability and caring

One of the consequences of inadequate social services support, whether as a result of insufficient funding, oppressive policies or poor social work, is that it will cause disabled people of all ages to be dependent on family and friends for personal assistance. It can, of course, be argued that rather than viewing the lack of such services as being the cause of dependent relationships, their provision at whatever level should be seen as a contribution towards reducing the dependency that results from the presence of an impairment. This, however, does not stand up to the scrutiny of comparison with many other services that are provided collectively to ensure the comfort, security and mobility of the non-disabled population; for example, utilities such as water and fuel suppliers, or services such as road maintenance or snow clearance. While disabled people also benefit from such services, the efficiency with which they are provided to a level that affords non-disabled people the opportunity to enjoy a satisfying lifestyle is in contrast to the social commitment to services that would allow disabled people to live independently (Finkelstein and Stuart, 1996).

In the 1990s, those who provide the assistance within dependent relationships received official recognition and succeeded in having their own needs considered to be deserving of welfare support through the Carers (Recognition and Services) Act, 1995. The early case for this was made by a combination of arguments: that carers save the state a considerable sum of money (Nissel and Bonnerjea, 1982); that the task of caring falls disproportionately on women (Equal Opportunities Commission, 1982); and through highlighting the consequences of lack of support for families that take on the role (Oliver, J., 1982).

There is no denying that a great deal of stress can arise from being on either side of this dependency relationship, but what is problematic are solutions that do not accord with the aims of independent living for disabled people. The recognition of carers is itself part of the problem, because it reinforces the helper–helped relationship that lies at the heart of the creation of dependency, by seeing carers' needs as relative to the 'burden' caused by the disabled person. As a result, the solutions that have been advocated, in particular by feminists seeking to reduce the exploitation of women (Finch, 1984), and which have been maintained by welfare services, have been to offer respite to carers by providing short- and long-term residential care to disabled people. Such solutions, which focus on the support of carers within the current policy context, clearly reinforce the exclusion of disabled people from full citizenship.

Others, however (Croft, 1986; Morris, 1991), have argued

that the interests of disabled people and women carers can be viewed as compatible if a social model analysis is applied to the issues. In this way, what is recognised is not so much the burden on one side of the relationship – that is, the carers – but that the aims of independent living are for disabled people to be free of the dependency it creates. Katbamna *et al.* (2000) argue that relationships are complex, and that both carers and disabled people experience stigma, love, exhaustion and commitment. The policy solution therefore lies in collective approaches that are based on the inclusion, not the exclusion of disabled people from mainstream social organisation: in other words the removal of disabling barriers.

Prior to 1997, much of the government guidance about carers focused on the social work task of mediating between their needs and those of disabled people. Since 1997, policy documents from the Department of Health have used the phrase 'users and carers' in such a way that suggests they wish both to have an equal status as participants in the design and delivery of social welfare. While this is laudable inasmuch as it does represent a definite attempt at involvement of both users and carers, it runs the risk of ignoring the potential conflicts of interest between these groups. On the one hand, carers are not being offered a favoured status over those they care for, but on the other it may diminish the voice of disabled people and hinder the struggle to achieve social inclusion.

At the level of the individual and families, which is where social workers are likely to be working, the creation of carers as a recognised, though unpaid, occupation is also problematic, because it ignores the reality of how people live:

> Rather than assuming that the presence of a non-disabled family member creates a relationship of carer and cared-for, it is the relationship between partners, parent and child, siblings, etc. which should be recognised. Some relationships can sustain the giving of personal assistance, some cannot. Some people can facilitate independence for their partner, parent or child, some cannot. Some relationships are abusive and exploitative, some are liberating. To categorise people as carers and dependants is to gloss over all of this.
> (Morris, 1993, p. 40)

This assumption of dependency can have profound effects on families, and in particular the tendency of social workers to see caring by a child for a parent as a form of role reversal. Keith and Morris (1995) argue that the construction of child carers within an individual model analysis, in which the provision of personal assistance determines dependency within a relationship, has the effect of denying the ability of disabled people to parent. Research in this area, they argue, has tended to assume that the presence of an impairment is the cause of the need to care rather than inadequate community support services. The demand therefore for more support on the basis of carers' needs is to both ignore the reality of the situation and to attribute blame to disabled people.

While the social model perspective of this debate has gained some recognition, its full implications have yet to be appreciated by the carers' lobby. In a review of research in this area by the director of the Carers National Association (Pitkeathley, 1996), the emphasis remains clearly on the needs of carers rather than on establishing the rights of disabled people to be free of these dependency relationships, and indeed, Aldridge and Becker (1996) argue that, unpalatable though it might be, this approach is necessary given the economic and political realities of a residual welfare system. However, what such arguments do is to reinforce the injustice of the individual model of disability with its acceptance that disability is a welfare, and not a civil rights, issue.

Clearly, some of these issues are beyond the ability of individual social workers to resolve, but their contribution to the administration of welfare can have a determining impact on individuals and families. The message for social workers in relation to the issue of carers is the same as it has been throughout this chapter; that is not to make assumptions about how different individuals might respond to similar situations, but to work with people from their own perception of the reality of their lives. Working within families is a privilege that requires sensitivity and open-mindedness rather than a professional judgementalism based on politically normative views of complex relationships.

putting it into practice

Exercise 1

There is a quote about the stages approach to loss from Avery (1997) in Chapter 2:

> I have seen a 5th stage, and it is not Acceptance or Hope of a Cure. It is learning that an unborn perfect child was one conceived by society, not me, and that the actual child I was gifted with is perfectly fine.

What strategies could you employ to help overcome the pressures placed on parents to view their children as imperfect?

Exercise 2

Respite care is a common provision of social services departments and often takes the form of institutionalising older and disabled people in order to provide their families with a break from caring for them. However, this suggests that the individual in need of support is the source of the problem and that their removal resolves it. Think creatively about what alternatives you could offer the family carers of (a) an older person; (b) a person with learning difficulties; and (c) a person with physical impairments. The aim of your alternatives should be to avoid institutionalising one person in order to provide respite to another.

Further reading

Ahmad, W. (ed.) (2000) *Ethnicity, Disability and Chronic Illness*, Buckingham: Open University Press. Useful perspectives on the impact of disability within ethnic minority families.

Keith, L. and Morris, J. (1995) 'Easy Targets: A Disability Rights Perspective on the "Children as Carers" Debate', *Critical Social Policy*, 15(2/3), pp. 36–57. A social model perspective of the construction of caring as a problem of dependence when it involves young people.

Middleton, L. (1999) *Disabled Children: Challenging Social Exclusion*, London: Blackwell Science. A child-centred and

social model approach to the issues facing social workers working with disabled children.

Wates, M. (2002) *Supporting Disabled Adults in their Parenting
Role*, York: Joseph Rowntree Foundation. Report of a survey
carried out to investigate the problems disabled people face as
parents in getting support from social services.

5 | Living with disabilities

From the discussion in Chapter 4, it is apparent that one of the main difficulties that disabled people face at all ages is how to maintain relationships with their families while also achieving a level of independence and autonomy. Leat (1988) suggests that the pressure of dependency within families is the most significant cause of disabled people having to enter residential care. Hence in discussing the living options of disabled people, it is necessary to consider the impact of poor community services on these relationships. This impact may also account for the fact that disabled adults are far more likely than non-disabled people to be living alone. In 1986, 30 per cent of disabled adults were living alone (Martin et al., 1989) which compares with just 12.5 per cent of the whole population at the time of the 2001 census. As would be expected, the proportion rises with age, but even if only those under 65 years are considered, some 16 per cent of disabled adults were living alone. This has significant implications for the provision of both housing and the personal assistance that would enable these individuals to live independently, but also for the provision of support to those who live within families. This chapter considers the living options for younger disabled people, generally taken to mean under 65 years old, and discusses the issues of residential and nursing homes, day centres, accessible housing, and personal assistance.

Residential care

While independent living is the preferred option for most people, it has often been the case that the only option available to disabled people is residential care:

> In Great Britain we have a habit of providing for 'difficult' minority groups in segregated institutions and those suffering traumatic tetraplegia are no exception. It is a tradition which

has roots in the Poor Law and which comes down to us today virtually unchanged. Only rarely can someone who depends heavily on others for personal help, and who for some reason does not have the support of – or wishes to live independently of – his or her family, find an alternative system of accommodation and care.
(Davis, 1981, p. 322)

While methodological differences between overall estimates of disabled people and the occupancy of residential and nursing homes make it difficult to compare data directly, it is clear that less than 5 per cent of younger disabled people with physical or sensory impairments are living in this type of accommodation. However, according to the Personal Social Services Current Expenditure 2002/03, 32 per cent of gross expenditure for this group was spent on residential care. Table 5.1 shows that, in 2003, there were 11,500 disabled adults under 65 years of age supported in residential and nursing homes in England.

In addition to this, it should be noted that a significant proportion of people with learning difficulties, and elderly people, of whom 36,320 and 218,500, respectively, were in such accommodation,

Table 5.1 Numbers of adults supported in residential and nursing homes in England, 2003

	Total of all supported residents	Council staffed	Registered care homes		Unstaffed and other
			Independent residential	Independent nursing	
People aged 18–65 years					
Physically/ sensorily disabled adults	11,500	655	6,195	4,485	160
People with mental health problems	13,210	775	9,530	2,540	365
People with learning disabilities	36,320	4,505	28,940	1,855	1,020
Other people	1,785	50	1,440	240	60
People over 65 years	218,500	28,130	120,235	69,275	855
All ages	284,135	37,115	166,340	78,400	5,280

Source: Department of Health, 2003.

will also have physical impairments. It is clear from the OPCS disability surveys that the proportion of disabled people living in institutions rises with age, and as we noted in the previous chapter this is a fear of some disabled people when growing older. While there has been little research concerning younger disabled adults in residential care, if the circumstances of their admission are in any way similar to those of older people, these fears may well be justified. Booth concluded from a comprehensive review of studies about elderly residents that 'Most people do not themselves make a positive choice to enter residential care, and the majority are admitted (often with little consultation and sometimes under pressure) as the result of arrangements by someone else' (Booth, 1992, p. 2).

From the little that is known, disabled people living in residential homes tend to have one of four particular medical conditions – multiple sclerosis, cerebral palsy, stroke or rheumatoid arthritis. While this is reflective of the whole population of disabled people, those with multiple sclerosis formed a disproportionately high part of the population (over half) of health authority Young Disabled Units (YDUs) while local authority homes seemed to cater primarily (about 40 per cent) for people with cerebral palsy (Leat, 1988). Both the increase in likelihood of residential care with age and the preponderance of certain impairments among residential home residents can perhaps be accounted for by dominant social attitudes towards the provision of welfare. Dalley (1996) argues that residential care reflects the ideological attitudes of society as to what form care should take at any given time. It appears, however, that the application of this ideology may be selective, according to medical conditions. This suggests that people with particular types of impairments may be more vulnerable to being institutionalised, as are older disabled people.

Dalley considered, however, that the climate in the mid-1990s was in favour of home care and, indeed, there has been a gradual acknowledgement that the most appropriate place to live is in the community, even for those people with severe impairments. Alf Morris, when opening the Sunningdale conference on disability in the late 1970s, gave voice to this view when he said that 'Happily, more and more people are coming to see that it is undesirable to institutionalise even severely disabled people, that their needs must increasingly be met in the community.' This philosophy was enshrined in official documents (DHSS, 1976, 1981; Department of

Health, 1998), endorsed in reports such as the Snowdon Report, and given parliamentary approval through a series of legal measures, notably the Chronically Sick and Disabled Persons Act, 1970 and the Community Care (Direct Payments) Act, 1996. If, as Drake (1999) argues, 'disability policy in Britain has expressed several objectives: the desire to contain, to compensate, to "care" and, latterly, to achieve citizenship' (p. 67), then the move away from residential or nursing care is certainly necessary for the latter.

This change of attitude may be insufficient in itself, though, to replace the physical legacy of the centuries of development of institutions. Furthermore, while the rhetoric of community care may be dominant, in practice there has been a massive growth in residential provision since 1948, when the NHS inherited just 55,000 beds for chronically sick people from the Poor Law infirmaries and workhouses (Barnes, 1991). This rose to 506,500 places in residential and nursing homes in 1996, housing just over 428,000 people (Department of Health, 1996), though, as we noted above in Table 5.1, the total number of supported residents has now fallen to 284,000. Langan (1990) had argued that current community care legislation, which encourages the expansion of the independent sector, would cause this growth of institutional care as it is more profitable than any of the alternatives.

The continued use of residential care may also be a result of personal economic factors. Schorr (1992) pointed to the correlation that exists, in both Britain and the USA, between the use of residential care and income. It is only when the spending power of elderly people has increased relative to the incomes of others in the population that there has been any reduction in the trend of increasing numbers of people entering residential homes. Schorr argued that changes in welfare policy must include income maintenance issues as well as personal social services policy if community care is to succeed. This was also the position taken in 1976 by the Union of Physically Impaired Against Segregation (UPIAS) in its statement of Fundamental Principles of Disability:

> Of course the Union supports and struggles for increased
> help for physically impaired people, there can be no doubt
> about our impoverishment and the need for urgent change.
> However, our Union's Aims seek the 'necessary financial . . .
> and other help required from the State to enable us to gain

the maximum possible independence in daily living activities, to achieve mobility, undertake productive work and to live where and how we choose with full control over our lives'. (UPIAS, 1976, p. 15)

These trends have important ramifications for the shape and future of residential care facilities for disabled people. Some, like the UPIAS, have called for nothing less than the complete disappearance of all segregated and segregative institutions: 'The Union's eventual object is to achieve a situation where as physically impaired people we all have the means to choose where and how we wish to live. This will involve the phasing out of segregated institutions maintained by the State or Charities.' And while stopping short of a demand for the closure of all existing institutions, they stated that 'The Union is opposed to the building of any further segregated institutions' (UPIAS policy statement, *Disability Challenge*, May 1981). At the same time, however, Topliss was arguing the need for additional residential facilities: 'The real issues are the desperate shortage of facilities and the fact that standards and variety in the provision of residential accommodation are not commensurate with expectations and variety of needs of disabled individuals' (in Topliss and Gould, 1981, p. 118). However, in 1996, the Department of Health (1996) statistics showed that there were about 900 vacant places (just over 8 per cent of the total) in residential homes for physically/sensorily disabled people, which suggests that this type of provision has been grossly over-supplied. Although overall numbers of residents may not have been increasing over this period, the growth in numbers of homes may be problematic if the purchasing of services remains supply-led.

Residential care for all client groups has been criticized heavily for many years, and this is equally true in respect of disabled people. From the perspective of the social model of disability, there is little doubt that the experience of residential care further disables impaired individuals. Before considering the implications of the social model of disability and the possible tasks of social workers in relation to independent living, it is necessary to fill out some of the background to residential care, outline some of the criticisms of it, and then consider some of the alternatives.

The legal situation of residential care

Social services departments have a duty under part III, section 21, of the National Assistance Act, 1948 'to provide residential accommodation for persons who by reason of age, illness, disability or any other circumstances are in need of care and attention which is not otherwise available to them' and they must also 'have regard for the welfare of all persons for whom such accommodation is provided'. Despite subsequent amendment, in particular by the NHS and Community Care Act, 1990, the statutory duty remains, though it must now be achieved through the purchase of the majority of such services from the private and voluntary sectors.

The 1948 Act recognized a powerful historical tradition for charitable agencies to be involved in such provision, and thereby permitted local authorities to delegate their powers to approved agencies if they so wished. Some authorities chose to do this, and the largest agency providing residential accommodation for disabled people was the Leonard Cheshire Foundation, which has a network of eighty-five Cheshire homes throughout Britain. The NHS also had responsibility for providing residential accommodation for disabled people, and its powers in this area stemmed from section 12 of the Health Services and Public Health Act, 1968 and section 2 of the National Health Service Reorganisation Act, 1973. These powers enabled the NHS to provide residential accommodation for physically handicapped people, but the medical emphasis is often retained, even in the title, where they are called 'young chronic sick units'.

While the first of these units was opened in 1968, the building programme for new units was accelerated after the passage of the Chronically Sick and Disabled Persons Act, 1970, as section 17 required that: 'In any hospital a person who is suffering from a condition of chronic illness or disability is not cared for in the hospital as an in-patient in any part of the hospital which is normally used wholly or mainly for the care of elderly persons, unless he is himself an elderly person'. According to one national survey (Bloomfield, 1976) there were forty-one operational YDUs in Britain in 1975 in comparison with thirty purpose-built local authority homes (Goldsmith, 1976). By 1986, the figures had risen to seventy-two YDUs and fifty-eight local authority homes (Leat, 1988). In the early 1980s, both social services and health authorities had plans for a considerable number of additional units, but economic circumstances and consumer resistance slowed down building programmes. This was effectively halted in 1983 by the amendment to the supplementary benefit regulations regarding board and lodging payments, which led instead to a massive increase in the number of private residential and nursing homes. This change permitted the then DHSS to pay the fees for people in voluntary and private residential and nursing homes, thereby transferring much of the responsibility for these costs away from local authorities and the NHS. These payments eventually constituted the sums that were transferred from the Department of Social Security to local authorities under the NHS and Community Care Act, 1990, placing the responsibility for all residential and nursing home funding with social services departments, since when some YDUs and local authority residential homes have passed into private ownership.

There are effectively three main sectors providing residential accommodation for disabled people: local authorities; the health service; and the independent sector, including voluntary organizations such as the Cheshire Foundation and a large number of private establishments. There is no clear distinction between them, and while some are registered as residential homes, others are registered as nursing homes. In practice, those establishments registered as nursing homes are able to charge higher fees, and while they in theory may take people requiring greater levels of assistance, this is not necessarily the case. Small homes, those with fewer than four residents, have also been required to register since 1993 under the Registered Homes (Amendment) Act, 1991.

Residential accommodation for disabled people: a discredited provision

Since the publication of *Asylums* (Goffman, 1961) a considerable amount of work on the effects of institutionalization has been done. 'Total institutions', as Goffman called them, are characterized by a loss of privacy, a lack of freedom of choice, and the individuals within them miss the opportunity to make meaningful personal relationships. The institution provides a highly structured routine where the lives of the individual residents are regulated by management, and all tend to be treated alike. This gives rise to what has been identified as institutional neurosis:

a disease characterised by apathy, lack of initiative, loss of interest more marked in things and events not immediately personal or present, submissiveness, and sometimes no expression of feelings or resentment at harsh or unfair orders. There is also a lack of interest in the future and an apparent inability to make practical plans for it, a deterioration in personal habits, toilet and standards generally, a loss of individuality, and a resigned acceptance that things will go on as they are – unchangingly, inevitably and indefinitely. (Barton, 1959)

Such studies as are concerned specifically with institutions for disabled people have tended to see the effects of institutionalisation on the residents in less dramatic terms than does Goffman. The 'warehousing' model of residential care described by Miller and Gwynne (1971), and which they call the conventional approach to residential care, approximates to Goffman's total institution in its requirement that the inmate remains dependent and depersonalised, and subjugated to the task of the institution. The authors were 'captured by the plight of intelligent cripples . . . who were forced to lead stunted lives in institutions that do not provide opportunities for their development'. But they do not portray the residents they met in the negative terms used by Barton, for example; two possible differences are that the heavily medicated patients with schizophrenia studied by Barton were particularly vulnerable to institutionalisation, and that the psychiatric hospital is more of a 'closed' community than is a residential home for disabled people. In another study of a home for disabled people, Musgrove (1977) described a visit to a Cheshire Home, which he saw as fitting Goffman's picture of a total institution only in a very superficial way, as the residents were not completely regimented, and he was struck, contrary to his expectation, by the extent to which they had managed to maintain their sense of identity.

However, in a view from the inside, Battye, who experienced life as a resident in both the chronic ward of a long-stay hospital and a Cheshire Home, saw the difference between the two, in spite of the more favourable lifestyle of the latter, as one only of degree, not of kind:

Unless he fights a constant battle to retain his intellectual integrity and sense of purpose, as the years go by he will

gradually feel the atmosphere of the place closing in on him
as it did in the chronic ward . . . in spite of efforts to arouse
or retain his interest in life he will feel boredom and apathy
creeping over him like a slow paralysis eroding his will,
dulling his critical wits, dousing his spirit, killing his independence . . . In a subtler, more civilised way than in the
chronic ward, he will have become institutionalised.
(Battye, 1966, p. 14)

Miller and Gwynne (1971) drew the distinction between 'warehousing' and 'horticultural' models of residential care. The warehousing model expresses the humanitarian or medical value that
the prolongation of life is a good thing, but the question concerning the purpose of the life that is prolonged is never asked. The
emphasis is on medical care and the minimisation of risk – the
main aim is to keep the gap between social death (the point when
the disabled person enters the institution) and physical death as
long as possible. Alternatively, the horticultural model emphasises
the uniqueness of each inmate, the importance of individual
responsibility, and the potential to realise unfulfilled ambitions
and capacities.

However, Miller and Gwynne (1971) failed to fully endorse the
horticultural model because of their concerns that it was problematic because of the overvaluing of independence, the denial of
disability and the distortion of staff–resident relations where the
real facts of the situation are ignored or distorted. Paul Hunt and
other residents of Le Court quickly came to realise that, regardless
of changes that might be made to the operation of residential
homes, the process of segregation would continue to be a process
of social death that could only be countered by living options integrated within the community.

It is not just voluntary and local authority homes that have come
in for such criticism, but YDUs also. Bloomfield, in her national
survey, argued:

By focusing on this one aspect of the inmates' requirements,
the Younger Chronic Sick Unit systematically robs the individual of the opportunity for achieving satisfaction and
purpose in the life remaining to him. The unavoidable
emphasis on his physical dependence on authoritative
personnel frequently leads all but the strongest individuals to

an accepting, apathetic state with little interest in life and
even less initiative.
(Bloomfield, 1976)

When the health authority in Rochdale attempted to build a YDU,
it met with such resistance that it had to abandon their plans
(Finlay, 1978), and the same happened in Surrey (North Surrey
CHC, 1978). Internal and external criticisms of the residential care
sector, coupled with consumer resistance, have forced providers to
look to possible alternatives, but despite a few changes, the
numbers of disabled people entering residential care remains
constant, as do the criticisms. Laurie summarises the attitudes of
many disabled people towards residential care:

> Residential institutions can become virtual prisons for
> disabled people if and when denied any choice in daily deci-
> sions – what to eat and when, when to get up and go to bed,
> who provides assistance and how that is provided. Thus,
> residents in institutions often find themselves stripped of
> their privacy, dignity and individuality, with no locks on
> bathroom or bedroom doors, staff entering rooms without
> knocking, and the right to form relationships denied.
> (Laurie, 1991, p. 51)

The social model analysis of institutionalised care, both in segregated homes and in the community, has also highlighted the issue
of violence towards disabled people. Just as children are made
vulnerable to abuse by being placed in institutions, disabled adults
have also become victims of criminal assaults and other acts of
violence that are not deemed by society to be illegal. In a Canadian
study of violence towards disabled people, the Roeher Institute
found that:

> people with disabilities are more likely than others to be
> subjected to acts of violence and abuse that are proscribed by
> criminal and civil acts. They are also subjected to acts of
> violence and abuse that do not meet legal definitions of
> violence but that the survivors perceive as harmful. These
> may include acts that are perpetrated in places where the
> abuse is shielded from the arm of the law. Contributing to
> the vulnerability is society's inability or unwillingness to
> clearly name and prohibit the problem. But equally important

are the often radically unequal social and economic position
of persons with disabilities that place them at a dispropor-
tionate risk, as well as the lack of individual control and
choice that makes it difficult for the individual to avoid and
escape situations of risk.
(Rioux *et al.*, 1997, p. 203)

Many criticisms of residential care implicitly and explicitly draw
upon the social model of disability in that they see institutional
regimes as adding to, rather than alleviating many of the problems
that disabled individuals face, but in terms of translating this into an
active social policy, there have been some pitfalls in the alternatives.
At the time of writing, it is clear that autonomy and citizenship can
only be achieved by independent living, but it is worth examining
some of the approaches that have been tried along the way.

Alternatives to residential care on the path to independent living

The disabled village

This was based on the village settlement at Het Dorp in The
Netherlands, where around 400 severely disabled people were
accommodated in a single colony. Approximately 80 per cent of the
residents were single, but there were a number of married couples
where both parties were severely impaired. Each resident had a self-
contained flat, and services such as meals and staff care were
provided on site.

The argument in favour of this sort of development was that it
allowed severely handicapped residents to take control of their own
lives. However, the village was not integrated successfully into the
wider community and it became a 'cripples' colony', with little mixing
of disabled and non-disabled people. There are a couple of similar
settlements in Britain, most notably the Thistle Foundation Village in
Edinburgh and the Papworth Settlement in Cambridgeshire. The idea
of villages is probably discredited for people with physical impairments, but there are still those who would advocate that they are suitable for people with learning difficulties.

Collective houses

A number of these sprang up in Denmark, where the tenancies of
blocks of flats are allocated on the approximate ratio of one

disabled person to three non-disabled ones. Consumer services such as restaurants were situated within the blocks and the aim was to move away from institutions and colonies. This ratio of disabled to non-disabled people was found to be rather high, however, and internal social divisions occurred between the two groups. Additionally, the outside world continued to regard the blocks of flats as institutions for the disabled.

While collective houses were not developed on a large scale outside Denmark, there have been a few isolated experiments in Britain where severely disabled people have lived in flats where other, non-disabled, tenants provided physical assistance in exchange for lower rents. Probably the most successful example of this kind of development, though on a smaller scale than the Danish collective houses, was the Grove Road scheme (Davis, 1981). Not only did it provide an appropriate housing environment, but the disabled tenants were able to manage with less than one-third of the direct physical assistance they had needed while in residential care, and were also able to prove wrong all the professional assessments that had labelled them 'too disabled to live in the community'.

Fokus housing

This developed in Sweden and was an attempt to integrate severely disabled people into ordinary housing schemes. Supportive services were provided and there were a range of communal facilities available. It is estimated that in 1983 there were over 2,000 severely disabled people living in this type of accommodation in Sweden.

While these schemes have moved a long way towards the integration of disabled people, it has been suggested that some of the trappings of institutionalisation remain, and that not all of the tenants became part of the community. Ratzka (1991) argued that not only did individual disabled people have no choice in who provided their personal assistance in these schemes, but that the lack of control over when it would be provided meant that Fokus is based on the 'house-arrest principle' of care.

In Britain, following the Chronically Sick and Disabled Persons Act, 1970, many housing authorities attempted to integrate housing for disabled people into their new schemes. However, as disabled people relied on community medical and nursing services for support, and these were often too remote or inflexible to allow severely impaired people to live in the community without a great deal of family support, the utility of such schemes was limited. Furthermore, since the late 1970s, policy towards public-sector housing led to a rapid decline in construction and has effectively ended this programme.

British housing association schemes

The early examples of these were assemblies of between twelve and twenty-five flats grouped together to form a 'mini-colony', often with a warden or caretaker to oversee the residents. Special housing has its roots in the medieval almshouses (Borsay, 2005) which were associated with hospitals, though the modern dwellings are usually built in an urban setting close to main services, and are purpose-designed to maximise independent living.

It is interesting to note that some of the most important voluntary organisations in the residential care sector set up their own housing associations to provide suitable accommodation in the community – notably the Spastics Society (now Scope), John Grooms and the Cheshire Foundation. While many of these schemes may have removed the worst effects of institutionalisation, it has been suggested that they did not truly integrate disabled people into the community, but rather provided a more sympathetic, though still isolated, physical environment. Thus they only go some way towards removing the disabling effects of institutionalisation.

Wood's (2004) study of supported housing did conclude, however, that it was favoured over residential care, and that housing associations have become the major source of new, accessible dwellings for disabled people. Some, such as Habinteg, have been commended for their good practice (Laurie, 1991). Habinteg build integrated estates in which approximately 25 per cent of properties are wheelchair-accessible, while the others are built to a mobility standard. They also avoid the mistake of only building single-bedroomed properties, recognising that disabled people have, and are part of, families. However, it must also be recognised that this has not been the general pattern of either housing association or local authority building (Morris, 1990) and that inappropriate policies and practices concerning the size, nature and location of properties may be major factors in the fact that only 24 per cent of lettings of housing association wheelchair dwellings in 1996 were to wheelchair users (Harris *et al.*, 1997).

Supporting People

Supporting People was introduced in April 2003 as a means of funding care provided in conjunction with social-rented housing. In the late 1990s, legal concerns were raised about the use of Housing Benefit to fund rents that included more than the 'bricks and mortar' costs of housing. Many sheltered and supported housing schemes for a wide range of people had included the costs of support in their rents. The Supporting People project was set up in 1998 and in each local area social services and housing authorities formed partnerships which now deliver the service. In practice, what happens to people in supported housing is that they receive the 'bricks and mortar' element of their rent from Housing Benefit and the care is paid for through Supporting People. Both are, of course, subject to means testing.

The process of the Supporting People project has been compared to the implementation of community care a decade earlier, in that the transfer of responsibility for funding was used as a means of placing budgetary limits on spending that was previously unlimited, at least in terms of the number of applicants. However, Watson *et al.* (2003) do emphasise that the government appears to have been motivated to use this opportunity to increase the amount and effectiveness of services for marginalised groups, although they warn that underfunding of the service, problems related to tenure and a failure so far to reach some of the most marginalised people may undermine these aims. However, as we noted earlier, the numbers of older people living in residential or nursing homes has been reducing, and it may be that in many parts of the UK, local policies to use Supporting People to provide more specialised support in social rented housing may be having some effect.

Lifetime Homes

Lifetime Homes describes a standard of building which means that all housing would have the potential to be adapted for use by a disabled person. The standard was first recommended by the United Nations in 1974, but by twenty years on, only Italy, the

Netherlands, Spain, Sweden and Norway had adopted it, and only Norway was offering any incentives through building loans (Ambrose, 1997). Studies in the UK (Bonnett, 1996; Cobbold, 1997) have shown that this policy would be cost-effective, and the Labour government finally accepted the standards into building regulations for private dwellings in March 1998. Effectively, what this means is that all new private dwellings must be built to an accessible standard, although that may mean that the property is adaptable to the individual requirements of a particular tenant rather than already adapted for any eventuality. It is hoped that this will increase the opportunities for independent living of disabled people by widening their choice in housing, though it must be noted that it will take decades for this to mean that disabled people would have as much choice as non-disabled people.

Personal assistance schemes and direct payments

These are schemes where individual disabled people obtain cash payments from the state in order to employ others directly to act as personal assistants to them. In 1988, the Independent Living Fund (ILF) was set up, which gave large numbers of disabled people access to funds for this purpose, and in 1993 this responsibility was absorbed by local authorities following implementation of the NHS and Community Care Act, 1990. In support of this trend, the Greenwich Association of Disabled People (GAD) employed a Personal Assistance Adviser to help individuals with the problems they might encounter by becoming an employer. An evaluation of this scheme after three years in operation concluded that

> developing independent living options like Personal Assistance Schemes is not just morally desirable and professionally appropriate, but also offers the possibility of providing more cost effective and efficient services through switching from the overproduction of services that people don't want or need and the underproduction of those that they do, to a situation where the services that are produced and purchased by statutory providers are precisely the services that users want and need.
> (Oliver and Zarb, 1992, p. 13)

The Community Care (Direct Payments) Act, 1996 made it legal for local authorities to support individual personal assistance schemes with cash payments to disabled people rather than by providing them with services. This helped to overcome many of the problems experienced in relation to the provision of adequate support services, but the transfer of employer responsibilities from local authorities to individual disabled people also requires a transfer of skills in the recruitment, management and administration of the service. A very useful guide to setting up such schemes has been written by Simpson and Campbell (1996). It is aimed at helping disabled people, voluntary organisations and social services staff to understand what these responsibilities are and how to undertake them.

Since 1996, direct payments have been extended to all those who are eligible for community care services, with two exceptions. The first exception is people whose entitlement is under section 117 of the Mental Health Act, 1983, where the law places a specific responsibility on the social services authority to provide aftercare. The second is those people who are deemed by the social service authority to be incapable of managing the payments, although anyone may appoint an advocate to do this on his or her behalf. Initially, the scheme was not mandatory, but in April 2004 the Secretary of State for Health required local authorities to provide direct payments under powers granted in the Health and Social Care Act, 2001.

The experience of direct payments has so far been mixed, with many disabled people clearly benefiting from the additional autonomy and independence they have achieved by being in control of their own personal assistance. As we noted earlier (see Chapter 3) direct payments have the potential to make radical changes in the relationship between disabled people and those who provide their personal assistance, very much part of the citizenship approach. However, many local authorities have been slow to provide direct payment schemes and some have attempted to impose restrictions on its use so that little is permitted in addition to what was previously provided. Barnes et al. (2004) found 'a general pattern whereby many traditional Labour controlled local authorities have failed to develop direct payments. Conversely, in Conservative administrations – particularly where there is a strong user-led support organisation – recipients have increased significantly'

(Barnes *et al.*, 2004, p. 10). This resistance, which typifies the compliance approach, has meant that the take up of direct payments by older people and people with mental health problems has been negligible in most areas of the country, and many other disabled people are being denied the advantages the scheme could offer them.

Although the Department of Health has consistently promoted direct payments as being central to the delivery of empowering services, by 2003 only 12,585 people in England were in receipt of this service, and the majority of these were people aged 16 to 25 with physical impairments (Commission for Social Care Inspection, 2004). This contrasts sharply with the 22,000 people in receipt of payments from the Independent Living Fund when it closed in 1992 (Morris, 1993) and shows the effectiveness of local authorities' resistance in denying disabled people independence. In their most recent inspection report, the Commission for Social Care Inspection (CSCI) identify certain barriers to direct payments:

- a lack of clear information for people who might take advantage of direct payments
- low staff awareness of direct payments and what they are intended to achieve
- restrictive or patronising attitudes about the capabilities of people who might use a direct payment and a reluctance to devolve power away from professionals to the people who use the service
- inadequate or patchy advocacy and support services for people applying for and using direct payments
- inconsistencies between the intention of the legislation and local practice
- unnecessary, over-bureaucratic paperwork
- problems in recruiting, employing, retaining and developing personal assistants and assuring quality.

(Commission for Social Care Inspection, 2004, p. 5)

So, while social workers make much of their commitment to anti-oppressive practice and their value base, the body responsible for inspecting their activities describes them as holding 'restrictive or patronising attitudes', of being unaware of what they should be doing, or worse, erecting barriers in order to maintain power over the services that disabled people need to use. However, Stainton

(2002) found that individual social workers were sympathetic to the schemes, and that the main barriers were in the structures within which they operated. Glasby and Littlechild (2002) provide a comprehensive list of barriers, which they discuss in depth. These include:

- The tensions between consumerism and public expenditure which, as we have seen, is played out in the different approaches of councils according to their political control.
- The actions of social workers as gatekeepers of services. Glasby and Littlechild (2002) say that 'time and time again, a major barrier to the extension of direct payments has been shown to be the anxiety and ignorance of frontline social workers' (p. 104).
- Local authorities' financial concerns may prevent direct payment users from exercising real choice.
- The potential for inequalities, especially concerning the exploitation of women. Leece (2004, p. 220) also argues 'that women could be disadvantaged by changing employment conditions, and that present inequalities in society may be reinforced'.
- Social workers' concerns over the risks involved in independent living, concerns that have been central to the humanitarian approach.
- Overcoming the practical problems, especially the need for support mechanisms. This has been a key concern of disabled people's organisations, as the next section on 'Centres for Independent Living' explains, and in particular needs to be extended and made available to people with learning difficulties (Bewley and McCulloch, 2004).

Centres for Independent Living

Centres for Independent Living (CILs) began in the USA in the early 1970s. At Berkeley University, Ed Roberts and other students started the Physically Disabled Students Program with the help of a small Federal grant, and later, in 1972, when many of them had left the university campus, they formed the first Centre for Independent Living (CIL) so that disabled people could help each other to find jobs, housing and personal support. In the USA the CILs were able to bid for Federal and State funds and to take over the provision of services for disabled people. By doing this on the basis of disabled people being in control of the way services were provided, the CILs were able to reject the institutional solutions that had been provided in the past (Shearer, 1984). Their campaigning eventually led to a more radical outcome than the restructuring of welfare, with the passing of comprehensive anti-discrimination legislation in the Americans with Disabilities Act, 1990 (Oliver, 1996). However, despite this success, at the end of the twentieth century welfare policy in the USA still ensured that 80 per cent of the Medicaid budget for support to disabled people was spent on nursing homes.

In the UK, the National Assistance Act, 1948 placed the responsibility and funds for providing personal care services with local authorities. While they were permitted to, and did, fund the provision of care in registered homes run by voluntary organizations, it was illegal for them to make payments to individuals for personal care, and their institutional practices meant that the only contracting of services undertaken was with established charities. In effect, this prevented groups of disabled people from taking over in the way that the CILs had in the USA. Despite this, since 1984, CILs have developed in the UK, and by the year 2000 there were fourteen (Barnes *et al.*, 2000a), though this is clearly not on quite the same scale as in the USA, where there are now more than 400 (National Council on Independent Living, www.ncil.org).

The National Centre for Independent Living in the UK describes CILs as organizations controlled by and for disabled people. They provide a range of services including:

● information;
● advocacy;
● peer support;
● housing advice;
● personal assistance support; and
● work training and advice.

While CILs may be few in numbers in the UK, their impact on the lives of those who have used their services contrasts markedly with their experience of social work (Barnes *et al.* 2001). CILs enable disabled people to be in control of the way in which their services are provided, and to have a real say in the reasons for receiving personal assistance. Unlike the institutionalised approach of social services departments, which often result in moral judgements about what disabled people may or may not expect from the welfare system, CILs are notable developments because they do listen and respect the service user as a citizen, with all that entails.

Social work, the social model and independent living

The social model suggests that disability is imposed on impaired individuals as a consequence of the way society is organised. There can be little doubt that residential care does indeed further disable impaired individuals, and from this viewpoint residential care offers an unacceptable form of provision. In its Civil Rights Charter, the Disabled People's Direct Action Network (DAN) calls for the closure of all long-stay institutions and hospitals.

It is easy to see how, by working within the individual model of disability, those involved in planning and providing services for disabled people are led to see residential provision as a suitable option when an individual is no longer able to continue living as previously, either as a consequence of family break up, lack of community support and/or increasing impairment. The question for those charged with responsibility for providing a service from within the individual model then automatically becomes: what does the individual need? The answer simplistically is food, clothing, shelter and personal assistance, and when individual needs are aggregated it seems not unreasonable to meet these needs through the provision of residential accommodation for a number of individuals, especially given the social and economic pressures from the care industry to make such a choice.

The question service providers should ask from within the social model, however, is a different one, and becomes: in what ways does the physical and social environment prevent this individual from remaining in the community, from continuing to live an independent life, and from achieving his or her aspirations? This obviously produces a different answer along the lines of the need for suitable and adequate housing, a reasonable income to ensure access to food, clothing and personal assistance, the provision of community support and so on.

The first social work task, then, is to ensure that those who are at risk of being forced to go into residential care are given the option of remaining in the community with adequate support. It continues to be argued that some may wish to go into residential care, and as such it should be a real choice available to them. But, as we have argued, this choice is disabling and too often it is the only option available. Neither should it be assumed that a disabled person is in fact making a free choice if they opt for residential care as this may be an act of desperation following their experience of inadequate support in the community. Also, the argument commonly put forward by local authorities that this is the cheaper option for certain individuals does not itself stand up to scrutiny, given the disproportionately high amount of Personal Social Services budgets that are spent on a relatively small proportion of disabled people. Social services departments and social workers must aim to provide independent living options if they are to be of any value to disabled people.

Resistance to independent living is widespread in society, and this reflects the functions of residential care, which does not exist solely to meet the needs of residents. Goffman drew attention to this when he wrote:

> If all the institutions in a given region were emptied and closed down today, tomorrow parents, relatives, police, judges, doctors and social workers would raise a clamour for new ones: and these the true clients of the institution would demand new institutions to satisfy their needs.
> (Goffman, 1961, p. 334)

The aims of the disabled people's movement and the essential difference of the citizenship approach to welfare provision are that disabled people should be able to experience the same degree of independent living as any non-disabled person. Traditional approaches to welfare including residential care and many of the semi-independent alternatives that we have reviewed fail to provide this. Attempting to improve such services can only ever amount to the treatment of symptoms rather than the cause, which is the use of such services in the first place. What is required of social workers is that they first understand the meaning and implications of independent living, and second, that they use their skills and their role within the welfare system to support disabled people in pursuit of this.

While many models of care have been provided over the years, the key to independent living is that full control of the provision of personal assistance should be handed over to the disabled person who is to receive it. Within the new market structures of welfare in Britain this means giving disabled people the finances to resource their own personal assistance schemes, and then supporting them in that task in ways that they determine as being of use.

With the implementation of direct payments, social workers and care managers are be required to relinquish part of their responsibility for the purchasing or provision of community care services, and to support individuals in running their own personal assistance schemes. Just as senior managers and councillors have found it difficult to delegate the responsibility for budgets to caseworkers as envisaged in the White Paper, *Caring for People* (Department of Health, 1989), social workers are resisting handing over such responsibility to disabled people (Sapey and Pearson, 2002). The immediate task of the social worker will therefore be one of working with disabled people to put the case for this change within their agencies. If social workers are committed to the delivery of non-stigmatised services, then this piece of legislation probably offers them their best opportunity since 1948 to humanise the relationship between disabled people and the state.

Once its implementation has been achieved, it will be for social workers to ensure that the administration of these monies and the ways in which disabled people are required to account for their use, is managed in a manner that is helpful to the aims of independent living and not in ways that replicate the barriers of institutionalised care.

Conclusion

In this chapter we have reviewed a number of developments in welfare, many of which have proved to be unacceptable, though they form a history of the road to independent living. At the time that the early changes were occurring Hunt (1981) argued that, 'The liberal growth approach, whatever criticisms may be made of some of its theories and assumptions, represents a genuine advance towards securing the rights and freedoms of a civilised life for many handicapped people.' We would now argue that it is time for the history of both humanitarian and compliance approaches to welfare to be brought to an end, and that radical changes are required to ensure the that citizenship approach gains dominance in social work. In the next chapter we shall examine the legal context of social work practice.

putting it into practice

Exercise 1

Using your local library and the internet, make a list of all the disability organisations operating in your locality. Find out if these are organisations led by disabled people or not, and whether they offer any support to disabled people in respect of independent living. As a social worker you will now possess an invaluable resource which you can share with disabled people about where they can seek support.

Exercise 2

Find our how many carers, older people and people with physical impairments, learning difficulties, or mental health problems are in receipt of direct payments within local authority close to you. This information may be available from the social services department or it may be found at the Department of Health's website as part of the RAP project (Referals, Assessments and Packages of Care, for adults) – you will need to look at the Excel tables for the number of clients receiving community-based services. Compare this with the numbers receiving other services in the same area and consider which of the barriers described in this chapter apply to this authority.

Further reading

Glasby, J. and Littlechild, R. (2002) *Social Work and Direct Payments*, Bristol: The Policy Press. A study of how direct payments work and the barriers created by poor social work practice.

Morris, J. (1993) *Independent Lives: Community Care and Disabled People*, London: Macmillan. A study of the impact of disabled people being able to pay for personal assistance on to run their lives.

Priestley, M. (1999) *Disability Politics and Community Care*, London: Jessica Kingsley. A study of how a disabled people's organisation was and is able to improve the quality of community care.

6 | The legal and social context of disability

Living within a family or in residential accommodation can be disabling for impaired people. In the wider context, all impaired people are disabled to a greater or lesser degree by the society in which they live. The social model of disability suggests that people with impairments in Britain may face educational disability, employment disability and economic disability, and it is perhaps somewhat ironic that some of the legal measures taken to combat such disadvantages actually in fact contribute further to the disabling process. This chapter will focus on some aspects of this relationship between disabled people and society, and consider some of the possible intervention strategies for social workers. To begin, the discussion needs to be placed in the context of legislation relating to disability.

The legal rights of disabled people

While it is possible to trace state involvement and concern regarding physically disabled people back to 1601 and beyond – Borsay (2005) takes it back to 1247 – there is little need to go back further than the 1940s, when the foundations of the welfare state were laid in Britain. Prior to this, statutory provision for disabled people had been made on a piecemeal or *ad hoc* basis, and often only related to specific types of impairment or the way in which impairments had been caused. While this specificity has not been completely eradicated, state provision is now geared towards 'disabled people' as a single group.

The first Act of Parliament to treat disabled people as one single category of persons was the Disabled Persons (Employment) Act, 1944. Not only did this attempt to ensure that companies employed a certain number of disabled workers, it also made provision for the assessment of employment potential, the establishment of rehabilitation centres and the provision of vocational training courses and maintenance grants for those selected to attend them. Subsequently, the National Health Service Act, 1946, while providing for the acute medical needs of disabled people, also made it possible for local authority health departments to provide any medical equipment or aids necessary to support people in their own homes. The National Assistance Act, 1948 made some provision for meeting the financial needs of disabled people and imposed a duty on local authorities to provide residential accommodation, and in addition gave local authorities the power to provide certain services for 'persons who are blind, deaf or dumb and other persons who are substantially and permanently handicapped by illness, injury or congenital deformity'. This was extended in 1974 to include 'persons suffering from a mental disorder of any description' (Local Authority Circular 13/74). In addition the Education Act, 1944 stated that every child should receive education suitable for his age, ability and aptitude, and to provide special educational treatment for those thought to need it.

These Acts formed the cornerstone of statutory provision for disabled people, and until the Disability Discrimination Act, 1995, subsequent legislation tended to alter, modify or extend existing provision. The current situation regarding education and employment will be discussed separately, as will discrimination, first, consideration needs to be given to the provision of social welfare.

Perhaps the most publicised piece of legislation in this area is the Chronically Sick and Disabled Persons Act, 1970 (CSDPA). This sought to give disabled people the right to live in the community, by providing appropriate support services. Section 1 of the Act imposes two duties on local authorities:

(a) The duty to inform themselves of the number and needs of handicapped persons in their areas.
(b) The duty to publicise available services.

The latter duty originally applied only to those services provided by the local authority itself, but this was extended by the Disabled Persons (Services, Consultation and Representation) Act, 1986 to include any services known to them.

Further, Section 2 lists various services which should be provided for those whose needs have been assessed, and these may include:

- Practical assistance in the home;
- Recreational facilities, both in the home and outside;
- Travel facilities, either free or subsidised;
- Social work support to families;
- Adaptations to the home and special equipment including telephones;
- Holiday arrangements; and
- Meals.

Since the Children Act, 1989 these services apply only to adults, but do include asylum seekers. As Roberts and Harris (2002) have noted, disabled asylum seekers may be denied access to other sources of help, but they do have rights under these welfare enactments.

The 1970 Act was regarded by some (Topliss and Gould, 1981) as nothing less than 'a charter for the disabled', its very presence constituting nothing less than public acknowledgement of the social rights of disabled people. However, the evidence for this is somewhat tenuous, and Topliss and Gould argue that

> Society may in fact have expended too little in the way of resources and effort to adjust the environment, as much as many would wish, to meet the needs of disabled people, but the acceptance of an obligation to move in this direction has never been challenged since the passing of the Act.
> (Topliss and Gould, 1981, p. 142)

It was further claimed that the passage of the Act and its subsequent presence increased public awareness of disability and changed attitudes towards disabled people. Finally, it is claimed that the Act at last laid down a statutory framework for services to which disabled people were entitled.

There are a number of criticisms that can be levelled at this evaluation of the Act. To begin with, one commentator has noted that 'In the main, Section 2 of the Chronically Sick and Disabled Persons Act . . . is only Section 29 of the National Assistance Act, 1948 writ large' (Keeble, 1979, p. 40).

There has certainly been concern expressed that the Act promised more than it actually delivered, and one national survey concluded: 'The CSDPA surveys found handicapped people requiring and wanting help who were not in regular contact with any of the professional caring services and some who, although in contact with one service, needed help from another' (Knight and Warren, 1978, p. 70). Numerous economic crises and subsequent cutbacks have exacerbated these problems as local authorities have often withdrawn services previously provided.

Another criticism (Knight and Warren, 1978; Shearer, 1981a) was that services were often provided on the basis of locality rather than of need. There was considerable variation between local authorities about what services they provided and, unfortunately, it is still true that the best professional advice for some disabled people is to 'move'! This problem was perhaps best summed up in the title of Fiedler's (1988) report for the Prince of Wales' Advisory Group on Disability, *Living Options Lottery*.

Another serious criticism of the 1970 Act stems from the Royal Association for Disability and Rehabilitation (RADAR) project undertaken by fifteen major disability organizations which attempted to clarify the duties of local authorities (Cook and Mitchell, 1982). One of the major flaws that arose with the CSDPA was that local authorities argued that, while they might have a duty to provide services to meet an individual's need, they did not have such a duty if they were unaware of that need. Their tactic was to delay assessment until resources were available. Despite some limited success in individual cases which was accounted for by the local authorities taking action to avoid a precedent-setting court case, it was clear that, given the current economic climate and the often uneasy relationship between central and local government, the Act was neither implementable nor enforceable. The position was to some extent corrected by section 4 of the 1986 Act, which clarified beyond doubt the local authorities' responsibility to carry out assessments if requested to do so either by a disabled person or her/his carer, while sections 5 and 6 laid down detailed procedures for children with special educational needs to be assessed under the 1970 Act when they reached school-leaving age.

What remained unresolved was the extent of the duty to provide services. As the 1970 Act had begun life as a private Members' bill, it could not constitutionally cause local authorities to incur additional costs. However, a Money Order Resolution passed by the government did make provision for this, but it remained unclear as to the extent of the duty (Topliss and Gould, 1981). The position was clarified by the 1990 Act, which placed clear budgetary limits on all local authority spending in relation to both residential/nursing homes and community care. The duty to provide services is now restricted by the budget.

Furthermore, Shearer (1981a) is not just critical of the Act's failure to meet need and provide services, but also of its underlying philosophy, which, she suggests, takes away from disabled people the crucial element of choice:

> The substitution of kind for cash sits no less uneasily with aspirations to enhance the self-determination and dignity of people with disabilities, in a society where status and respect has so much to do with purchasing power. The potential public outcry against a paternalistic state which attempted to deliver, say, child benefit in the form of nappies, creams and baby foods, does not take much imagining.
> (Shearer, 1981a, pp. 82–3)

Borsay (2005), whose historical analysis is concerned with the extent to which legislation and policy has excluded disabled people systematically as citizens concluded that 'The Chronically Sick and Disabled Persons Act thus failed to liberate disabled people from inadequate, needs-based services that compromised their status as citizens' (Borsay, 2005, p. 195).

Most of these criticisms remain valid despite the passing and implementation of the National Health Service and Community Care Act, 1990, which certainly claimed the intent to tackle many of them, although the more recent Community Care (Direct Payments) Act, 1996 does allow for cash rather than payment in kind. The needs-led assessment that is central to the 1990 Act was intended to get away from the 'MOT test' approach (Middleton, 1992) of Section 2 of the CSDPA, while specifying financial responsibilities and charging arrangements was supposed to clarify rights to services. Legislating for collaboration between agencies was also meant to ensure that the gaps between services were plugged, and that people could make use of single points of entry into the welfare system. None of these have proved to be effective as the focus on budgets that also accompanied this Act ensured that local authorities and the NHS have now institutionalised their boundaries and made assessment a far more instrumental process. Following the Audit Commission's (1986) report into community care, Kenneth Clarke, then Secretary of State for Health, described the supplementary benefit payments for residential care as offering a 'perverse incentive' to local authorities not to provide alternative services. In 1997, after four and a half years of the Act that was supposed to take away those incentives, the Audit Commission reported that the situation between local authorities and the NHS was like a 'Berlin wall'. Furthermore, charging policies have multiplied since the Act's implementation in 1993, and while the structural inequalities within authorities have lessened, those between them grew until the government intervened some ten years later. In a direct return to the Poor Law, local authorities even charge each other if the person requiring a service has lived in their area for less than an agreed length of time.

Shearer suggested that the 1970 Act's underlying philosophy was a step in the wrong direction, and that what disabled people in fact needed was more cash and strong anti-discrimination legislation to ensure that they could buy the kinds of services they needed. While neither of these have been achieved in full, both the Community Care (Direct Payments) Act, 1996 and the Disability Discrimination Act, 1995 have gone some way towards addressing the problem.

The 1996 Act initially gave local authorities the power, though not a duty, to provide disabled people with the cash to purchase their own community care services. This was extended to people over 65 via the Community Care (Direct Payments) Amendment Regulations, 1999, and to carers and young people through the Carers and Disabled Children Act, 2000. Section 57 of the Health and Social Care Act, 2001 confirmed this position and gave the Secretary of State the authority to require local authorities to implement the scheme, rather than leaving it to their discretion, and this was done in April 2004. While the assessment of need remains with the local authority, rather than providing or purchasing services to meet that need they must, if requested, provide the equivalent in cash, which is then used by the disabled person to pay for their own personal assistance. In effect, the 1996 Act makes use of the market principles within the 1990 Act, but shifts the role of customer from care managers to disabled people. While social workers will retain some responsibility for monitoring the use of this money, they should act in a supporting role, not a policing one. The importance of working with the spirit of this Act was voiced by the Director of the National Centre for Independent Living, who is now the chair of the Social Care Institute for Excellence:

When the Act comes into force from 1 April 1997 local authorities have been given the choice whether they offer Direct Payments. In my view it will be disastrous if they do not. There is an explicit expectation embodied within the disabled people's movement that Direct Payments will be on offer. All reasoned arguments against it have been demolished throughout the campaign and nowhere better exemplified than on the floor of the House of Commons and the House of Lords where we finally won our victory. It would be a foolish waste of time if we had to repeat that process, because the arguments have been won.
(Campbell, 1997, p. 23)

More will be said of anti-discrimination later in the chapter, but it is worth remembering that, whatever its defects, the Chronically Sick and Disabled Persons Act, 1970 with its subsequent amendments and changes, provides a significant part of the legal framework within which social workers, particularly those employed in social services departments, have to work. A crucial problem for social workers is that very often they know there are not the resources available to meet the needs they encounter, and yet to acknowledge these needs may well place a legal obligation on their employer to meet them. It is scarcely credible to imagine doctors refusing to diagnose illnesses because there are not sufficient resources available to treat all those so diagnosed, and neither should social workers shy away from identifying social need.

There are a number of informal solutions to this dilemma: social workers may suggest that clients take their complaints to politicians, and can assist by drafting letters. Others have contacted organizations such as RADAR, and if necessary have done so anonymously. However, while such tactics may resolve discrepancies between need and provision in individual cases, they do not make the Act ultimately more implementable or enforceable. To be a client (or indeed a social worker) in a service where expectations and needs far outweigh available resources can be a disabling experience in itself. None the less, one cannot help feeling that more disabled people would get the services to which they are entitled if professionals were to act as advocates of that need rather than as the rationing agents of their employers.

Education

The Education Act, 1944 laid a duty on local authorities to have regard 'to the need for securing that provision is made for pupils who suffer from any disability of the mind and body by providing, either in special schools or otherwise, special educational treatment'. It also obliged the authorities to ascertain the numbers of children in their areas who required special educational support. The Act was important for disabled children and their families, in that it gave them legal rights to education, but unfortunately it left it to the authorities and to professionals to determine exactly what kind of education was appropriate.

Even more unfortunately, responsible authorities chose to make provision for the special needs of disabled children in segregated establishments of one kind or another. Despite mounting criticism of special education over many years, both on the grounds of its failure to provide an adequate or comparable education to that provided in ordinary schools, and the social implications of segregating large numbers of children from their peers, the percentage of the school population in special schools grew steadily until the mid-1980s, and the overall proportion appears to have levelled at a point that is still higher than it was fifty years ago. In 2004, the total number of children in special schools was just over 90,000 (see Table 6.1).

In recognition of the growing controversies surrounding the educational needs of disabled children, the government set up a Committee of Enquiry, which produced the Warnock Report in 1978. The Report made numerous recommendations, including replacing the original categories of disabled children with the broader concept of 'special educational needs', and the government issued a White Paper in 1980 called *Special Needs in Education*, which broadly endorsed the proposals of the Warnock Report. While Warnock, the White Paper and the subsequent Education Act, 1981 favoured the idea of integration, it made no extra resources available to facilitate such a move. The 1981 Act left the legal rights of parents and their disabled children unchanged, and it was still the local authority which decided what educational provision was appropriate. The Education Act, 1993, which placed a duty on local education authorities to accept parental preference for a particular school, still left the final decision with that authority if they either

Table 6.1 Maintained schools: number and percentage of pupils by type of need, England, January 2004

	Special schools as % of all	Special schools	All schools
Specific learning difficulty	0.9	750	83,790
Moderate learning difficulty	16.6	28,520	171,930
Severe learning difficulty	67.5	21,620	32,030
Profound & multiple learning difficulty	81.9	6,380	7,790
Behaviour, emotional & social difficulties	9.8	12,390	126,890
Speech, language and communications needs	4.8	3,040	63,890
Hearing impairment	13.4	1,740	12,960
Visual impairment	13.9	1,000	7,170
Multi-sensory impairment	19.8	170	860
Physical disability	21.6	5,330	24,660
Autistic spectrum disorder	27.5	8,610	31,260
Other difficulty/disability	3.9	990	25,540
Unclassified	0.0	0	40
Total	**15.4**	**90,540**	**588,780**

Source: National Statistics Office, 2004, table 9.

found the placement would be unsuitable for a child's special educational needs, or incompatible with the education of other children or the use of resources (Braye and Preston-Shoot, 1997). The influence of the individual model of disability, in which the disabled child is seen as being the problem, and his or her exclusion from mainstream schooling as the solution is clear, and sets boundaries around what might be achieved in changing the environment of education.

There are important implications in the continued commitment to special schools, because, as Tomlinson has shown, this is not based solely on the humanitarian ideal of providing what is best for disabled children, but also 'to cater for the needs of ordinary schools, the interests of the wider industrial society and the specific interests of professionals' (Tomlinson, 1982, p. 57). Indeed, in October 1997, when launching the White Paper, *Excellence for All Children*, David Blunkett, then Secretary of State for Education and Employment, made clear his opposition to segregated education and announced his intention to reduce the numbers of children in special schools. The initial response of National Association of Schoolmasters and Union of Women Teachers was to threaten 'not to teach' certain children if integration were to go 'too far'. It is simply unimaginable that such a threat would ever be made on the basis of gender, religion, race or virtually any other characteristic of children, but it was largely accepted as a responsible position in relation to disability. Indeed, while race and sex discrimination laws apply to education, it was specifically excluded from the provisions of the Disability Discrimination Act, 1995 at that time.

Since then, the Special Educational Needs and Disability Act, 2001, which amended the Disability Discrimination Act, 1995, prohibits 'all schools from discriminating against disabled children in their admissions arrangements, in the education and associated services provided by the school for its pupils or in relation to exclusions from the school' (Department for Education and Skills, 2001). The move has been towards an inclusive approach to education in which all schools are expected to be accessible. This is an anticipatory duty, which has meant a move away from the statementing of individual children followed by individual adjustments to a position where barriers are removed in order that all children should be able to go to the school of their family's choice.

It could be argued that all this is of little relevance to social work. However, it is clear that more and more parents are beginning to demand that their children are educated in ordinary schools, and in order to achieve those demands against the opposition of vested interests, talked about by Tomlinson, then parents will need help. Furthermore, the tendency of some schools to use special educational needs as a means of permanently excluding children (ACE, 1996) ran counter to the intentions of the process to ensure inclusion. Parents and children will perhaps need advocates to intercede on their behalf, and argue that it is not in the best interests of the child, either educationally or socially, that he or she be deprived of family life and links with peers and community for substantial periods during the formative years. Social workers may be ideally placed by virtue of regular contact since the birth of the disabled child to help families negotiate with the education authorities, though at present it seems that they are reluctant to take on this advocacy role and to challenge decisions made by their local authority colleagues.

What is clear is that, in the future, with or without help, increasing numbers of parents will demand the social rights to an ordinary education for their children, for it is clear that, for many impaired children, segregated education adds educational and social disability to existing disadvantages.

Employment

The Disabled Persons (Employment) Act, 1944, which was substantially repealed by Part II of the Disability Discrimination Act, 1995, laid a framework for the provision of a variety of employment rehabilitation and resettlement services. Alongside the numerous day centres and Adult Training Centres run by social services and health authorities, the Department of Employment operated up to twenty-seven rehabilitation centres at their peak in the 1980s. The Department of Employment was subjected to the same market-type reforms, as were the health and social services, leading to its reorganisation in 1990 along the lines of a purchaser–provider split. This signalled a move away from the operation of rehabilitation services to contracting individual courses for disabled people. It was justified economically in terms of the under-use of these centres – by the time that Ingol, one of only two regional residential Employment Resettlement Centres, closed at the end of 1991, the numbers using it had fallen to single figures – and by the changing aspirations of disabled people:

> People with disabilities increasingly insist on their right to be treated as individual people, not categorised; to be served and not managed by services; not to be unnecessarily segregated in training and work from their non-disabled colleagues; to have their full potential and its development fairly recognised by employers and public services.
> (Employment Department Group, 1990, p. 4)

The 1944 Act also gave disabled people legal rights to employment, in that it placed an obligation on all employers with more than twenty workers to employ a quota of 3 per cent of the work-force who were registered as disabled, but in practice this was never enforced, and disabled people have experienced a higher level of unemployment than non-disabled people. Those who do find employment are often in less skilled jobs and earn lower wages than their non-disabled counterparts.

Grover and Gladstone (1982, p. 1) reported that 'in 1965 the general unemployment rate was well below 2 per cent but among registered disabled people, over 7 per cent'. By 1982, the general rate was 'something over 12 per cent while among registered disabled people it is nearly 16 per cent'. By 1989, both the gap and the actual position of disabled people had worsened, with 5.4 per cent and 20.5 per cent, respectively (Barnes, 1991). The ways in which unemployment is measured changes according to political interpretations, so measurements across time are not always reli-able. However, the data persistently shows vast inequalities in rela-tion to employment: only 49 per cent of disabled adults were in employment in 2003, compared to 81 per cent of non-disabled people; while 4 per cent of each group were officially unemployed, 15 per cent of disabled people were economically inactive and seek-ing a job compared with only 4 per cent of non-disabled people (*Social Trends*, Table 4.6)

Clearly, the opportunities for disabled people are limited, but this is made worse by the tendency to direct assistance towards people who are economically active, that is, actively seeking work. This works against disabled people, who may have withdrawn from what they have experienced as a futile task. Barnes (1991) reported that the 1986 OPCS disability surveys revealed that 85 per cent of the men and 65 per cent of the women who were not look-ing for work and who defined themselves as 'unable to work' had previously taken steps to find work, but had later given up.

The Disability Discrimination Act, 1995 replaced the quota system and registration of disabled people in favour of defining lawful and unlawful discrimination in employment. There are two ways in which employers would be acting unlawfully: first, if they treated a disabled person less favourably than a non-disabled person, and could not show that this is justified; and second, if they fail to provide reasonable adjustments to the working environment. Lawful discrimination results from the definitions of what might be justified in terms of treatment of a disabled person and what would be unreasonable in terms of adjustments to the environment. Justification is a complex issue and is likely to be settled through the Code of Practice issued by the Secretary of State and through case law – Gooding (1996) provides a useful and comprehensive guide to how the Act might be interpreted based on comparable experience in the USA. Certainly one aspect of such a justification would be first to show that no reasonable adjustment could be made. Here, section 6(3) of the Act provides an illustrative list of what might be considered reasonable:

- making adjustments to premises;
- allocating some of the disabled person's duties to another person;
- transferring him/her to fill an existing vacancy;
- altering his/her working hours;
- assigning him/her to a different place of work;
- allowing him/her to be absent during working hours for rehabilitation, assessment or treatment;
- giving him/her, or arranging for him/her to be given, training;
- acquiring or modifying equipment;
- modifying instructions or reference manuals;
- modifying procedures for testing or assessment;
- providing a reader or interpreter; and
- providing supervision.

However, as Gooding (1996, p.21) points out, 'an employer will not necessarily be expected to take any of these steps. He or she will be obliged to take only such steps as are reasonable in all the circumstances' and section 6(4) of the Act provides a further list of five factors that would have to be considered in determining that

1. the extent to which taking the step would prevent the effect in question;
2. the extent to which it is practicable for the employer to take the step;
3. the financial and other costs that would be incurred by the employer in taking the step, and the extent to which taking it would disrupt any of his/her activities;
4. the extent of the employer's financial and other resources; and
5. the availability to the employer of financial or other assistance with respect to taking the step.

While the effectiveness of this Act remains to be seen, what is certain, as far as social work intervention is concerned, is that often the major problem that many disabled people face is that of unemployment, and again the question arises as to whether it is part of the social work task to attempt to alleviate such problems. While the formal responsibility may lie with the Disability Employment Advisers (DEAs) from JobCentre Plus, their effectiveness can be enhanced if social workers are prepared to work in an advocacy role with disabled people. Interestingly, social workers have tended to be more critical of DEAs than they have of other professionals working in the area of special education, but have not taken their task much beyond criticism. This is perhaps unfortunate, because if unemployment is assessed as the major problem, more than criticism may be needed.

They can also advocate good practice within their own organisations, which may have a tendency to view disabled people as dependent clients rather than potential employees. Most local authorities themselves were below their quota for disabled employees when this existed and it is therefore perfectly justified for social workers to attempt to get disabled people employed in their own departments and agencies, rather than simply seeing employment as being the responsibility of the DEA. Social workers who have unemployed disabled clients should be prepared to see finding a job as part of their task, and should be much more imaginative and practical about how they go about it, ensuring that their own employers meet their obligations as well as criticising others who fail to do so. This is one way in which social workers might contribute to the task of reducing unemployment disability among their clients.

Welfare rights

The term 'welfare rights' can be interpreted in two ways: in its broadest sense, it can mean the rights of the individual to all the services provided by the welfare state; while in its narrower sense, it might mean the social security benefit entitlements that individuals may have. While recognising the broad use of the term, which might also encompass legal and social rights, in this section the term will be confined to its usage in reference to the financial benefits and entitlements of disabled people.

The 2004 *Benefits and Tax Credits Checklist* provided by the Disability Alliance (www.disabilityalliance.org) reveals that twenty-two separate welfare benefits are available to disabled people. Despite this seemingly generous provision, numerous studies have shown the clear connection between poverty and disability. For example, Townsend showed that half of the appreciably or severely disabled people in the United Kingdom were living in poverty, compared with only a fifth of able-bodied people, and he further showed that even where disabled people were in work they were poorer than their able-bodied counterparts. He concluded:

> Not only do disabled people have lower social status. They also have lower incomes and fewer assets. Moreover, they tend to be poorer even when their social status is the same as the non-disabled . . . With increasing incapacity, proportionately more people lived in households with incomes below, or only marginally above that standard. Fewer lived in households with relatively high incomes.
> (Townsend, 1979, p. 711)

This level of dependency on state benefits was confirmed by the 1986 OPCS disability surveys, when 78 per cent of all disabled people and 54 per cent of those below retirement age were living in households with no wage earners (Barnes, 1991), and in 2002/3 the Department for Work and Pensions concluded that disabled people were at particular risk of poverty:

> individuals in families containing one or more disabled people were more likely to live in low-income households than those in families with no disabled person, with around 22 per cent of individuals in households with a disabled adult lived in low income [*sic*] Before Housing Costs and 27 per cent After Housing Costs. The risk of low income for individuals in households with a disabled child were 23 per cent BHC and 29 per cent AHC. Risk of low income was significantly higher where there was both an adult and a child with disabilities.
> (National Statistics First Release; www.dwp.gov.uk)

There are a number of reasons that have been suggested for the persistence of chronic poverty among disabled people. It is sometimes argued that the level of benefits is set at too low a level, and certainly evidence produced by the Royal Commission on the Distribution of Income and Wealth, which reported in 1978, indicates that despite a proliferation of benefits throughout the 1970s the relative position of disabled people as a group had not changed significantly. As was noted in Chapter 2, official estimations of poverty such as the 1986 OPCS disability surveys have failed to recognise the real additional costs of impairment, which is then reflected in the level at which benefits are set.

Another reason concerns the 'take-up' of various benefits, as some people may not know of their existence, while others may feel that application (and certainly appeal) is a stigmatising business and therefore refuse to claim. A final reason concerns the complexity of the system, with its overlapping benefits, different eligibility criteria and other administrative problems that often make claiming a nightmare.

Given that these criticisms are valid, there seem to be three fairly simple solutions to the problems of poverty and disability: (i) raise the level of benefits; (ii) make them available as a right and reduce the number of eligibility tests; and finally (iii) simplify the system. However, these are not realistic possibilities in the short term, and even where change has been forced as in the case of the European Court's ruling that the additional housework test for disabled women claiming Non-Contributory Invalidity Pension was discriminatory, it resulted in a tightening of criteria to the Severe Disability Allowance that replaced it in order to ensure no overall additional expenditure.

In April 1992, there was an attempt to rationalise some benefits when the Mobility and Attendance Allowances were merged into the Disability Living Allowance (DLA), though Attendance Allowances were retained for those over 65 years old. The mobility component is paid at two rates, and the attendance component at three, resulting in eleven possible levels at which this might be paid, plus refusal. One of the aims of the introduction of the DLA was to extend the reach of these benefits to people with 'moderate' disabilities, as research had showed that they fared worse than those with either 'severe' or 'mild' impairments. Within twelve months of its introduction it had overshot its target of 300,000 claimants and by November 1994 had reached 430,000 (Burgess, 1996). However, despite this apparent success, the evaluation of the DLA carried out for the Department of Social Security also showed that less than 30 per cent of people who requested claim packs in fact returned them, though the researchers were unable to follow any of these up and could only speculate that it might have had much to do with the forms being too long and complex for many people to complete (Burgess, 1996).

This explanation is supported by a study (Daly and Noble, 1996) which sought to examine the effectiveness of the DLA by looking at a representative sample of disabled people and their take-up of this benefit, which did allow them also to examine the characteristics of people who were not in receipt of DLA. They found that 43 per cent of their sample did not receive DLA, and that this did not correlate with any measure of severity of disability. Daly and Noble concluded that the best advice for disabled people was 'Don't fill in this form yourself!' (p. 49) as claims were more likely to succeed if someone experienced in completing the 40-page application form were to do so on their behalf.

In addition to the widespread problem of non-receipt of DLA, Daly and Noble found considerable variations in the rates that were paid to those in receipt, which led them to conclude that 'the only confident statement to be made about benefit reach is that those who cannot walk at all, the utterly immobile, will be in receipt of the mobility award, if this condition set in before their 65th birthday' (p. 48).

For the social worker, who has a disabled client whose poverty is current, immediate action is necessary and social workers have a record of being effective advocates when they do help their clients with benefits issues. The first approach is to make sure that the client is receiving all entitled benefits, and in order to do that the social worker may need additional help – otherwise the myths that some professionals subscribe to, such as 'you can't get the attendance component if you work', or 'you can't get the mobility component if you can walk', will continue to abound. The first place to start is with the *Disability Rights Handbook*, which is produced every year by the Disability Alliance and is the simplest yet most accurate and comprehensive guide to welfare benefits. And it is a guide that both social workers and disabled people can use. This will also keep social workers up to date with the tribunal and court rulings that may have relevance for disabled people who have previously had claims rejected. If more expert advice is needed then the Disability Alliance or other local organisations such as

Disablement Information and Advice Line (DIAL) may be able to help, not just with information, but also possibly with representation at appeals or tribunals. In short, in order to minimise poverty and reduce economic disability, it is important that disabled people receive all the benefits to which they are entitled. A second approach is to set up a disability rights project, where a number of disabled people in a particular area or day centre are assessed by welfare rights experts to see whether they are getting all the benefits to which they are entitled.

Since 1993, with the transfer of some of the Income Support functions and the Independent Living Fund to local authorities, social workers themselves have taken on a much larger role in income maintenance. With the Community Care (Direct Payments) Act, 1996 this role has grown and it is essential that, as well as advocating for and assisting disabled people with state benefits, social workers work similarly within their own organizations. Depending on the level to which budgets have been devolved, this may mean challenging the decisions of managers, or having their own decisions challenged by others. The basis on which social workers either challenge decisions or respond to such challenges is a matter of professional practice as much as it is procedural, as this area of payments is one that is directly related to an assessment of need rather than rights-based eligibility criteria.

A similar situation applies to district council improvement grants and Disabled Facilities Grants, which, because they are outside the main benefits system, do not have the clear review and appeals procedures of other benefits. There is evidence (Sapey, 1995) that this leads to officials exercising their judgements in a subjective manner which requires different skills to challenge than with the rule-bound decisions of an adjudication officer.

A longer-term solution involves working with established disability organisations towards the eventual provision of a national disability income as of right. Both the Disablement Income Group (DIG) and the Disability Alliance have in the past put forward proposals for such a scheme, and while both organisations would argue that their proposals are radically different, to the outsider they look broadly similar. Part of the conflict may stem from the fact that the Alliance is part of the 'poverty lobby', and thus to the left politically, whereas the DIG was avowedly non-political.

Not all organisations are united in this 'incomes approach' to disability. The Union of the Physically Impaired Against Segregation (UPIAS) suggested that poverty was a symptom of disabled people's oppression and not the cause, and consequently it may be inappropriate to attack the symptom without dealing with the cause. UPIAS advanced three fundamental principles:

disability is a social situation, caused by social conditions, which requires for its elimination
(a) that no one aspect such as incomes, mobility, or institutions is treated in isolation
(b) that disabled people should, with the help and advice of others, assume control over their own lives, and
(c) that professionals, experts and others who seek to help must be committed to promoting such control by disabled people.
(UPIAS, 1976, p. 3)

It could be argued that as financial benefits fall within the province of the Department for Work and Pensions (DWP), social workers should not get involved. However, there are two arguments that can counter this: it is clear that the DWP cannot be relied on to ensure that disabled people receive their entitlements; and as poverty is a major problem for many disabled people, it is an abrogation of professional responsibility not to make any attempt to alleviate it. Both individual welfare rights advice, provided it is accurate, and the establishment of welfare rights projects, are thus part of the social work task. Involvement in the incomes approach to disability, however, can be viewed as a personal rather than a professional responsibility, and while social workers may join organisations in their spare time, active involvement in the politics of disability might be considered beyond their professional duty. The difficulty with this position, however, is that it involves sitting on the fence, which has the effect of supporting the status quo, which in turn implies support for the continuation of policies that leave disabled people in poverty.

The rights of disabled people: ways forward?

It is clear, then, that disabled people currently do have certain limited rights not to be discriminated against in the employment market, to education commensurate with need, and to a whole range of benefits and services. However, it is also plain that many disabled people do not get these rights, and there are furious arguments about how best the rights of disabled people should be safeguarded and extended. These arguments have been characterised as 'persuasion versus enforcement' or 'the carrot versus the stick' (Oliver, 1982). The persuasionist view suggests that discrimination against disabled people arises as the result either of negative attitudes or the failure to consider particular 'special' needs. From this point of view what is needed is more information, public education campaigns and research.

The enforcement view, on the other hand, suggests that strong legal action is necessary, as it is only then that disabled people will achieve their rights. There are three problems with this view, however:

(a) Even if legislation is passed, it may not be enforced the Disabled Persons (Employment) Act 1944 is a good example of this.

(b) Even if legislation is passed and enforced, it may not achieve its aim of ending discrimination. Both the Equal Pay and Race Relations Acts are examples of this.

(c) Such legislation tends to operate to the benefit of certain sections of the professional classes rather than serve to protect the interests of all the groups for whom the legislation was designed.

(Oliver, 1982, p. 78)

Thus Shearer (1981a) suggested that what is needed is some additional anti-discrimination legislation. This call was picked up by a number of disabled people and their organisations, and up to 1995 there were thirteen unsuccessful attempts to get such an enactment through Parliament (Barnes and Oliver, 1995). After the last attempt, the Civil Rights (Disabled Persons) Bill was defeated in 1994 with the connivance of the Minister for Disabled People, the government was effectively forced to introduce its own bill, which became the Disability Discrimination Act, 1995 (DDA). Initially, it did not meet the aspirations of the disabled people's movement, partially because it based its understanding of disability on an individual, rather than a social model, but also because it appeared to be intended to be ineffective. Gooding summarised the problems:

The Disability Discrimination Act 1995 is indeed a confusing, contorted and unsatisfactory piece of legislation. It signally fails to establish the clear principle of equal treatment which should be the essence of a law countering discrimination. (It has, for example, three separate definitions of what constitutes discrimination applying in different sections). The Act's fatal equivocation towards the principle of equality for disabled people has produced an extremely complicated and unclear law, hedged around with exceptions and justifications. Lord Lester, the prominent civil liberties lawyer, described it as 'riddled with vague, slippery and elusive exceptions making it so full of holes that it was more like a colander than a binding code' [Hansard, 22 May 1995, 813].

The Act's exclusion of crucial areas of social life, such as education and small businesses, makes no logical sense, and can be understood only as the product of inter-Cabinet compromises, and a concern to control potential Treasury Costs.

Above all, the Act's lack of any effective enforcement mechanism undermines any claim to be a sincere attempt at ending a social evil.
(Gooding, 1996, p. 1)

When the incoming Labour government of 1997 announced that it would act in respect of two of these criticisms, namely ensuring the early implementation of Part III of the Act and in setting up a Disability Rights Commission (DRC) to ensure its effectiveness, the British Council of Disabled People (BCODP) responded by calling for the Act to be repealed and replaced with legislation set in a social, and not a medical framework. Their view of the Commission was that it would simply be policing a bad piece of legislation rather than protecting and enforcing the rights of disabled people.

Since that time, the DRC has been established and the 1995 Act has been extended and strengthened in several ways. Since December 1996 it has been unlawful for businesses and organizations to treat disabled people less favourably than other people for a reason related to their disability, and since October 1999 they have had to make reasonable adjustments for disabled people, such as providing extra help or making changes to the way they provide their services, and from 2004 they have had to make reasonable adjustments to the physical features of their premises to overcome physical barriers to access. Services here include social work and social care services. The provisions for preventing discrimination in employment have been extended to employers with fewer than fifteen employees. For education providers, new duties came into effect in September 2002 under Part IV of the DDA, amended by the Special Educational Needs and Disability Act, 2001 (SENDA). These require schools, colleges, universities and providers of adult education and youth services to ensure that they do not discriminate against disabled people. Under Part IV of the DDA, the duty to provide auxiliary aids, through reasonable adjustment, came into force in September 2003 (Disability Rights Commission website [www.drc.org.uk]).

At the time of writing, the Disability Discrimination Bill, 2003 is still making its way through the parliamentary process. This is intended to extend the DDA in several ways:

i.   provide powers to enable the exemption for transport vehicles in Part 3 of the Act to be lifted;

ii. extend the Act to cover the exercise of functions of public bodies, so that it would apply to most of their activities, not just those which consist of the provision of services;

iii. introduce a new duty on public bodies to promote equality of opportunity for disabled people, so they would be required to consider the needs of disabled people as early as possible and at every stage in their policy and decision making;

iv. extend the definition of disability to cover more people with HIV, cancer or multiple sclerosis, so that more disabled people would benefit from the Act's protection;

v.   require those who manage or let premises to make reasonable adjustments to their policies and practices for disabled tenants or prospective tenants;

vi. make clear that insurance provided on group terms to an employer's staff is covered as a service under the Act;

vii. bring within scope of the DDA private clubs with 25 or more members, so that such clubs would be unable to discriminate against disabled members or prospective members or others who have rights to use such clubs;

viii. allow disabled people to issue a questionnaire in relation to discrimination complaints, not just in employment cases as now, but also cases concerning service providers, private clubs, landlords or public bodies carrying out their functions; and

ix. make third party publishers (e.g. newspapers) liable for publishing discriminatory advertisements, so that they would be acting unlawfully if they published a discriminatory job advertisement.

(www.disability.gov.uk)

In addition to the DDA, the European Convention on Human Rights was incorporated into British domestic legislation in 2000 through the Human Rights Act, 1998. This provides simpler access to redress under the Convention and places a range of obligations on public bodies, including the employers of most social workers. Clements and Read (2003) argue that good practice in respect of the Human Rights Act should not simply follow a checklist of what must be done as a minimum, but that practitioners and their employers should seek to provide best practice by working towards the spirit of the Convention.

Although the DDA bases its definition of disability on an individual model, increasingly it is requiring organisations to make themselves accessible in similar ways to the anticipatory duty in education discussed earlier. However, implementation has been far from simple. Some employers have been quite successful in defending themselves when discriminating against people with mental health problems, by arguing that the individuals concerned are not covered by the DDA (Gooding, 2003), and many people fear the DRC will be weakened by the proposed merger with the Equal Opportunities Commission and the Commission for Racial Equality. Grass-roots political activism is still required to ensure the DDA is effective.

The development of the BCODP and of similar organisations in other countries in recent decades, including the formation of Disabled People's International, represents an important challenge to the dominance of the individual model of disability. In the disabled people's movement, individuals have been able to assert their own positive self-identity, organise collectively in political campaigns, develop arts and literature that reflect the experience of disability, and to refine the analysis of disability that challenges quite fundamentally the way we all see ourselves. It is from this growing consciousness and political power of disabled people that solutions to the problems of disability may ultimately emerge.

In conclusion, it may be difficult for social workers as professionals to participate fully in the growing political movement of disabled people, though there may be scope for working with these emergent organisations. However, this will have implications for the 'professional attitude' to professional practice in general, and disabled people in particular, and it is a theme that will be considered further in the final chapter. Clearly, however, there are a number of important social work tasks to be tackled in a society not totally committed to the ultimate goal of removing the disabling consequences of impairment.

---

putting it into practice

Exercise 1

Visit the Disability Rights Commission website at www.drc.org.uk and read about the duties your organisation (employer, university, etc.) has under the Disability Discrimination Act. With this information, evaluate whether your organisation is meeting its duties by considering what barriers would exist to a disabled person occupying your role. (If you are disabled then consider what barriers would exist to someone with different access needs.)

Exercise 2

List the services that are available for disabled children in your locality and, using the three approaches to welfare described in Chapter 1 – Humanitarian, Compliance and Citizenship – determine whether these contribute or detract from disabled children achieving citizenship as compared to non-disabled children.

Further reading

Borsay, A. (2005) *Disability and Social Policy in Britain since 1750*, Basingstoke: Palgrave. A comprehensive and critical history of disability policy in Britain and its impact on the citizenship status of disabled people.

Clements, L. and Read, J. (2003) *Disabled People and European Human Rights*, Bristol: Policy Press. A legal textbook which promotes the idea of positive, rather than defensive practice.

Gooding, C. (1996) *Blackstone's Guide to the Disability Discrimination Act 1995*, London: Blackstone Press. Though the DDA has since been amended, this book still provides a useful guide to understanding the debates and reasoning that took place during its passage through Parliament.

7 | Conclusions and implications for practice

This final chapter will attempt to bring together some of the issues raised by applying the social model of disability to social work as an organised professional activity. We start with some theoretical and professional issues, then move on to look at organisational aspects before ending with a range of strategies for the future.

Theoretical and professional developments

As we noted in Chapter 1, there have been some significant changes in the design and avowed purpose of welfare since the late 1990s. The introduction of direct payments; the emphasis on independent living, autonomy and empowerment in policy documents from the Department of Health; and the appointment of Jane Campbell, the former Director of the National Council for Independent Living, as Chair of the Social Care Institute for Excellence all suggest that the government is serious about following a social model analysis of disability. However, their implementation strategy also needs to be based on a social model, and the changes need to be accepted by those with responsibility for the delivery of social care if it is to make a real difference to the lives of disabled individuals – and it is here that resistance persists.

The main professional problem in trying to develop an adequate conceptualisation of social work in this area has been that there were few, if any, models or frameworks adequate for the purpose. While both the Central Council for Education and Training in Social Work (CCETSW) (the predecessor to the social care councils and training organisations – see the Introduction to this book) and the British Association of Social Workers (BASW) have made attempts to define the roles and tasks of social workers with disabled people, and to recommend levels of training that are needed (CCETSW, 1974; BASW, 1982, 1990; Stevens, 1991), they have proved inadequate for a number of reasons, and two in particular.

The first of these was that, with the exception of Stevens' (1991) report, both organisations were developing their guidance from an individual model of disability that led them to assume a causal relationship between impairment and disability. This was clearly inappropriate from a social model analysis, as someone with a very severe impairment may only be mildly disabled, whereas someone with a minor impairment may be totally disabled by poverty, poor housing, the attitudes of employers, or hostile social treatment. A scarce resource such as professional expertise should be allocated on the extent of disability, not on the extent of impairment.

The second reason was that most attempts to lay a professional basis for the practice of social work with disabled people have never really come to grips with the perennial problem of the relationship between theory and practice, and the individual and social models of disability are dependent on that relationship, either overtly or covertly. Thus it could be said that the individual model stems from the 'personal tragedy theory of disability', whereas the social model stems from 'the social problem theory of disability'.

An attempt to look at this problem in the context of social work generally was made by Lee (in Bailey and Lee, 1982, p. 16), who distinguished between three levels:

Level 1 Actual task;
Level 2 Technical knowledge; and
Level 3 Theoretical knowledge.

While, ideally, good social work practice should be based on an integration of all three levels, in reality there is often a polarisation between 'academics' and 'practitioners', with each group seeing its sphere of activity as being unrelated to the other. Lee, however, suggests that 'speculative theory with scant regard for practice (level 1) is of little utility, and practice insulated from theoretical questions (level 3) while perfectly permissible in car maintenance, is downright dangerous in social work' (p. 17).

The problem with both the CCETSW and BASW attempts to establish a framework was that they had been concerned almost totally with the relationship between Levels 1 and 2, whereas the social model of disability is concerned primarily with the relationship between Levels 2 and 3. There were a number of reasons for this. Until the 1980s, articulated theories about disability were few and far between, as were considerations of their relationship to technical knowledge. Also, it is extremely difficult to draw up a skills manual for social workers as one might for plumbers, electricians or car mechanics. Finally, much work with disabled people has been atheoretical, either based covertly on the individual model of disability, or simply orientated to the immediate practical task at hand. This approach has problems, because, as Lee has argued:

theory must have regard for practice but it should not be 'tailored' for it. Practical contingencies must not be allowed to dictate the terms of theoretical speculation, for if they do a most anaemic form of theorising will result. Such theory, raised in a protected environment to fit necessity, is the stuff of car maintenance manuals; and people informed by such manuals might be able to perform reasonably efficiently, but then so could unreflexive automatons.
(in Bailey and Lee, 1982, p. 41)

While the social model of disability would provide an adequate and appropriate base for developing social work practice with disabled people, much social work was, and is, inherently conservative and does not challenge existing social relations. Deeply embedded as it is in social consciousness generally, the individual model or personal disaster theory of disability can only be replaced or superseded by a radical change in both theoretical conceptualisation and practical approach. This has fundamental implications both for the training needs of social workers and for the professional organisation of generic social work. It was, and is, not enough merely to increase knowledge about disability on basic training courses; this must be tackled alongside a reversion towards specialist practice and away from the generic approach.

Both BASW and CCETSW have made some attempt to recognise, at least in terms of official policy, that disability arises as a consequence of social forces, but neither responded fully to the need to develop a practice that is informed by such theorising. In the case of BASW, while their 1990 Annual General Meting (AGM) unanimously passed a motion recognising that disability resulted from the social reactions to impairment, their policy documents continued to reflect an individual model understanding of the problem. In a discussion document on the subject (BASW, 1990) they describe the nature of disability as being caused initially by impairment, but that the impact of this on individuals and families depends on severity, prognosis, origin, social barriers, age, social impact, changes in personal functioning and changes in social functioning. This paper goes on to describe the social work role in terms of a series of functional tasks, including taking responsibility for 'whether the disabled person can appreciate danger and act accordingly', clearly viewing independent living as potentially at odds with a societal responsibility to protect 'vulnerable' individuals. This description is little more than a reiteration of what is happening within an individual model of practice, leaving the recommendations clearly at the technical knowledge/actual task levels.

Following the launch of the Diploma in Social Work (DipSW) in 1989, the CCETSW formed a number of working parties to develop detailed performance criteria for social work students in a range of areas of particular practice. Their report (Stevens, 1991) recommends that disability should be viewed in terms of the social model, but the CCETSW were immersed simultaneously in the development of a competence-based social work training that is based on a functional analysis of social work activity within local authority agencies; this 'car maintenance' approach to social work is dominated by an individual model of disability. The result is a failure to get to grips with the perennial problem of the relationship between theory and practice. Some even argue that the CCETSW rejected this relationship as being irrelevant to social work practice (Jones, 1994).

Avoiding the dangers of an 'anaemic form of theorising' (Bailey and Lee, 1982), little was stated by Stevens about the social work task, and instead his report concentrated on the issue of participation by producing guidelines for the training of disabled people as social workers. A similar approach to widening participation in the new degree in social work was taken by Sapey et al. (2004b) endorsed by the General Social Care Council (GSCC). While this is in accordance with aspects of a citizenship approach, more needs to change in terms of altering the relationships between service providers and service users for the social model to be truly integrated into social work practice.

The paradox is that the CCETSW and the GSCC have placed considerable importance on such values as empowerment, participation and choice in welfare, and have taken a lead in this respect through the development of anti-oppressive practice in the social work curriculum. The foundation of such practice is that the social problems that individuals, families and communities face are often the result of systematic oppression within the structures of British society. At the same time, their adoption of a competence model of education has, according to some, left social work

> foundering in the mechanistic application of a political correctness which represents an ill-digested, prescriptive and rule-bound approach to which students must submit or rebel, but which they have little scope to interrogate and own, and the original point of which may well elude them.
> (Froggett and Sapey 1997, p. 50)

A further contradiction, which suggests that the term 'anti-oppressive social work' is little more than an oxymoron, is the nature of social work values. Holman argues that the ideology that underpins the BASW's *Code of Ethics for Social Work* is in fact intensely individualistic, and that while it may be correct to uphold the value of individuals

> a focus which minimizes considerations of mutual obliga-tions, of environment and structures, contains certain draw-backs. For a start it opens the door to explanations of human problems which stress the inadequacy of individuals regardless of their circumstances. This individualism has something in common with that of the New Right and its conception of an underclass of feckless individuals to be condemned and controlled. Then it diminishes the resolve to campaign against poverty and other societal forces, for they are regarded as outside the real scope of social work, which is just to deal with individuals. Not least, the climate that social work is to do with a professional coping with an indi-vidual client is a barrier to social workers acting collectively with user organizations and residents of communities.
> (Holman, 1993, pp. 51–2)

For Holman, the solution lies in the development of mutuality as the basis of the relationship between the state (and hence social workers as administrators of its welfare functions), and the recipi-ents of welfare. Mutuality is a development of the socialist value of fraternity, and a social work practice that was underpinned by this might be capable of responding to the criticisms of the social model analysis. Not only would it imply a mutual sharing of responsibility with disabled people, and that the social work role was one of supporting individuals to achieve their own aspirations; it would also mean that for social workers to be truly effective in helping people to be less disabled, they would have to view the struggle of the disabled people's movement as also affecting them also directly. The model of social work that would follow from this ideology would be based on the notion that a world in which particular groups of people are systematically oppressed is oppressive to all people.

The individual model of disability and its associated themes of deviancy and abnormality are very much the product of the modernist project and the search for scientific certainty, yet still influenced by the traditional need for strong social hierarchies. In such a world, people are identified, and develop a self-identity, as normal or abnormal, and the social model helps us to understand how this has become a systematic process of oppression. In the struggle against oppression, the oppressed will challenge the identity bestowed upon them, but what is also required is a similar challenge from the oppressors. Stuart Hall argues, in relation to race, that this may be happening:

> with globalisation comes the growing recognition that
> nobody has one identity. There isn't anyone who doesn't
> have complex cultural roots. The Brits suddenly discover
> half of them are really French, they speak a language partly
> based on Norse, they came from Scandinavia, they're
> Romans, many have gone to live in Australia and the
> Himalayas.
> (quoted in Jacques, 1997, p. 34)

The result of this is to break down some of the notions that underpin racism, and in particular the ideology of superiority that permits white people to justify their oppression of black people. What is required in relation to disability is for non-disabled people to discover that they may be as different from the ideal human body as those they had considered to be impaired, and as such are not part of a distinct and superior group.

Thus, to professionalise social work on the basis of an expertise in impairment as a cause of social need would be an act of oppression as this would serve to reinforce theories of individual inadequacy and blame, whereas what is required is for social workers and social work to develop a commitment to the removal of disabling barriers, in partnership with disabled people. This requires a fundamental shift towards a radical rather than an individualistic practice – the problems of disabled people, or social workers, are not resolved by the incorporation of empowerment as an instrumental competence within the curriculum. In part this is because of the anti-theoretical approach of competence-based education, but primarily it is because this in fact represents part of the process of disempowering disabled people by providing bureaucratic measures to limit the effectiveness of protest and self-empowerment.

Organisational issues and structural developments

Three organisational concerns can be levelled at the services for disabled people:

● First, that social workers act as arbiters of need between disabled people and the state;
● Second, that the responsibilities for services for disabled people are unco-ordinated and distributed across a large number of organisations and rehabilitation professions; and
● Third, the services that are available tend to reflect the professional interests and aspirations of those workers rather than being based on any analysis of disability and the needs of disabled people.

The issue of the relationship between the needs of disabled people and the services provided is a complicated one in which there is no direct link between the two (see Figure 7.1). From this diagram it is clear that disabled people have their needs defined and interpreted by others, and the services provided to meet these needs are often delivered by large, bureaucratic organisations.

Social workers tend to be defensive about their role, often looking to their organisations as constraining their practice. However, the problem for social workers in social services departments is not merely one of a lack of opportunities to work in different ways, but is also exacerbated by the failure of the profession to distinguish between professional and administrative criteria for decision-making, or to

Figure 7.1 The relationship between needs and services

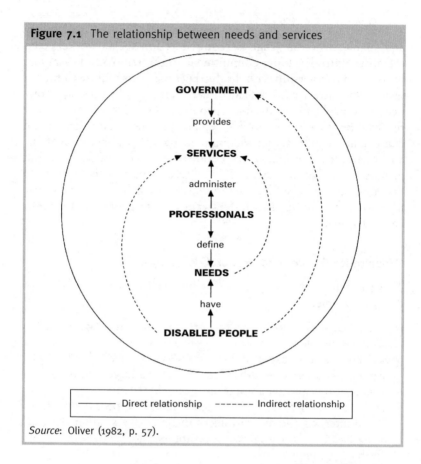

                          Direct relationship   - - - - - - Indirect relationship

Source: Oliver (1982, p. 57).

support workers who wish to make decisions based on the former rather than the latter. The administrative approach received official sanction through the National Health Service and Community Care Act, 1990, which, by introducing quasi-markets also placed budget control at the top of local authority priorities.

While the Seebohm reorganisation of welfare was one that focused on the organisation of the institutions through which social work was delivered, without challenging the basic principles of welfare that had been laid down in 1948, the changes that followed the Griffiths Report into community care were aimed at the structure of the relationship between the government and the bureaucracy. Through the purchaser–provider split, its architects hoped to use market mechanisms, rather than professional judgement, as the major mechanism for rationing services and keeping costs down. Community care plans of local authorities, and strict controls over the size and use of budgets, were the mechanisms through which this control would be exercised directly, while the disciplines of the market would control the actions of individual practitioners and managers. We should question the extent to which this has been conducive to the development of a social work practice based on the social model of disability.

Some writers (for example, Le Grand and Bartlett, 1993) have argued that these changes were necessary if the business of welfare was to be conducted efficiently and equitably, but their analysis starts from traditional or individual model assumptions about the causes of social need. Others, such as Holman, are very clear that a system based on the ideologies of the New Right has failed and will continue to fail:

> New Right policies have failed to revive the economy . . .
> they have made a god out of Mammon so that personal gain
> and material selfishness are regarded as virtues while the
> compassion for the disadvantaged and a readiness to share
> goods and power are sneered at as weaknesses.
> (Holman, 1993, p. 26)

This argument suggests that, to enable the organization of welfare to support the practice of social work within a social model analysis of disability, there would need to be a fundamental change to the ideologies that informed the structures of welfare.

The New Labour vision of welfare is as a mechanism to support people during periods of risk – for example while they are temporarily unemployed. Rather than changing the system fundamentally, this builds on the New Right idea of individuals being responsible for their own welfare, but in need of support from time to time so that more flexible employment markets can operate within the globalised capitalist economy. At a level of rhetoric the government appears keen to promote

> disabled people's inclusion in the paid labour market with
> policies to revise the benefits system, and to make radical
> changes in the operation of the labour market. All these

sound like social model solutions to the problem of high unemployment rate amongst disabled people. However, when the
government talks about mechanisms to implement these
changes, it focuses on two things: a small number of special
schemes, and job coaches for individual disabled people. So
while the government accepts that the problems are external to
disabled people, its solutions target individual disabled people.
(Oliver, 2004, p. 21)

Within social work it is the Community Care (Direct Payments)
Act, 1996 that is significant because, while it exploits the method
of the market for the provision of care, it has the potential to shift
the control and power over the purchase of services from local
authorities to disabled people. Furthermore, with the anticipated
change to self-assessment of need, disabled people would gain the
opportunity not only to determine the best services, but also their
purpose. Within this structure there is potential for social workers
to practice from a social model understanding of disability,
although the evidence tends to suggest considerable resistance to
the direct payments system (Commission for Social Care
Inspection, 2004). The social work task would be one of supporting disabled people in the processes of assessing their own needs
and purchasing their own personal assistance. Inevitably, this will
affect the relationship between the helped and helper, as personal
assistants will be employees, not carers, and in the long term this
has the potential to change the ways in which society views
disabled people as being dependent.

However, while the potential for change exists, it currently
remains dependent on the local authority's assessment of need, and
there are some barriers to this being conducted within a social
model of disability. First, the tendency to require that disabled
people have to come to terms with their impairment and disability
before they can be helped successfully places a precondition on the
assessment of need that reinforces normative assumptions about
disability based on an individual model. This problem was integral
to the analysis that led CCETSW to assert that self-assessment of
need is essential to good social work practice (Stevens, 1991).
Second, the continued emphasis on budgets limits the extent to
which local authorities are prepared to relinquish their control in
the determination of individual need – self-assessment requires a

partnership between social workers and disabled people which threatens that control. There is mounting evidence in reviews of direct payment schemes that local authorities are quite creative in finding ways of resisting the changes the schemes were designed to achieve. Furthermore, social workers may be motivated to hold on to the assessment role in a non-participatory way as it is a significant source of power. While the Barclay Report may have placed an emphasis on social care planning, community social work and counselling, for many social workers in local authorities their role has become one of social care administration, and a profession under threat may not be willing or able to assist others who are attempting to empower themselves.

Figure 7.1 is in itself simplistic, and two additional aspects are important: first, the overlapping organizational context in which services are delivered; and second, the people who deliver the services. Blaxter (1980) found that services for disabled people could be provided by more than a dozen different organisations. These tended to be large, bureaucratic and remote, and consequently found it difficult to respond to individual needs in a personalized way. Furthermore, there was considerable overlap as to the services provided, and demarcation lines were often blurred. As a consequence, disabled people were passed from one department to another, or asked the same questions many times, and this did little to enhance their quality of life.

Because of these complexities and overlapping services, it was often suggested that 'co-ordination' is a major problem in providing services for disabled people. However, the real problem is not co-ordination but, as Wilding says, the consequences of services that had been built up around professional skills rather than client need:

> Services organised around professional skills are a tribute to the power of professionals in policy making. They also bear witness to a failure of professional responsibility. This is a failure to recognise that services organised around particular skills may be logical for professionals but may not meet the needs of clients and potential clients. *The real sufferers, for example, from the multiplicity of professionals actually or potentially involved in the care and rehabilitation of the physically handicapped are the handicapped.*
> [emphasis added] (Wilding, 1982, p. 98)

Finkelstein also suggested that the problem is not one of co-ordination, but rather one of a need for a change in the professional role – the professional must change from being an expert definer of need and/or rationer of services to become a resource that the disabled person might use as he or she chooses:

> The endemic squabbles between rehabilitation workers about professional boundaries and the familiar farce of professional 'teamwork' can only be put at an end when all the workers and facilities in rehabilitation become resources in a process of self-controlled rehabilitation.
> (Finkelstein, 1981, p. 27)

More recently, Finkelstein (1999a and 1999b) has called for an abandonment of professions allied to medicine in favour of professions allied to the community. These workers would replace existing services and service providers and be immersed within disability culture and politics, an essential ingredient in Finkelstein's view, if real change is to be achieved for and by disabled people. Thompson (2002b), in analysing the impact of the disabled people's movement, also calls for radical change:

> In some respects, this user participation movement has had the effect of challenging the complacency of a traditional model of professionalism based on the notion of 'we know best'. The notion of professionalism is an ambiguous one. It can refer to a commitment to high standards, to learning and development, to ethical practice and to accountability. In this regard, it is compatible with emancipatory practice and the pursuit of social justice. However, it can also refer to elitism and relations of dominance and subordination, in which case it is far from compatible with social justice . . . The challenge social work faces, therefore, is to develop forms of professionalism which are consistent with, and welcoming of, user participation and a commitment to equality and social justice – that is, professionalism based on partnership.
> (p. 717)

For social workers in local authority social services departments (SSDs), however, the problems are not only those of a service organised around narrow professional skills, or even lack of co-ordination and teamwork, but also of working in departments where there was little or no recognition of the exercise of professional skills in working with disabled people. It could be argued that Seebohm did not create generic departments, but rather specialist child care ones, where the needs of children were met by trained professionals, and other needs and obligations were met by unqualified staff, welfare assistants and the like, or passed on to occupational therapists employed by SSDs.

Despite this low priority, a disabled person can be confronted with many different professionals from health and social welfare agencies. A major problem for disabled people and their families therefore is not just a matter of which particular agency to approach, but also of which particular professional to contact. Furthermore, even when professionals are in contact, disabled people and their families are often unclear as to which department the professional represents, and consequently what services may, or may not, be offered. To overcome this, the idea of a 'named person' has variously been built into practice.

There are a number of problems related to this idea, particularly about whether the named person would in fact be the 'key worker' or simply someone given nominal responsibility, such as the head of a special school. There is also the question about whether most professionals have sufficient knowledge and skills to act in this capacity. Both in terms of their strategic position and Finkelstein's principle of self-controlled rehabilitation, the disabled person is the logical choice as both named person and key worker. The professional task, therefore, should not be to usurp the key worker position from the disabled person, but rather to work with him or her to ensure that the required knowledge is acquired, and thereby allay fears that a new profession of 'named persons' could arise, with its own career structure, salary increments and enhanced professional status.

There are a number of other problems to which the professional relationship can give rise. Some writers (McKnight, 1981; Davis, 2004) have suggested that the very relationship is itself disabling, and others (Fox, 1974; Robinson, 1978; Gibbs, 2004; Harris, 2004; Priestley, 2004) have pointed to the fact that very often professional definitions of need do not coincide with the needs defined by disabled people themselves. Consequently, where professional and personal definitions of need conflict, the quality of life for disabled people is unlikely to be enhanced. Scott, who had written perceptively on the topic, stated that the professional

> has been specially trained to give professional help to impaired people. He cannot use his expertise if those who are sent to him for assistance do not regard themselves as being impaired. Given this fact, it is not surprising that the doctrine has emerged among experts that truly effective rehabilitation and adjustment can occur only after the client has squarely faced and accepted the 'fact' that he is, indeed, 'impaired'.
> (Scott, 1970, p. 280)

And it was not just in terms of acceptance of disability, but also in the assessment of needs and services that professionals sought to impose their definitions, though not always with total success. Thus many disabled people have had their needs met (or not) by professionalised welfare bureaucracies which very often do not provide an appropriate service in an acceptable fashion.

Hence there are organisational pressures, embedded in the structures of the welfare system, that have prevented social work practice from developing the radical approach necessary for working within a social model:

> The social model then, has had no real impact on professional practice, and social work has failed to meet disabled people's self-articulated needs. Twenty years ago [in the first edition of this book], I predicted that if social work was not prepared to change in terms of its practice towards disabled people it would eventually disappear altogether. Given the proposed changes by the New Labour government in respect of modernising social services, it seems likely that that forecast is about to come true. We can probably now announce the death of social work at least in relation to its involvement in the lives of disabled people.
> (Oliver, 2004, p. 25)

While that may seem to be an appropriate point at which to end this book, this death is likely to be a lingering one, and for those individuals who are able to embrace the changes required, there are likely to be opportunities of working with disabled people within a citizenship approach, perhaps as professionals allied to communities. The final section of this chapter therefore considers the strategies that social workers may need to employ in order to practise with and alongside disabled people in their struggle to remove disabling barriers.

Some strategies for social work

While the traditional role of social workers with disabled people may be dying, there are aspects of professional social work that have the potential to be of use within a citizenship approach, but this is dependent on the ideologies that inform practice. A profession built upon an expertise model, such as medicine or law, which ignores the voices and experiences of the people they purport to serve, will do little to change the unequal and debilitating power relationships between the welfare state and disabled people. Neither will codes of ethics, based on individualistic ideologies, help to achieve progress in the struggle against social barriers, as they tend to value people despite, rather than because of, their difference. What is required is a form of professionalism that is capable of asserting itself in the face of oppressive social policies, but which does so with disabled people rather than for them. A social work profession that might achieve this would need several features in its curriculum. The five that follow are not an exhaustive list, though they are important.

First, disability equality training and disability studies would need to be integral to the education of social workers. Disability equality training is essential because of the depth to which negative assumptions about dependency and impairment are embedded in the culture of our society. Anti-disablist social work cannot be taught from textbooks alone, as the hegemony of the individual model prevents even those who are aware of oppression from developing a full understanding of what is involved. This was seen in the debate concerning carers, and the proposition that institutional care would provide a non-sexist solution to the problem of dependency (Finch, 1984). The construction of such an argument arises from an awareness and politicisation of the oppression of women, and while such theorising might be transferred to other issues, such as racism or homophobia, the dominance of the individual model of disability prevents even the most politically aware people from transferring their understanding to the oppression of people with impairments. The struggle against disablism is not one of simply asserting equal rights, but of also challenging basic concepts of normality. As Jenny Morris put it:

> I think that the challenge that it makes to the rest of society is absolutely fundamental. I just think it's extraordinary the changes that it's trying to bring about. The whole way that people think about themselves and about their impairment. These things are very, very significant and they are changing society very fundamentally.
>
> (cited in Campbell and Oliver, 1996, p. 139)

In terms of the social work curriculum, such an awareness-raising exercise would not be aimed simply at the individual level of practitioners and students, but at the cultural assumptions that inform the design of the syllabus for the degree in social work. The focus on normality and deviancy through the inclusion of the study of human growth and development within this syllabus typifies the way in which, despite the exhortation of the social model within the context of anti-oppressive practice, social work education is still dominated by the theories based on the individual model of disability.

Although awareness-raising is essential, it is not enough to bring about an informed social work practice. What is also required is that social workers have a knowledge of the social model of disability that will inform their actions as practitioners and managers within a welfare system that has itself been seen to be oppressive. This can be achieved by the incorporation of disability studies as a central, even foundational, aspect of the curriculum for social work education. Disability studies should be on a par with childhood studies in all social work degrees.

In their inaugural conference in 2003, the Disability Studies Association stated that

> Disability Studies is concerned with the inter-disciplinary development of an increasing body of knowledge and practice, which has arisen from the activities of the disabled people's movement, and which has come to be known as 'the social model of disability'. The social model of disability locates the changing character of disability, which is viewed as an important dimension of inequality, in the social and

economic structure and culture of the society in which it is found, rather than in individual limitations. Disability Studies seeks to advance teaching, research and scholarship that is concerned with:

● the analysis of disability and the exclusion of disabled people as a social consequence of impairment;
● the identification and development of strategies for fundamental social and political changes that are necessary for the creation of an inclusive society in which disabled people are full participants, and are guaranteed the same rights as non-disabled people. (www.lancs.ac.uk/fss/apsocsci/events/dsaconf2003/dsa2003. htm)

It is still the case that only a few social work degrees in the UK teach disability studies, and few social workers attend postgraduate courses on the subject. As a result, while many disability studies academics and researchers are developing the knowledge base and practice strategies that would be required to improve the lives of disabled people, they have too little impact on social work practice (Harris, 2003). As a consequence, social workers continue to make applications for their clients to enter residential and nursing homes, and managers continue to spend very large proportions of their budgets on such unwanted services, while local authorities continue to argue that they lack the funding for the services people in fact want. If social workers and their managers are to act differently in their professional lives, they need to be educated differently.

Second, social workers and social service agencies need to give their full support to schemes designed to promote independent living, especially direct payments. There is evidence to suggest (Sapey and Pearson, 2002) that social workers regard people who choose direct payments as opting out of the collective welfare system, and some social workers regard these people as no longer eligible for their support. There is also evidence to show that social workers actively discourage people from using direct payments as they see this as a loss of their budgets, and should they not be successful in this dissuasion, then they and their agencies will try to place restrictions on the use of the payments. For example, the third national objective of *Modernising Social Services* is

to ensure that people of working age who have been assessed as requiring community care services, are provided with these services in ways which take account of and, as far as possible, *maximise their and their carers' capacity to take up, remain in or return to employment.*
[emphasis added] (Department of Health, 1998)

The Social Services Inspectorate found progress to be poor in this respect, however, particularly for people with physical or sensory impairments, and indeed the eligibility criteria might specifically be a barrier (Griffiths, 2001).

Social workers and their managers need to view direct payment schemes as an integral part of a collective approach to the provision of personal assistance. Implementing these schemes positively would provide social workers with the means of promoting independent living and helping disabled people to access mainstream economic and social life (Priestley, 1999).

Third, the most common area in which disputes will arise is that of assessment of need. While local authorities currently retain the right to determine the needs of individuals, there will always be a level of conflict over the interpretation and assessment of need. This was discussed in detail in Chapter 3, and various strategies were proposed for practitioners to undertake assessments within a social model. At the core of these were the issues of empowerment and self-assessment. However, what may also be required is that social workers adopt a position of 'determined advocacy' in relation to supporting the rights of individual disabled people to participate and to define their own needs.

Determined advocacy implies not making judgements about whether the self-assessment of need is correct by some normative criteria, but to advocate for that assessment without reservation. This is not to relinquish any form of professional judgement or involvement with the individual concerned, as the advice and experience of the social worker may be of immense value in helping disabled people to develop strategies in their self-assessment. Rather, it is to ensure that the social work role is not to act as yet another barrier to independent living – it is to enable rather than to disable.

Fourth, is the role of counselling in social work practice with disabled people. This is a matter that social workers often dispute as to whether it is part of their task, with some viewing it as the only therapeutic skill that they can genuinely possess, while others consider it to be a specialist activity and not part of the administration of welfare. There are good arguments for both positions.

Those who support the practice of counselling would suggest that social work is not simply a matter of administering the delivery of material and personal services, but rather one of helping people who are failing to realise their potential within the social sphere of their lives. As such counselling becomes a useful skill to either raise the consciousness of individuals or, in a less radical manner, to help people to understand the meanings of their own actions.

A counter to this argument is that, because of the position social workers occupy within the power structures of the welfare system, it would be wrong to employ skills that may blur the transparency with which their actions should be conducted, if they are to enable the full participation of their clients. This view may see counselling as a manipulative process, or simply as a matter that should be kept separate from the provision of social services.

To some extent, both these arguments are conducted within an individual model of understanding of disability in which counselling is used either to help people come to terms with their impairment, or not if it is seen as an inadequate response to the request for material help. From the perspective of the social model, what is required is to evaluate the usefulness of counselling in the struggle to remove disabling barriers. One piece of research into what might constitute counselling in a social model of practice concluded that

> The focus of counselling physically disabled people seems to be one of very consciously giving control back to the client or enabling the client to empower themselves through practical, emotional and social means. This is found to be necessary as many disabled people have had difficult and often painful experiences at the hands of the medical and allied professions or in their families or in interactions with the public at large. Due to their circumstances they have had to rely on others for their practical needs and sometimes the 'professionals' or family members have taken over the decision making for the disabled person. The result of feeling out of control, in a practical sense, has led to emotional difficulties for some

disabled people. The emotional cost for them of not feeling empowered is having low self esteem, low self confidence and a feeling of worthlessness.
(Oliver, 1995, p. 275)

Thus counselling can play a useful and necessary role in countering the impact of many of the disabling barriers that people with impairments face. While it would certainly be right for social workers to refuse to counsel people with the aim of getting them to accept the non-provision of material resources, it would be wrong to reject counselling *per se*.

Fifth, there is a need to rediscover the role of community social work within community care. The beginning of care management has had the effect of neutralising social work as a radical activity. The development of procedures and regulations for the provision of services, along with the limitation of the legitimate role of social work to this instrumental activity, has curtailed many of the roles of social workers that were previously undisputed. Social work within local authorities tends to be viewed as a purely administrative process, and one that might legitimately be undertaken by people with some other form of training. However, this would be to accept that the current organisation of disability services, and of welfare in general, is appropriate and that there is no need for it to be challenged from within the system.

Community social work has always meant working with and within communities to assist them to realise greater benefits from the welfare state, and it is to these roles of advocacy and development that social work must return. The struggle against disability is a collective one, as the solutions are social rather than individual. If social work is to be an effective ally to the struggle and to use its influence within the welfare state to alter and modify disability policies, it must do so from a position that is informed by its work with collective organisations of disabled people. It may, in Finkelstein's terms, need to become a profession allied to the community.

Individual disabled people who are isolated from these developments may be in touch with social workers who can help by making them aware of the collective nature of their problems. Social workers can also help groups of disabled people to be heard in preference to the traditional organisations *for* the disabled that have established access to social service managements. It is impossible, and would be quite wrong to attempt, to reproduce the instrumentalism of care management by providing a list of social work tasks that flow from an acceptance of the social model of disability. The issues that have been highlighted here are the most obvious and perhaps most urgent that need to be addressed by the social work establishment – its professional bodies, education providers and principal employers. It is only by examining and re-examining the implications of the social model analysis for the structures of social policy, the management of the welfare system and the actual practice of social work, that social workers will be able to formulate a means of working that is meaningful and useful to disabled people as citizens, not clients.

Conclusion

The first edition of this book was written in the early 1980s, in the hope that the social model of disability would provide a useful basis for constructing an effective social work practice with disabled people. In the years since then, economic and political changes, coupled with a less than inspired professional leadership of the social work profession, has meant that many of our earlier hopes have not materialised. However, the emergence of a strong and committed movement of disabled people based on the social model of disability has meant that an enabling professional practice remains firmly on the agenda.

In this third edition of the book, we have reviewed the changes that have taken place within social work and society over the past two decades, and concluded that the individual model of disability is so embedded in social work practice that in its current form the profession is unlikely to retain its role of working with disabled people as citizens. The citizenship approach to welfare seeks to change fundamentally the relationship that disabled people have with the welfare state, and this requires the administrators of welfare also to change fundamentally.

We hope that this book will be a vehicle for such a change, and that those social workers who understand and appreciate the need for change will join in the struggle by the disabled people's movement.

putting it into practice

Exercise

Oliver (2004, p. 25) has argued that 'We can probably now announce the death of social work at last in relation to its involvement in the lives of disabled people.' Examine the curriculum of the social work course you undertook, or are undertaking, and decide how much is relevant or not to working with disabled people. What additional knowledge and skills do you think you would require that were/are not on this course? On completing this final exercise you should have the basis for identifying your own professional development needs.

Further reading

Barnes, C. and Mercer, G. (eds) (2004a) *Implementing the Social Model of Disability: Theory and Research*, Leeds: The Disability Press.

Barnes, C. and Mercer, G. (eds) (2004b) *Disability Policy and Practice: Applying the Social Model*, Leeds: The Disability Press.

These two books consist of papers presented at an Economic and Social Research Council (ESRC)-funded seminar series on the topic of putting the social model of disability into practice.

Appendix: disability studies resources on the internet

UK websites

Centre for Disability Studies, University of Leeds

www.leeds.ac.uk/disability-studies/
The CDS is the first and most active research centre in the UK. Much of its work can be viewed at this site.

Disability Archive

www.leeds.ac.uk/disability-studies/archiveuk/index.html
The Disability Archive is an ever-expanding collection of hundreds of papers that are not easily available elsewhere.

Disability Studies Association

http://www.disabilitystudies.net
Since 2003, Lancaster University have been hosting the DSA conferences, and many of the papers presented are available on this site.

Disability Rights Commission

www.drc-gb.org/
The DRC is the most authoritative source for up-to-date information about the Disability Discrimination Act and what it means.

Disabling Imagery at the British Film Institute

www.bfi.org.uk/education/resources/teaching/disability/
The BFI provides a wide range of critical materials related to the portrayal of disability on film. The accompanying DVD is very reasonably priced.

Social Care Online

www.socialcareonline.org.uk
Social Care Online has a range of resources including Caredata, the most extensive database of social work and social care literature in the UK.

Social Care Institute for Excellence

www.scie.org.uk
SCIE produce a wide range of practice guides for social workers which are all available electronically.

UK Government Disability Website

www.disability.gov.uk/
Many links and other resources giving access to most official documents related to disability.

International websites

Nordic Network on Disability Research

http://www.nndr.dk/
NNDR is a multidisciplinary network of disability researchers interested in cultural, societal and environmental dimensions of disability and marginalisation.

Society for Disability Studies

http://www.uic.edu/orgs/sds/
For nearly two decades, the Society for Disability Studies has worked to explore issues of disability and chronic illness from scholarly perspectives. Its membership includes social scientists, health researchers, and humanities scholars, as well as artists and those active in the disability rights movement.

European Disability Forum

http://www.edf-feph.org/
EDF is a European umbrella organisation representing more than 50 million disabled people in Europe. Its mission is to ensure disabled citizens' full access to fundamental and human rights through their active involvement in policy development and implementation in the European Union.

Independent Living Institute

http://www.independentliving.org/
The Independent Living Institute offers resources for persons with extensive disabilities and develops consumer-driven policies for self-determination, self-respect and dignity.

Bibliography

Abberley, P. (1992) 'Counting Us Out: A Discussion of the OPCS Disability Surveys', *Disability, Handicap & Society*, 9(2), pp. 139–55.

Abbott, D., Morris, J. and Ward, L. (2000) *Disabled Children at Residential School*, York: Joseph Rowntree Foundation.

Abrams, P. (1978) 'Community Care: Some Research Problems and Priorities', in J. Barnes and N. Connelly (eds) *Social Care Research*, London: Bedford Square Press.

ACE (1996) *Special Education Handbook: The Law on Children with Special Needs*, London: Advisory Centre for Education.

Ahmad, W. (ed.) (2000) *Ethnicity, Disability and Chronic Illness*, Buckingham: Open University Press.

Ahmad, W., Atkin, K. and Chamba, R. (2000a) ' "Causing Havoc Among Their Children": Parental and Professional Perspectives on Consanguinity and Childhood Disability', in W. Ahmad (ed.), *Ethnicity, Disability and Chronic Illness*, Buckingham: Open University Press.

Ahmad, W., Darr, A. and Jones, L. (2000b) ' "I Sent My Child to School and He Comes Back an Englishman": Minority Ethnic Deaf People, Identity Politics and Services', in W. Ahmad (ed.), *Ethnicity, Disability and Chronic Illness*, Buckingham: Open University Press.

Albrecht, G. L. (ed.) (1976) *The Sociology of Physical Disability and Rehabilitation*, Pittsburg, Pa.: University of Pittsburgh Press.

Albrecht, G. and Levy, J. (1981) 'Constructing Disabilities as Social Problems', in G. Albrecht (ed.), *Cross National Rehabilitation Policies: A Sociological Perspective*, Beverly Hills, Calif.: Sage.

Aldridge, J. and Becker, S. (1996) 'Disability Rights and the Denial of Young Carers: The Dangers of Zero-sum Arguments', *Critical Social Policy*, 16(3), pp. 55–76.

Allen, C., Milner, J. and Price, D. (2002) *Home Is Where the Start Is*, Bristol: Policy Press.

Ambrose, I. (1997) *Lifetime Homes in Europe and the UK: European Legislation and Good Practice for Ensuring Accessibility of Domestic Dwellings*, Housing Research Findings, York: Joseph Rowntree Foundation.

Audit Commission (1986) *Making a Reality of Community Care*, London: HMSO.

Avery, D. (1997) Message to disability-research@mailbase.ac.uk discussion group, re: age onset of disability, 9 June.

Bailey, R. and Lee, P. (ed.) (1982) *Theory and Practice in Social Work*, Oxford: Basil Blackwell.

Baistow, K. (1995) 'Liberation and Regulation? Some Paradoxes of Empowerment', *Critical Social Policy*, 42, pp. 34–46.

Bajekal, M., Harries, T., Breman, R. and Woodfield, K. (2004) *Review of Disability Estimates and Definitions*, London: Department of Work and Pensions.

Barclay Committee (1982) *Social Workers: Their Role and Tasks*, London: Bedford Square Press.

Barnes, C. (1991) *Disabled People in Britain and Discrimination. A Case for Anti-Discrimination Legislation*, London: Hurst & Co.

Barnes, C. (1997) 'A Legacy of Oppression: A History of Disability in Western Culture', in L. Barton and M. Oliver (eds), *Disability Studies: Past, Present and Future*, Leeds: The Disability Press.

Barnes, C. and Oliver, M. (1995) 'Disability Rights: Rhetoric and Reality in the UK', *Disability & Society*, **10**(1), pp. 111–16.

Barnes, C., Mercer, G. and Morgan, H. (2000a) *Creating Independent Futures: An Evaluation of Services Led by Disabled People, Stage 2 report*, Leeds: The Disability Press.

Barnes, C., Mercer, G. and Morgan, H. (2000b) 'Creating Independent Futures' website; www.leeds.ac.uk/disability-studies/projects/independentfutures/stageone/semreport.pdf.

Barnes, C., Mercer, G. and Morgan, H. (2001) *Creating Independent Futures: An Evaluation of Services Led by Disabled People, Stage 3 report*, Leeds: The Disability Press.

Barnes, C., Jolly, D., Mercer, G., Pearson, C., Priestley, M. and Riddell, S. (2004) 'Devolving Direct Payments: A Review of Policy Development in the UK', Paper at the Disability Studies: Putting Theory into Practice conference, Lancaster University, 26–28 July; www.lancs.ac.uk/fss/apsocsci/events/ds_archive.htm.

Barnes, M. (1997) *Care, Communities and Citizens*, Harlow: Longman.

Barton, R. (1959) *Institutional Neurosis*, London: John Wright.

BASW (British Association of Social Workers) (1982) *Guidelines for Social Work with the Disabled*, Draft Paper, London: BASW.

BASW (British Association of Social Workers) (1990) *Managing Care: The Social Work Task*, Birmingham: BASW.

Battye, L. (1966) 'The Chatterley Syndrome', in P. Hunt (ed.), *Stigma*, London: Geoffrey Chapman.

Beardshaw, V. (1993) 'Conductive Education: A Rejoinder', in J. Swain, V. Finkelstein, S. French and M. Oliver (eds), *Disabling Barriers – Enabling Environments*, London: Sage.

Becker, H. (1963) *Outsiders: Studies in the Sociology of Deviance*, New York: The Free Press.

Begum, N., Hill, M. and Stevens, A. (eds) (1994) *Reflections: The Views of Black Disabled People on their Lives and on Community Care*, London: CCETSW.

Bell, L. and Klemz, A. (1981) *Physical Handicap*, Cambridge: Woodhead-Faulkner.

Bentall, R. (1998) 'Why There Will Never Be a Convincing Theory of Schizophrenia', in S. Rose (ed.), *From Brains to Consciousness? Essays on the New Sciences of the Mind*, London: Penguin.

Beresford, B. and Oldman, C. (2002) *Housing Matters*, Bristol: Policy Press.

Beresford, P. (2004) 'Madness, Distress, Research and a Social Model', in C. Barnes and G. Mercer (eds), *Implementing the Social Model of Disability: Theory and Research*, Leeds: The Disability Press.

Berger, R. (1988) 'Helping Clients Survive a Loss', *Social Work Today*, 19(34), pp. 14–17.

Bewley, C. and McCulloch, L. (2004) *The Importance and Availability of Peer Support for People with Learning Difficulties Accessing Direct Payments*, York: Joseph Rowntree Foundation.

Blaug, R. (1995) 'Distortion of the Face to Face: Communicative Reason and Social Work Practice', *British Journal of Social Work*, 25(4), pp. 423–39.

Blaxter, M. (1980) *The Meaning of Disability*, 2nd edn, London: Heinemann.

Bloomfield, R. (1976) *Younger Chronic Sick Units: A Survey and Critique*, Unpublished paper.

Bone, M. and Meltzer, H. (1989) *The Prevalence of Disability Among Children*, London: HMSO.

Bonnett, D. (1996) *Incorporating Lifetime Homes Standards into Modernisation Programmes*, Housing Research Findings, York: Joseph Rowntree Foundation.

Booth, T. (1992) *Reasons for Admission to Part III Residential Homes*, London: National Council of Domiciliary Care Services.

Borsay, A. (2005) *Disability and Social Policy in Britain since 1750*, Basingstoke: Palgrave.

Boswell, D. M. and Wingrove, J. M. (eds) (1974) *The Handicapped Person in the Community*, London: Tavistock.

Braye, S. and Preston-Shoot, M. (1997) *Practising Social Work Law*, 2nd edn, London: Macmillan.

Brechin, A. and Liddiard, P. (1981) *Look at it this Way: New Perspectives in Rehabilitation*, London: Hodder & Stoughton.

Brechin, A., Liddiard, P. and Swain, J. (eds) (1981) *Handicap in a Social World*, London: Hodder & Stoughton.

Brown, H. and Craft, A. (eds) (1989) *Thinking the Unthinkable: Papers on Sexual Abuse and People with Learning Difficulties*, London: Family Planning Association.

Buckle, J. (1971) *Work and Housing of Impaired People in Great Britain*, London: HMSO.

Burgess, P. (1982) 'In Benefit', *Community Care*, 1 July 1982.

Burgess, P. (1996) 'Social Security', *Research Matters*, April–October 1996, pp. 22–4.

Bury, M. (1996) 'Defining and Researching Disability: Challenges and Responses', in C. Barnes and G. Mercer (eds), *Exploring the Divide: Illness and Disability*, Leeds: The Disability Press.

Cabinet Office (2005) *Improving the Life Chances of Disabled People*, London: Strategy Unit.

Campbell, J. (1997) 'Implementing Direct Payments: Towards the Next Millennium', in S. Balloch and N. Connelly (eds), *Buying and Selling Social Care*, London: National Institute for Social Work.

Campbell, J. and Oliver, M. (eds) (1996) *Disability Politics*, London: Routledge.

Carroll, T. J. (1961) *Blindness – What It Is, What It Does, and How To Live with It*, Boston, Mass.: Little, Brown.

Carver, V. (1982) *The Individual Behind the Statistics*, Milton Keynes: Open University Press.

Casserly, J. and Clark, B. (1978) *A Welfare Rights Approach to the Chronically Sick and Disabled*, Glasgow: Strathclyde Regional Council.

Cavet, J. (1999) *People Don't Understand: Children, Young People and Their Families Living with a Didden Disability*, London: National Children's Bureau.

CCETSW (1974) *Social Work: People with Handicaps Need Better Trained Workers*, London: Central Council for Education and Training in Social Work.

Clark, F. le Gros (1969) *Blinded in War: A Model for the Welfare of all Handicapped People*, Royston: Priory Press.

Clements, L. and Read, J. (2003) *Disabled People and European Human Rights*, Bristol: Policy Press.

Cobbold, C. (1997) *A Cost Benefit Analysis of Lifetime Homes*, York: Joseph Rowntree Foundation.

College of Occupational Therapists (1996) *National Prosthetic and Wheelchair Service Report*, London: College of Occupational Therapy.

Commission for Social Care Inspection (2004) *Direct Payments: What Are the Barriers?* London: CSCI.

Cook, J. and Mitchell, P. (1982) *Putting Teeth in the Act: A History of Attempts to Enforce the Provisions of Section 2 of the Chronically Sick and Disabled Persons Act 1970*, London: RADAR.

Corker, M. and French, S. (eds) (1998) *Disability Discourse*, Milton Keynes: Open University Press.

Corrigan, P. and Leonard, P. (1979) *Social Work Practice Under Capitalism*, London: Macmillan.

Crawshaw, M. (2002) Disabled People's Access to Social Work Education – Ways and Means of Promoting Environmental Change, *Social Work Education*, **21**(5), 503–14.

Creek, G., Moore, M., Oliver, M., Salisbury, V., Silver, J. and Zarb, G. (1987) *The Social Implication of Spinal Cord Injury*, London: Thames Polytechnic.

Croft, S. (1986) 'Women, Caring and the Recasting of Need – A Feminist Reappraisal', *Critical Social Policy*, 16, pp. 23–39.

Crow, L. (1996) 'Including All of Our Lives: Renewing the Social Model of Disability', in C. Barnes and G. Mercer (eds), *Exploring the Divide: Illness and Disability*, Leeds: The Disability Press.

Cypher, J. (ed.) (1979) *Seebohm Across Three Decades*, London: BASW.

d'Aboville, E. (1991) 'Social Work in an Organisation of Disabled People', in M. Oliver (ed.), *Social Work, Disabled People and Disabling Environments*, London: Jessica Kingsley.

Dalley, G. (1996) *Ideologies of Caring*, London: Macmillan.

Daly, M. and Noble, M. (1996) 'The Reach of Disability Benefits: An Examination of the Disability Living Allowance', *Journal of Social Welfare and Family Law*, **18**(1), pp. 37–51.

Dartington, T., Miller, E. and Gwynne, G. (1981) *A Life Together*, London: Tavistock.

Davis, K. (1981) '28–38 Grove Road: Accommodation and Care in a Community Setting', in A. Brechin, P. Liddiard and J. Swain (eds), *Handicap in a Social World*, London: Hodder & Stoughton.

Davis, K. (2004) 'The Crafting of Good Clients', in J. Swain, S. French, C. Barnes and C. Thomas (eds), *Disabling Barriers – Enabling Environments*, 2nd edn, London: Sage.

Davis K. and Woodward, J. (1981) 'DIAL UK: Development of the National Association of Disablement Information and Advice Services', in A. Brechin, P. Liddiard and J. Swain (eds) *Handicap in a Social World*, London: Hodder & Stoughton.

Dawson, C. (2000) *Independent Success: Implementing Direct Payments*, York: Joseph Rowntree Foundation.

Department for Education and Skills (2001) *Special Educational Needs Code of Practice*, London: DfES Publications.

Department for Education and Skills (2004) *Youth Cohort Study: The Activities and Experiences of 18 Year Olds: England and Wales 2004*, London: DfES.

Department of Health (1989) *Caring for People – Community Care in the Next Decade and Beyond*, London: HMSO.

Department of Health (1996) *Statistical Bulletin: Residential Accommodation Statistics 1996*, London: Department of Health.

Department of Health (1998) *Modernising Social Services: Promoting Independence, Improving Protection, Raising Standards*, London: Department of Health.

Department of Health (2000) *A Quality Strategy for Social Care*, London: Department of Health.

Department of Health (2002) *Requirements for Social Work Training*, London: Department of Health.

Department of Health (2003) *Community Care Statistics 2003: Supported Residents (Adults), England*, London: Department of Health.

Department for Work and Pensions (2005) *Department for Work and Pensions Five Year Strategy: Opportunity and Security Throughout Life*, London: DWP.

DHSS (Department of Health and Social Security) (1968) *Report of the Committee on Local Authority and Allied Social Services* (Seebohm Report), London: HMSO.

DHSS (Department of Health and Social Security) (1976) *The Way Forward: Priorities for Health and Personal Social Services in England*, London: HMSO.

Department of Health and Social Security (1981) *Care in Action*, London: HMSO.

Despouy, L. (1993) *Human Rights and Disability*, New York: United Nations Economic and Social Council.

Douglas, J. (ed.) (1970) *Deviance and Respectability: The Social Construction of Moral Meanings*, New York: Basic Books.

Doyal, L. (1980) *The Political Economy of Health*, London: Pluto Press.

Doyal, L. and Gough, I. (1991) *A Theory of Human Need*, London: Macmillan.

Drake, R. (1999) *Understanding Disability Policies*, London: Macmillan.

Ellis, K. (1993) *Squaring the Circle: User and Carer Participation in Needs Assessment*, York: Joseph Rowntree Foundation.

Employment Department Group (1990) *Employment and Training for People with Disabilities*, London: Employment Department Group.

Equal Opportunities Commission (1982) *Caring for the Elderly and Handicapped*, London: Equal Opportunities Commission.

Family Policies Study Centre (1997) *A Guide to Family Issues: Family Briefing Paper 2*, London: Family Policies Study Centre.

Fiedler, B. (1988) *Living Options Lottery*, London: King's Fund Centre.

Fiedler, B. (1991) *Tracking Success: Testing Services for People with Severe Physical and Sensory Disabilities*, London: King's Fund Centre.

Finch, J. (1984) 'Community Care: Developing Non-sexist Alternatives', *Critical Social Policy*, 9, pp. 6–18.

Finkelstein, V. (1980) *Attitudes and Disabled People: Issues for Discussion*, New York: World Rehabilitation Fund.

Finkelstein, V. (1981) *Disability and Professional Attitudes*, Sevenoaks: NAIDEX Convention.

Finkelstein, V. (1991) 'Disability: An Administrative Challenge? (The Health and Welfare Heritage)', in M. Oliver (ed.), *Social Work, Disabled People and Disabling Environments*, London, Jessica Kingsley.

Finkelstein, V. (1999a) *Professions Allied to the Community (PACs)*; http://www.leeds.ac.uk/disability-studies/archiveuk/index.html.

Finkelstein, V. (1999b) *Professions Allied to the Community: The Disabled People's Trade Union*; http://www.leeds.ac.uk/disability-studies/archiveuk/index.html.

Finkelstein, V. and Stuart, O. (1996) 'Developing New Services', in G. Hales (ed.), *Beyond Disability*, London: Sage.

Finlay, B. (1978) *Housing and Disability: A Report on the Housing Needs of Physically Handicapped People in Rochdale*, Rochdale Voluntary Action.

Fitzgerald, R. G. (1970) 'Reaction to Blindness: An Exploratory Study of Adults', *Archives of General Psychiatry*, **22**(April), Chicago: American Medical Association.

Fox, A. M. (1974) *They Get this Training but They Don't Really Know How You Feel*, London: RADAR.

Freire, P. (1972) *Pedagogy of the Oppressed*, Harmondsworth: Penguin.

Froggatt, A. (1990) *Family Work with Elderly People*, Basingstoke: Macmillan.

Froggett, L. and Sapey, B. (1997) 'Communication, Culture and Competence in Social Work Education', *Social Work Education*, 16(1), pp. 41–53.

Fruin, D. (2000) *New Directions for Independent Living: Inspection of Independent Living Arrangements for Younger Disabled People*, London: Department of Health.

Gibbs, D. (2004) 'Social Model Services: An Oxymoron?', in C. Barnes and G. Mercer (eds), *Disability Policy and Practice: Applying the Social Model*, Leeds: The Disability Press.

Gilson, S and DePoy, E. (2002) 'Theoretical Approaches to Disability Content in Social Work Education', *Journal of Social Work Education*, 38(1), pp. 153–65.

Glasby, J. and Littlechild, R. (2002) *Social Work and Direct Payments*, Bristol: The Policy Press.

Glastonbury, B. (1995) 'Risk, Information Technology and Social Care', *New Technology in the Human Services*, 8(3), pp. 2–10.

Gleeson, B. (1999) *Geographies of Disability*, London: Routledge.

Glendinning, C. (1981) *Resource Worker Project: Final Report*, Social Policy Research Unit, University of York.

Goffman, E. (1961) *Asylums*, New York: Doubleday.

Goffman, E. (1963) *Stigma: Some Notes on the Management of Spoiled Identity*, Englewood Cliffs, NJ: Prentice-Hall.

Goldberg, M. and Warburton, C. (1979) *Ends and Means in Social Work*, London: George Allen & Unwin.

Goldsmith, S. (1976) *Designing for the Disabled*, 3rd edn, London: Royal Institute of British Architects.

Gooding, C. (1996) *Blackstone's Guide to the Disability Discrimination Act 1995*, London: Blackstone Press.

Gooding, C. (2003) 'The Disability Discrimination Act: Winners and Losers', Paper at the Working Futures seminar, University of Sunderland, 3–5 December.

Goodinge, S. (2000) *A Jigsaw of Services: Inspection of Services to Support Disabled Parents in their Parenting Role*, London: Department of Health.

Grewal, I., Joy, S., Lewis, J., Swales, K. and Woodfield, K. (2002) *'Disabled for Life?' Attitudes Towards, and Experiences of, Disability in Great Britain*. Research Report 173. London: Department for Work and Pensions,.

Griffiths, G. (2001) *Making It Work: Inspection of Welfare to Work for Disabled People*, London: Social Services Inspectorate.

Griffiths, R. (1988) *Community Care – Agenda for Action*, London: HMSO.

Groce, N. (1985) *Everyone Here Spoke Sign Language: Hereditary Deafness on Martha's Vineyard*, London: Harvard University Press.

Grover, R. and Gladstone, G. (1982) *Disabled People: A Right to Work?*, London: Bedford Square Press.

Grundy, E., Ahlburg, D., Ali, M., Breeze, E. and Sloggett, A. (1999) *Disability in Great Britain*, Research Report 94, London: Department of Social Security.

Guelke, J. (2003) 'Road-kill on the Information Highway: Repetitive Strain Injury in the Academy', *The Canadian Geographer*, 47(4), pp. 386–99.

Hanks, J. and Hanks, L. (1980) 'The Physically Handicapped in Certain Non-occidental Societies', in W. Phillips and J. Rosenberg (eds), *Social Scientists and the Physically Handicapped*, London: Arno Press.

Hanvey, C. (1981) *Social Work with Mentally Handicapped People*, London: Heinemann.

Harris, A. (1971) *Handicapped and Impaired in Great Britain*, London: HMSO.

Harris, J. (1995) *The Cultural Meaning of Deafness*, Aldershot: Averbury.

Harris, J. (1997) *Deafness and the Hearing*, Birmingham: Venture Press.

Harris, J. (2003) 'Ostrich Politics: Exploring the Place of Social Care in Disability Studies', Paper at the Disability Studies: Theory, Policy and Practice conference, Lancaster University, September 4–6; www.lancs.ac.uk/fss/apsocsci/events/ds_archive.htm.

Harris, J. (2004) 'Incorporating the Social Model into Outcome-focused Social Care Practice with Disabled People', in C. Barnes and G. Mercer (eds), *Disability Policy and Practice: Applying the Social Model*, Leeds: The Disability Press.

Harris, J., Sapey, B. and Stewart, J. (1997) *Wheelchair Housing and the Estimation of Need*, Preston: University of Central Lancashire/ National Wheelchair Housing Association Group.

Hasler, F., Zarb, G. and Campbell, J. (2000) *Key Issues for Local Authority Implementation of Direct Payments*, London: Policy Studies Institute.

Hatch, S. (1980) *Outside the State*, London: Croom Helm.

Holdsworth, L. (1991) *Empowerment Social Work with Physically Disabled People*, Norwich: Social Work Monographs.

Holman, B. (1993) A New Deal for Social Welfare, Oxford: Lion.

Howe, D. (1987) *An Introduction to Social Work Theory*, Aldershot: Wildwood House.

Hughes, B. (1995) *Older People and Community Care: Critical Theory and Practice*, Buckingham: Open University Press.

Hunt, P. (1981) 'Settling Accounts with the Parasite People, a Critique of "A Life Apart" by Miller and Gwynne', *Disability Challenge*, 1, UPIAS.

Huntington, A. and Sapey, B. (2003) 'Real Records, Virtual Clients', in E. Harlow and S. Webb (eds), *Information and Communication Technology in the Welfare Services*, London: Jessica Kingsley.

Ibbotson, J. (1975) 'Psychological Effects of Physical Disability', *Occupational Therapy*, January.

Illich, I. (1975) *Medical Nemesis: The Expropriation of Health*, London: Marion Boyars.

Inkeles, A. (1964) *What is Sociology?*, Englewood Cliffs, NJ: Prentice-Hall.

Jacques, M. (1997) 'Les enfants de Marx et de CocaCola', *New Statesman*, 28 November, pp. 34–6.

James, S. and Hutchings, M. (2003) 'Social Model in Practice?, Paper at the Disability Studies: Theory, Policy and Practice conference, Lancaster University, 4–6 September; www.lancs.ac.uk/fss/apsocsci/events/ds_archive.htm.

Jones, C. (1994) *Dangerous Times for British Social Work Education*, Paper at the 27th Congress of the International Association of Schools of Social Work, Amsterdam.

Katbamna, S., Bhakta, P. and Parker, G. (2000) 'Perceptions of Disability and Care-giving Relationships in South Asian Communities', in W. Ahmad (ed.) *Ethnicity, Disability and Chronic Illness*, Buckingham: Open University Press.

Keeble, U. (1979) *Aids and Adaptations*, London: Bedford Square Press.

Keith, L. and Morris, J. (1995) 'Easy Targets: A Disability Rights Perspective on the "Children as Carers" Debate', *Critical Social Policy*, 15(2/3), pp. 36–57.

Kelly, L. (1992) 'The Connections between Disability and Child Abuse: A Review of the Research Evidence', *Child Abuse Review*, 1(3), pp. 157–67.

Kennedy, M. (1989) 'The Abuse of Deaf Children', *Child Abuse Review*, 3(1), pp. 3–7.

Knight, R. and Warren, M. (1978) *Physically Handicapped People Living at Home: A Study of Numbers and Needs*, London: HMSO.

Kuhn, T. (1962) *The Structure of Scientific Revolutions*, Chicago: University of Chicago Press.

Lago, C. and Smith, B. (eds) (2003) *Anti-discriminatory Counselling Practice*, London: Sage Publications.

Langan, M. (1990) 'Community Care in the 1990s: The Community Care White Paper: "Caring for People" ', *Critical Social Policy*, 29, pp. 58–70.

Laurie, L. (ed.) (1991) *Building Our Lives: Housing, Independent Living and Disabled People*, London: Shelter.

Le Grand, J. and Bartlett, W. (eds) (1993) *Quasi-Markets and Social Policy*, London: Macmillan.

Leat, D. (1988) 'Residential Care for Younger Physically Disabled Adults', in I. Sinclair (ed.), *Residential Care: The Research Reviewed*, London: HMSO.

Leece, J. (2004) 'Money Talks, but What Does it Say? Direct Payments and the Commodification of Care', *Practice*, 16(3), pp. 211–21.

Lemert, E. (1967) *Human Deviance, Social Problems and Social Control*, Englewood Cliffs, NJ: Prentice-Hall.

Lenney, M. and Sercombe, H. (2002) ' "Did You See That Guy in the Wheelchair Down the Pub?" Interactions across Difference in a Public Place', *Disability & Society*, **17**(1), pp. 5–18.

Lenny, J. (1993) 'Do Disabled People Need Counselling?', in J. Swain, V. Finkelstein, S. French and M. Oliver (eds), *Disabling Barriers – Enabling Environments*, London: Sage.

Leonard, P. (1966) 'The Challenge of Primary Prevention', *Social Work Today*, 6 October.

Lonsdale, G., Elfer, P. and Ballard, R. (1979) *Children, Grief and Social Work*, Oxford: Basil Blackwell.

MacFarlane, A. (1994) 'On Becoming an Older Disabled Woman', *Disability and Society*, **9**(2), pp. 255–6.

Marchant, R. and Page, M. (1992) *Bridging the Gap*, London: National Society for the Prevention of Cruelty to Children.

Marks, D. (1999) *Disability: Controversial Debates and Psychosocial Perspectives*, London: Routledge.

Marshall, M. (1996) *"I Can't Place This Place At All." Working with People with Dementia and their Carers*, Birmingham, Venture Press.

Marshall, M. and Dixon, M. (1996) *Social Work with Old People*, 3rd edn, London: Macmillan.

Martin, J., Meltzer, H. and Elliot, D. (1988) *The Prevalence of Disability among Adults*, London: HMSO.

Martin, J., White, A. and Meltzer, H. (1989) *Disabled Adults: Services, Transport and Employment*, London: HMSO.

McCarthy, M. (1999) *Sexuality and Women with Learning Disabilities*, London: Jessica Kingsley.

McKnight, J. (1981) 'Professionalised Service and Disabled Help', in A. Brechin, P. Liddiard and J. Swain (eds) *Handicap in a Social World*, London: Hodder & Stoughton.

Merton, R. (1957) *Social Theory and Social Structure*, New York: Free Press.

Meteyard, B. (1992) *Assessment of Need, The OPAL Package*, London: NALGO Education.

Middleton, L. (1992) *Children First: Working with Children and Disability*, Birmingham: Venture Press.

Middleton, L. (1995) *Making a Difference: Social Work with Disabled Children*, Birmingham: Venture Press.

Middleton, L. (1997) *The Art of Assessment: Practitioners Guide*, Birmingham: Venture Press.

Middleton, L. (1999) *Disabled Children: Challenging Social Exclusion*, London: Blackwell Science.

Miller, E. and Gwynne, G. (1971) *A Life Apart*, London: Tavistock.

Morris, J. (ed.) (1989) *Able Lives: Women's Experience of Paralysis*, London: The Women's Press.

Moore, M., Skelton, J., and Patient, M. (2000) *Enabling Future Care*, Birmingham: Venture Press.

Morris, J. (1990) *Freedom to Lose: Housing Policy and People with Disabilities*, London: Shelter.

Morris, J. (1991) *Pride Against Prejudice*, London: Women's Press.

Morris, J. (1992) *Disabled Lives; Many Voices, One Message*, London: BBC Education.

Morris, J. (1993) *Community Care or Independent Living*, York: Joseph Rowntree Foundation.

Morris, J. (1997a) *Community Care: Working in Partnership with Service Users*, Birmingham: Venture Press.

Morris, J. (1997b) 'Gone Missing? Disabled Children Living Away from Their Families', *Disability & Society*, **12**(2), pp. 241–58.

Morris, J. (1998) *Still Missing?*, London: Who Cares? Trust.

Morris, J. (2002) *A Lot To Say*, London: Scope.

Musgrove, F. (1977) *Margins of the Mind*, London: Methuen.

Neimeyer, R. A. and Anderson, A. (2002) 'Meaning Reconstruction Theory', in N. Thompson (ed.), *Loss and Grief*, Basingstoke: Palgrave.

Nelson, G., Lord, J. and Ochoka, J. (2001) *Shifting the Paradigm in Community Mental Health: Towards Empowerment and Community*, Toronto: University of Toronto Press.

Nissel, M. and Bonnerjea, L. (1982) *Family Care of the Handicapped Elderly: Who Pays?*, London: Policy Studies Institute.

North Surrey CHC (1978) *Care and Facilities for the Younger Disabled*, Unpublished paper.

Oliver, J. (1982) 'Community Care: Who Pays?', *New Society*, 24 March.

Oliver, J. (1995) 'Counselling Disabled People: A Counsellor's Perspective', *Disability & Society*, **10**(3), pp. 261–79.

Oliver, M. (1982) *Disablement in Society*, Milton Keynes: Open University Press.

Oliver, M. (1983) *Social Work with Disabled People*, London: Macmillan.

Oliver, M. (1990) *The Politics of Disablement*, London: Macmillan.

Oliver, M. (ed.) (1991) *Social Work, Disabled People and Disabling Environments*, London: Jessica Kingsley.

Oliver, M. (1993) 'Conductive Education: If It Wasn't So Sad It Would Be Funny', in J. Swain, V. Finkelstein, S. French and M. Oliver (eds), *Disabling Barriers Enabling Environments*, London: Sage.

Oliver, M. (1996) *Understanding Disability, From Theory to Practice*, London: Macmillan.

Oliver, M. (2004) 'The Social Model in Action: If I Had a Hammer', in C. Barnes and G. Mercer (eds), *Implementing the Social Model of Disability: Theory and Research*, Leeds: The Disability Press.

Oliver, M. and Bailey, P. (2002) 'Report on the Application of the Social Model of Disability to the Services provided by Birmingham City Council', Unpublished.

Oliver, M. and Barnes, C. (1998) *Disabled People and Social Policy*, Harlow: Longman.

Oliver, M. and Sapey, B. (1999) *Social Work with Disabled People*, 2nd edn, Basingstoke: Macmillan.

Oliver, M. and Zarb, G. (1992) *Greenwich Personal Assistance Schemes: An Evaluation*, London: Greenwich Association of Disabled People.

Owen, T. (1981) 'How Remploy's Survey Helped Barclay', *Community Care*, 12 November.

Parsloe, P. and Stevenson, O. (1978) *Social Services Teams: The Practitioners' View*, London: HMSO.

Phillips, D. (2004) 'The Dynamics of Partnerships and Professionals in the Lives of People with Learning Difficulties', in C. Barnes and G. Mercer (eds), *Disability Policy and Practice: Applying the Social Model*, Leeds: The Disability Press.

Phillips, H. and Glendinning, C. (1981) *Who Benefits?*, London: The Disability Alliance.

Pitkeathley, J. (1996) 'Carers', *Research Matters*, April–October, pp. 58–60.

Powles, J. (1973) 'On the limitations of Modern Medicine', *Science, Medicine and Man*, 1, pp. 1–30.

Priestley, M. (1999) *Disability Politics and Community Care*, London: Jessica Kingsley.

Priestley, M. (2003) *Disability: A Life Course Approach*, Cambridge: Polity Press.

Priestley, M. (2004) 'Tragedy Strikes Again! Why Community Care Still Poses a Problem for Integrated Living', in J. Swain, S. French, C. Barnes and C. Thomas (eds) *Disabling Barriers – Enabling Environments*, 2nd edn, London: Sage.

Ratzka, A. (1991) 'The Swedish Experience', in L. Laurie (ed.), *Building Our Lives: Housing, Independent Living and Disabled People*, London: Shelter.

Read, J. (2000) *Disability, the Family and Society: Listening to Mothers*, Buckingham: Open University Press.

Read, J. and Clements, L. (2001) *Disabled Children and the Law: Research and Good Practice*, London: Jessica Kingsley.

Reeve, D. (2000) 'Oppression Within the Counselling Room', *Disability & Society* 15(4), pp. 669–82.

Reeve, D. (2002) 'Negotiating Psycho-emotional Dimensions of Disability and their Influence on Identity Constructions', *Disability & Society*, 17(5), pp. 493–508.

Reeve, D. (2003) 'The Impact of Psycho-Emotional Disablism on Disabled Children', *'I Feel: I Think'*, Warwick University, 13–14 November.

Reeve, D. (2004) 'Counselling and Disabled People: Help or Hindrance?', in J. Swain *et al.* (eds), *Disabling Barriers – Enabling Environments*, 2nd edn, London: Sage.

Rioux, M., Crawford, M. and Bach, M. (1997) 'Uncovering the Shape of Violence: A Research Methodology Rooted in the Experience of People with Disabilities', in C. Barnes and G. Mercer (eds), *Doing Disability Research*, Leeds: The Disability Press.

Roberts, K. and Harris, J. (2002) 'Disabled People in Refugee and Asylum Seeking Communities in Britain', York: Policy Press/Joseph Rowntree Foundation.

Robinson, T. (1978) *In Worlds Apart: Professionals and their Clients in the Welfare State*, London: Bedford Square Press.

Roith, A. (1974) 'The Myth of Parental Attitudes', in D. M. Boswell and J. M. Wingrove (eds), *The Handicapped Person in the Community*, London: Tavistock.

Rowlings, C. (1981) *Social Work with Elderly People*, London: George Allen & Unwin.

Rummery, K., Ellis, K. and Davis, A. (1999) 'Negotiating Access to Community Care Assessments: Perspectives of Front-line Workers, People with a Disability and Carers', *Health and Social Care in the Community*, 7(4), pp. 296–300.

Ryan, J. and Thomas, F. (1980) *The Politics of Mental Handicap*, Harmondsworth: Penguin.

Safilios-Rothschild, C. (1970) *The Sociology and Social Psychology of Disability and Rehabilitation*, New York: Random House.

Sainsbury, S. (1970) *Registered as Disabled*, Occasional Papers on Social Administration No. 35, London: Bell.

Salzberger-Wittenberg, I. (1970) *Psycho-Analytic Insights and Relationships: A Kleinian Approach*, London: Routledge & Kegan Paul.

Sapey, B. (1993) 'Community Care: Reinforcing the Dependency of Disabled People', *Applied Community Studies*, 1(3), pp. 21–9.

Sapey, B. (1995) 'Disabling Homes: A Study of the Housing Needs of Disabled People in Cornwall', *Disability & Society*, 10(1), pp. 71–85.

Sapey, B. (2004) 'Practice for What? The Use of Evidence in Social Work with Disabled People', in D. Smith (ed.), *Evidence-based Practice and Social Work*, London: Jessica Kingsley.

Sapey, B. and Hewitt, N. (1991) 'The Changing Context of Social Work Practice', in M. Oliver (ed.), *Social Work, Disabled People and Disabling Barriers*, London: Jessica Kingsley.

Sapey, B. and Pearson, J. (2002) *Direct Payments in Cumbria: An Evaluation of their Implementation*, commissioned by Cumbria Direct Payments Steering Group.

Sapey, B., Stewart, J. and Donaldson, G. (2004a) *The Social Implications of Increases in Wheelchair Use*, Lancaster: Lancaster University.

Sapey, B., Turner, R. and Orton, S. (2004b) *Access to Practice: Overcoming the Barriers to Practice Learning for Disabled Social Work Students*, Southampton: SWAPltsn.

Satyamurti, C. (1981) *Occupational Survival*, Oxford: Basil Blackwell.

Sayce, L. (2000) *From Psychiatric Patient to Citizen*, Basingstoke: Palgrave.

Schorr, A. (1992) *The Personal Social Services: An Outside View*, York: Joseph Rowntree Foundation.

Scott, R. A. (1970) 'The Constructions and Conceptions of Stigma by Professional Experts', in J. Douglas (ed.), *Deviance and Respectability: The Social Construction of Moral Meanings*, New York: Basic Books.

Scrutton, S. (1989) *Counselling Older People: A Creative Response to Ageing*, London: Edward Arnold.

Selfe, L. and Stow, L. (1981) *Children with Handicaps*, London: Hodder & Stoughton.

Shakespeare, T. (1996) 'Power and Prejudice: Issues of Gender, Sexuality and Disability', in L. Barton (ed.), *Disability & Society: Emerging Issues and Insights*, London: Longman.

Shakespeare, T. (1997) 'Researching Disabled Sexuality', in C. Barnes and G. Mercer (eds), *Doing Disability Research*, Leeds: The Disability Press.

Shakespeare, T., Gillespie-Sells, K. and Davies, D. (1996) *The Sexual Politics of Disability: Untold Desires*, London: Cassell.

Shearer, A. (1981a) 'A Framework for Independent Living', in A. Walker and P. Townsend (eds), *Disability in Britain*, London: Martin Robertson.

Shearer, A. (1981b) *Disability: Whose Handicap?*, Oxford: Basil Blackwell.

Shearer, A. (1984) *Centres for Independent Living in the US and the UK – an American Viewpoint*, London: King's Fund Centre.

Silburn, R. (1983) 'Social Assistance and Social Welfare: The Legacy of the Poor Law', in P. Bean and S. MacPherson (eds), *Approaches to Welfare*, London: Routledge & Kegan Paul.

Simpson, F. and Campbell, J. (1996) *Facilitating and Supporting Independent Living: A Guide to Setting up a Personal Assistance Scheme*, London: Disablement Income Group.

Social Services Inspectorate (1991a) *Care Management and Assessment: Managers Guide*, London: HMSO.

Social Services Inspectorate (1991b) *Care Management and Assessment: Practitioners Guide*, London: HMSO.

Social Services Inspectorate (1995) *Growing Up and Moving On: Report of an SSI Project on the Transition Services for Disabled Young People*, London, HMSO.

Social Services Inspectorate (1997) *Moving On Towards Independence: Second Report of an SSI Project on the Transition Services for Disabled Young People*, London: HMSO.

Social Services Inspectorate (1999) *Inspection Standards: Inspection of Services for Independent Living Arrangements*, London: Department of Health.

Social Services Inspectorate (2000) *New Directions for Independent Living: Inspection of Independent Living Arrangements for Younger Disabled People*, London: Department of Health.

Social Trends (2004) 'Social Trends No 34', London: National Statistics Online; www.statistics.gov.uk/downloads/theme_social/Social_Trends34/ Social_Trends34.pdf.

Stainton, T. (2002) 'Taking Rights Structurally: Disability, Rights and Social Worker Responses to Direct Payments', *British Journal of Social Work*, 32, pp. 751–63.

Stevens, A. (1991) *Disability Issues*, London: CCETSW.

Stewart, W. (1979) *The Sexual Side of Handicap*, Cambridge: Woodhead-Faulkner.

Stuart, O. (1994) 'Journey from the Margin: Black Disabled People and the Antiracist Debate', in N. Begum, M. Hill and A. Stevens (eds), *Reflections: The Views of Black Disabled People on their Lives and on Community Care*, London: CCETSW.

Stuart, O. (1995) 'Response to Mike Oliver's Review of "Reflections" ', *Disability & Society*, 10(3), pp. 371–3.

Sutherland, A. T. (1981) *Disabled We Stand*, London: Souvenir Press.

Swain, J. (1981) *Adopting a Life-Style*, Milton Keynes: Open University Press.

Swain, J., Finkelstein, V., French, S. and Oliver, M. (eds) (1993) *Disabling Barriers – Enabling Environments*, London: Sage.

Tate, D. G., Maynard, F. and Forchheimer, M. (1992) 'Evaluation of a Medical Rehabilitation and Independent Living Programme for Persons with Spinal Cord Injury', *Journal of Rehabilitation*, 58, pp. 25–8.

Taylor, D. (1977) *Physical Impairment – Social Handicap*, London: Office of Health Economics.

Thomas, C. (1999) *Female Forms: Experiencing and Understanding Disability*, Buckingham: Open University Press.

Thomas, C. (2004) 'How is Disability Understood? An Examination of Sociological Approaches', *Disability & Society*, **19**(6), pp. 569–83.

Thompson, N. (1993) *Anti-Discriminatory Practice*, London: Macmillan.

Thompson, N. (1998) *Promoting Equality*, London: Macmillan.

Thompson, N. (2001) *Anti-Discriminatory Practice*, 3rd edn, Basingstoke: Palgrave.

Thompson, N. (ed.) (2002a) *Loss and Grief*, Basingstoke: Palgrave.

Thompson, N. (2002b) Social Movements, Social Justice and Social Work, *British Journal of Social Work*, **32**, 711–22.

Tomlinson, S. (1982) *The Sociology of Special Education*, London: Routledge & Kegan Paul.

Topliss, E. (1979) *Provision for the Disabled*, 2nd edn, Oxford: Basil Blackwell, with Martin Robertson.

Topliss, E. and Gould, B. (1981) *A Charter for the Disabled*, Oxford: Basil Blackwell.

Townsend, P. (1979) *Poverty in the United Kingdom*, Harmondsworth: Penguin.

Trieschmann, R. B. (1980) *Spinal Cord Injuries*, Oxford: Pergamon Press.

Union of Physically Impaired Against Segregation (1976) *Fundamental Principles of Disability*, London: Union of Physically Impaired Against Segregation; www.leeds.ac.uk/disability-studies/archiveuk/index.html.

Walker, A. and Townsend, P. (eds) (1981) *Disability in Britain*, London: Martin Robertson.

Warren, M. D., Knight, R. and Warren, J. L. (1979) *Changing Capabilities and Needs of People with Handicaps*, Health Services Research Unit, University of Kent.

Wates, M. (2002) *Supporting Disabled Adults in their Parenting Role*, York: Joseph Rowntree Foundation.

Wates, M. (2004) 'Righting the Picture: Disability and Family Life' in J. Swain, S. French, C. Barnes and C. Thomas (eds), *Disabling Barriers – Enabling Environments*, 2nd edn, London: Sage.

Watson, L., Tarpey, M., Alexander, K. and Humphreys, C. (2003) *Supporting People: Real Change? Planning Housing and Support for Marginal Groups*, York: Joseph Rowntree Foundation.

Weller, D. J. and Miller, P. M. (1977) 'Emotional Reactions of Patient, Family, and Staff in Acute Care Period of Spinal Cord Injury: Part 2', *Social Work in Health Care*, **3**(1), pp. 7–17.

Westcott, H. (1993) *Abuse of Children and Adults with Disabilities*, London: NSPCC.

Westcott, H. and Cross, M. (1995) *This Far and No Further: Towards Ending the Abuse of Disabled Children*, Birmingham: Venture Press.

Wilding, P. (1982) *Professional Power and Social Welfare*, London: Routledge & Kegan Paul.

Willis, M. (1995) 'Customer Expectations of Service Quality at Community Team Offices', *Social Services Research*, no. 4, pp. 57–67.

Wilson, S. (2003) *Disability, Counselling and Psychotherapy: Challenges and Opportunities*, Basingstoke: Palgrave.

Wood, H. (2004) 'Sustaining Disabled People in the Community: Does Supported Housing Offer a Real Choice?' *Practice*, 16(3), pp. 185–96.

World Health Organization (WHO) (1980) *International Classification of Impairments, Disabilities and Handicaps*, Geneva: WHO.

World Health Organization (WHO) (2002) *Towards a Common Language for Functioning, Disability and Health: ICF*, Geneva: WHO.

Young, M. and Willmott, P. (1973) *The Symmetrical Family*, Harmondsworth: Penguin.

Ypren, T. A. van (1996) 'On Coding and Classification in Social Welfare', *New Technology in Human Services*, 9(3), pp. 3–10.

Zarb, G. (1991) 'Creating a Supportive Environment: Meeting the Needs of People who are Ageing with a Disability', in M. Oliver (ed), *Social Work, Disabled People and Disabling Environments*, London: Jessica Kingsley.

Zarb, G. (1993) 'The Dual Experience of Ageing with a Disability', in J. Swain, V. Finkelstein, S. French and M. Oliver (eds), *Disabling Barriers – Enabling Environments*, London: Sage.

Zarb, G. and Nadash, P. (1994) *Cashing in on Independence*, London: Policy Studies Institute for the British Council of Disabled People.

Zarb, G., Oliver, M. and Silver, J. (1990) *Ageing with Spinal Cord Injury: The Right to a Supportive Environment?*, London: Thames Polytechnic/Spinal Injuries Association.

Index